BOUNCING BACK

BOUNCING BACK

Rewiring Your Brain for
Maximum Resilience and Well-Being

LINDA GRAHAM, MFT

Foreword by Rick Hanson, PhD

New World Library

Novato, California

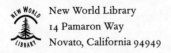

New World Library
14 Pamaron Way
Novato, California 94949

Grateful acknowledgment is given to Coleman Barks for the use of the Rumi poem "The
Guest House" on page 154 from his book *The Essential Rumi* and to Jack Kornfield for the
use of his forgiveness exercise on page 185 from his seminar "The Science and Practice of
Forgiveness" at the Greater Good Science Center. Every effort has been made to contact
rights holders for use of quoted material in *Bouncing Back*.

The material in this book is intended for education. It is not meant to take the place of
individual diagnosis and treatment by a qualified medical practitioner or therapist. No
expressed or implied guarantee as to the effects of the use of the recommendations can be
given nor liability taken.

Text design by Tona Pearce Myers

Library of Congress Cataloging-in-Publication Data
Graham, Linda, date.
Bouncing back : rewiring your brain for maximum resilience and well-being / Linda
Graham, MFT ; foreword by Rick Hanson, PhD.
    pages cm
Includes bibliographical references and index.
ISBN 978-1-60868-129-7 (pbk. : alk. paper) — ISBN 978-1-60868-130-3 (ebk.)
 1. Resilience (Personality trait) 2. Self-consciousness (Awareness) 3. Self-confidence.
4. Neuropsychology. I. Title.
BF698.35.R47G73 2013
158.1—dc23   2012048037

First printing, April 2013
ISBN 978-1-60868-129-7
Printed in Canada on 100% postconsumer-waste recycled paper

New World Library is proud to be a Gold Certified Environmentally
Responsible Publisher. Publisher certification awarded by Green Press
Initiative. www.greenpressinitiative.org

10   9   8   7   6   5   4   3   2

To James Baraz, Sylvia Boorstein,
Diana Fosha, Rick Hanson
— True Others to my True Self

More Praise for *Bouncing Back*

"A Japanese proverb tells us that 'the bamboo that bends is stronger than the oak that resists,' for when the monsoon strikes the oak breaks, while the bamboo bends but quickly recovers. In clear, accessible language, Linda Graham integrates insights from modern scientific psychology, ancient wisdom traditions, and neurobiology to show readers how to become more like bamboo. Filled with inspirational quotes, step-by-step exercises, and wisdom drawn from years of psychotherapeutic practice, this book can help anyone recover from sorrow and disappointment to live a richer, happier, more fulfilling life."

— **Ronald D. Siegel, PsyD**, assistant clinical professor of psychology
at Harvard Medical School and author of
The Mindfulness Solution: Everyday Practices for Everyday Problems

"Linda Graham shines clear light on one of the most vital skills we can develop — resilience — and takes the mystery out of how to get there. She offers beautiful, practical guidance on the underpinnings of 'bouncing back' and on how to rewire your brain's circuitry to increase your resilience. She includes real-life, relatable examples from her experience as a first-class psychotherapist and veteran mindfulness practitioner, as well as insights and road-tested practices you'll want to return to again and again."

— **Marsha Lucas, PhD**, author of *Rewire Your Brain for Love:
Creating Vibrant Relationships Using the Science of Mindfulness*

"Useful in a wide variety of contexts, *Bouncing Back* brings much-needed science to the subject of resilience via a wisdom-packed offering of simple yet effective insights and practices for growing through life's inevitable challenges."

— **Elisha Goldstein, PhD**, author of *The Now Effect* and coauthor of
A Mindfulness-Based Stress Reduction Workbook

"This book presents the neuroscience of self-healing in ways that make it totally accessible and applicable to our daily life concerns. Linda Graham shows us how to upgrade our old wiring to fit the new code of mental and spiritual health. I was personally touched by how *encouraging* her works and practices are."

— **David Richo, PhD**, author of *How to Be an Adult in Love*

"Linda Graham has written a remarkably clear, extraordinarily useful, and, yes, inspiring book. She brilliantly integrates cutting-edge neuroscience and the best of contemporary psychotherapy with the wisdom and practices of Buddhism. The result is both a sophisticated perspective on development and change and a practical program for healing and strengthening the psyche through exercises imaginatively designed to rewire the brain."

— **David Wallin, PhD**, author of *Attachment in Psychotherapy*

"Linda Graham provides a masterful integration of novel research findings in neuroscience and psychology with deep clinical insight into optimal human functioning. A joy to read and full of easy-to-follow exercises, this book offers a deceptively simple yet rich and complex road map for building and maintaining emotional resilience."

— **Kristin Neff, PhD,** associate professor of human development and culture at the University of Texas at Austin and author of *Self-Compassion*

"Having researched and cocreated a resilience training program for NASA, I can validate the breadth and power of *Bouncing Back*. Linda Graham has integrated the latest findings in neuroscience and emotionally focused therapies, along with perennial mindfulness practices, to provide us with a first-rate book on becoming more resilient. It may be premature to call a book a classic before it has hit the stands, but *Bouncing Back* has everything it takes: it is wise, helpful, compassionate, practical, and well researched.

— **Daniel Ellenberg, PhD,** leadership coach, psychotherapist, and seminar leader

"Filled with practical and powerful exercises that not only will deepen your capacity to deal with life's challenges but will lead to lasting change, *Bouncing Back* is a comprehensive and caring road map to a life of flourishing."

— **Ron Frederick, PhD,** author of *Living Like You Mean It*

"Wherever I go, and with all the populations I serve, I've discovered that nourishing resilience to counteract the stresses and strains of daily life is our number one priority. I'm therefore grateful to Linda Graham for weaving together this incredible tapestry of time-tested insights and exercises, which are vitally important for us to assimilate into our daily lives. *Bouncing Back* is a resource guide I will cherish and look forward to passing on to all my students, clients, and teachers-in-training."

— **Richard Miller, PhD,** clinical psychologist and president of the Integrative Restoration Institute

"A wealth of neuroscience research over the past ten years has told us much about how the brain works and what *change* really means. Linda Graham's *Bouncing Back* is the book we've all been waiting for that translates that knowledge into compassionate, down-to-earth language that inspires confidence and hope. Rather than rote skills for coping, she provides a brain-based understanding of how we became who we are and how we can use our brains to become who we want to be. With humor, warmth, and wisdom, she conveys how to use mindfulness practices to increase our tolerance for the ups and downs of human life."

— **Janina Fisher, PhD,** coauthor of the forthcoming *The Body as Resource*

"*Bouncing Back* reaches for and delivers more than a strategy for dealing with hard times. Its many practices are sure to be beneficial on a daily basis and can expand anyone's capacity to navigate the twists and turns that life inevitably presents us with. Linda Graham has written a very positive book that supports and encourages everyone to engage in life consciously, with an open heart and an open mind. I highly recommend *Bouncing Back*."

— **Peter Baumann,** coauthor of *Ego* and founder of the Baumann Foundation

"One of the most exciting discoveries of the age we are living in is the growing understanding that we can each consciously engage in practices, sometimes involving only shifts in our attention and intention, that directly influence the function and structure of our brains and bodies. Even better, we not only can do this for ourselves but can connect with others in ways that support resilience in our families, communities, and society. *Bouncing Back* is a heartfelt and comprehensive guide for how to use your mind to change your brain and, in the process, experience an amazing upward spiral of deep well-being."

— **Cassandra Vieten, PhD,** executive director of research at the Institute of Noetic Sciences, scientist at the California Pacific Medical Center Research Institute, coauthor of *Living Deeply*, and author of *Mindful Motherhood*

"We all know what it's like to feel stuck. Grounded in solid neuroscience and relational psychology, *Bouncing Back* is the perfect guidebook to help us not only get through hard times but develop the capacity for thriving in their midst. With extraordinary clarity, empathy, and depth, Linda Graham shows us how to navigate through life's challenges with confidence, trust, and the feeling of the wind in our sails. Highly recommended."

— **James Baraz,** coauthor of *Awakening Joy*

"In *Bouncing Back*, Linda Graham offers a beautiful and wise understanding of neuroscience combined with immensely practical tools for healthy living and genuine well-being."

— **Jack Kornfield, PhD,** author of *A Path with Heart*

"We each have the capacity to meet the most challenging life circumstances with deep intelligence and a courageous, open heart. Yet when our resilience is diminished, we suffer. In her pioneering new book, Linda Graham explores the psychological, relational, and neurological dynamics of resilience and offers a rich array of meditations and attentional practices that can help us navigate everything from daily stressors to deep trauma. Written with great lucidity and compassion, this book helps us cultivate a heart that is ready for anything."

— **Tara Brach, PhD,** author of *Radical Acceptance* and *True Refuge*

"Astoundingly brilliant! I've never read a book so packed with information and wisdom and so engagingly, imaginatively, and charmingly written. Every page is a pleasure and a delight to read. This is a must-read book for therapists, teachers, and everyone else (which means all of us) who are interested in how we bounce back amid life's many challenges."

— Sylvia Boorstein, PhD, author of
It's Easier Than You Think: The Buddhist Way to Happiness

"Linda Graham's *Bouncing Back* gives us what we most need to navigate through our rich, complex, and often challenging world: a fundamental understanding of how our brains work, a deep dive into the flexibility and changeability of the brain, and practical tools for meeting life's most difficult challenges. Whether you're currently dealing with trauma or in a joyful and unencumbered period of your life, this book will deepen your self-understanding as it moves your heart."

— Rick Foster, coauthor of
How We Choose to Be Happy and *Happiness and Health*

"Linda Graham has written the ultimate handbook for dealing with life's inevitable bumps, challenges, and, yes, even traumas. It is both practical and inspiring: Graham draws equally on modern science — neuroscience, psychology, and sociology — and contemplative philosophy to create a must-have resource for all those looking to make a full comeback."

— Christine Carter, PhD, author of *Raising Happiness*

"I highly recommend this intelligent and very readable book by Linda Graham. More than informative, it is a heartfelt conversation with a wise and compassionate friend — and we can all use more of those."

— Louis Cozolino, PhD, professor of psychology at Pepperdine University
and author of *The Neuroscience of Psychotherapy*

"*Bouncing Back* offers the rigor of science, the beauty of art, and the wisdom of deep reflection and contemplation. In this illuminating work, Linda Graham has given us a treasure that has the potential to transform our individual and collective lives."

— Shauna L. Shapiro, PhD, assistant professor of counseling psychology at
Santa Clara University and coauthor of *The Art and Science of Mindfulness*

CONTENTS

EXERCISES

FOREWORD

LIFE HAS MANY ENJOYABLE, even wonderful moments. Of course, as we all know, it contains other kinds of moments as well: times that are stressful, upsetting, depleting, tiring, even devastating and traumatic — or simply dull and dreary. These sometimes come with great intensity, but mainly they're woven into the fabric of everyday life: the frustrations of a long commute, a squabble with a roommate, trying to settle a squirming toddler into a car seat, an unexpected bill, a big push at work, a nagging illness, criticism from a boss, a painful breakup with a partner, sullen silence from a teenager... real life.

Faced with great challenges or a long accumulation of small ones, you may wonder: How hard will this hit me? How soon will I recover? And most important, how can I help myself?

Drawing on her many years of experience as a psychotherapist, meditation teacher, workshop leader, and writer, Linda Graham provides many excellent, even life-changing answers to these questions. She explores the intersection of brain science, relational psychology, and mindfulness practices to show us how to recover and develop our natural resilience.

The past several decades have produced a whole library's worth of research on stress, trauma, and recovery. We have learned how the body and mind react to threats, losses, and rejections, and we have discovered how some people are able to ride life's waves with skill and grace by developing new kinds of flexibility and strength.

In what's called the "stress-diathesis" model in health care, a person's response to the hard parts of life is shaped by three factors: the intensity of the challenges, his or her vulnerabilities, and compensating resources. We try to manage the challenges as best we can. Yet storms still come, bearing down on our vulnerabilities and taxing our resources.

We all have vulnerabilities, chinks in our mental and emotional armor. With the warm and accepting perspective of a seasoned therapist, Linda focuses on how we can protect our vulnerable points and strengthen them over time. Further, in a rich vein of gold running throughout this book, Linda offers down-to-earth perspectives and dozens of powerful, experiential practices for building up our inner resources. She knows these practices from the inside out, and she offers enthusiastic and creative ways to use them to help us develop new insights, inspirations, and capabilities. These resources — a kind of inner treasure — include greater mindfulness, empathy, self-understanding, self-compassion, security, confidence, interpersonal skills, comfort with the body, reservoirs of positive emotions, calm, courage, and flexibility. These help a person deal with life adaptively — to bend but not break, and then, as Linda puts it, to bounce back. In a word, they help a person become more *resilient*.

As the pace of social change accelerates, as negative developments emerge amid more positive ones, and as old bulwarks of protection fade or fracture, personal resilience is more valuable than ever. Rich or poor, child or adult, sick or healthy — we all need resilience. Besides helping us to help ourselves, resilience helps us to help others. In these pages, parents, teachers, therapists, managers, and health-care providers can learn many effective ways to support others in developing resilience of their own.

Linda Graham has seen up close what builds resilience and what tears it down. In language that is heartfelt, often lyrical, and always practical, and with a comprehensive approach to mind, body, heart, and spirit, she has distilled a lifetime of clinical practice and deep reflection into an authoritative and practical guide. Her work is creative in its groundbreaking integration of ancient contemplative wisdom, relational psychology, and modern neuroscience, and it is eminently useful in its compassionate focus on what will help you here and now.

Resilience is like the keel of a sailboat. As the winds of life blow, resilience keeps you balanced and moving forward. And when the really big squalls come — no life is without them — resilience lets you right your boat as soon as possible. Using the knowledge you gain from this book, you'll be able to chart your course with confidence across the great seas of this precious life.

RICK HANSON, PhD
Wellspring Institute for Neuroscience
and Contemplative Wisdom
San Rafael, California
November 26, 2012

What Resilience Is and How We Rewire Our Brains to Recover It

I'm not afraid of storms, for I am learning how to sail my ship.

— Louisa May Alcott

IN MY WORK as a psychotherapist, I hear many stories of resilience in action, such as this one from my client Deborah. Deborah had had a wonderful day at the beach during a heat wave last summer, luxuriating in the soft sleepiness of the day. She had no worries, no frets: she was just relaxing into a peaceful feeling that "God's in his heaven; all's right with the world."

Two hours later, stuck in gridlocked traffic and anxious about getting home in time to fix dinner for friends, she had to let go of the effortless good feeling of the day and click into the high-gear planning that she knew how to do so well: whom could she call and ask to pick up the salmon? Who had keys to let the others in? She was swiftly calculating and strategizing to navigate around this blip on the radar screen.

When Deborah arrived home, she encountered yet another setback: the dishwasher had flooded the kitchen. A good half inch of sudsy water covered the linoleum where people needed to be cooking dinner thirty minutes ago already.

Deborah's friends, who were already there to help pull the dinner together, pitched in to clear up the mess. Meanwhile, Deborah was able to quickly check her phone messages. Her sister-in-law Sheila had called with the news that her brother George in Detroit had been rushed to the emergency room...She didn't even wait for the end of the message. Her brother had had a heart attack four months before, and she was panicking right now.

She immediately called her brother's cell phone; Sheila answered at the hospital. George was alive; he was stable; he would probably be kept overnight and released in the morning. What they had suspected was his second heart attack was angina — severe enough to warrant calling the ambulance, but not life threatening. The doctors were glad he had come in so quickly this time; it looked as if he was going to be fine. Deborah talked with Sheila for a few more minutes, discussing whether she should fly out that night; they agreed she could come the next day.

After she hung up the phone, Deborah lost it. Her mother had had a heart attack when Deborah was eleven and her brother was eight. Memories of the panic and worry from the week their mother had been hospitalized flooded over her. Even with a house full of guests, she collapsed on the couch, shaking and crying. Her friend Gary came over and put his hands on Deborah's shoulders. Without even knowing the details of what Deborah was upset about, Gary reminded her of what she had often said to him in other circumstances: "You are big enough to hold this."

As Deborah remembers it, she could feel her awareness expanding back out from its implosion like a balloon expanding as breath is blown into it. "Oh, right. This is now; that was then. That then turned out fine. This now is fine." (Her mother lived another thirty-five years, well into her senior years and Deborah's own adulthood.) "George is okay. I'm okay. Right here, right now, everything is okay."

Deborah came back into a sense of presence, into compassion for herself and her brother. She remembered the peacefulness she had felt at the beach earlier in the day and reflected on all the modes of coping she'd shifted in and out of in just a few hours. She went out into her garden and breathed a prayer of relief and gratitude, for her brother, for the empathy of friends, for Gary's caring touch, for the calm that reconnected her to her inner resources and restored her resilience.

We are all called upon to cope with hiccups and hurricanes in our lives — losing our wallet and car keys, discovering mold in the bathroom, missing three days at the office to care for a sick child — and we do. We are resilient heroes in our own lives every day as we skillfully navigate the disruptive, unwanted changes of the washing machine going on the fritz or the car needing a new transmission.

Occasionally we have to respond with grace under pressure to greater troubles and tragedies: infertility or infidelity, a diagnosis of pancreatic cancer, losing a job, a son wounded in combat overseas. Sometimes too many things go disastrously wrong all at once: a daughter arrested for selling pot, a laptop left on a plane, finding out that the contractor repairing our roof is being sued for shoddy construction work, all in the same week we're placing an aging parent in a nursing home. We begin to feel as if we're drinking from a fire hose and about to go under.

Most of us feel internally stressed-out by some external stressor every single day. Few of us will get through an entire lifetime without our resilience being seriously challenged by the pain and suffering inherent in the human condition. None of us is immune to being asked to cope with what we never asked for, with what we deeply, deeply do not want.

The way we can respond with skill to such unwelcome challenges is through resilience. Resilience is the capacity to respond to pressures and tragedies quickly, adaptively, and effectively. Researchers have found that there's no single best or infallible way to cope with difficulties. Being able to adapt our coping to a specific challenge is the skill that allows us to find our footing when we're thrown off balance by the unknown, by stress, or by trauma. Responding flexibly can carry us through the ups and downs of our days. In the words of my yoga teacher, Debra McKnight-Higgins, "Blessed are they who are flexible, for they shall never be bent out of shape."

We now know, from the latest advances in neuroscience, that capacities for resilience are innate in the brain, hard-wired in by evolution. How well these capacities develop as we mature depends on our responses to our life experiences and how those experiences shape the neural circuitry and functioning of our brains — which in turn influence our responses. Whether we tend to bounce back from terrible setbacks or stay where we've been thrown depends on our learned patterns of response to other people and events. These patterns become fixed, not just incorporated into a behavioral repertoire but deeply encoded into our neural circuitry, from an early age. They shape not only the ways we cope with challenges but also the functioning of the brain itself.

Only in recent years have neuroscientists begun to understand how to harness the brain's capacities to radically rewire these neural circuits and rebuild the functioning of the brain to increase resilience. Science doesn't have all the answers yet. The technology that can look inside the "black box" of the brain and observe its functioning in real time, as it creates music, reacts to scenes of combat, or grieves over the death of a beloved pet, is a mere two decades old. The application of the findings of neuroscience to behavior in real time, as people cope with losing a job or flunking out of school, is even more recent.

New discoveries are reported daily, but the data are still far from complete. As in any new science, contradictions and controversies emerge, are resolved, and reemerge as new perspectives evolve. New understandings of the structures of the brain are allowing researchers to hypothesize about the dynamic and interrelated functions of those structures that can alter neural circuits, pathways, and networks created by those structures and even change the structures themselves. According to my friend neurologist Rick Mendius, "Modern neuroscience is so new that we must be comfortable venturing not only into the unknown but into error."

I'm neither a neuroscientist nor an academic researcher: I don't conduct laboratory research on brains or on people's behavior. My laboratory has been in the trenches. For twenty years I have worked every day with people earnestly seeking better ways to cope with the unexpected twists and turns of their lives, as a licensed psychotherapist, consultant and trainer, and workshop leader. For fifteen years I have been a dedicated practitioner of *vipassana* (insight) meditation in the Buddhist contemplative tradition. And for the past ten years I have also been a diligent student of the application of neuroscience to healing trauma and recovering resilience.

I've been privileged to study with some of the best thinkers and innovators in the emerging discipline of interpersonal neurobiology and in related, cutting-edge modalities of psychotherapy, particularly accelerated experiential dynamic psychotherapy, emotionally focused therapy for couples, and sensorimotor psychotherapy, a mindfulness- and body-based therapy for trauma. It's been a great privilege to study with the founders of Spirit Rock Meditation Center, masterful practitioners who bring Buddhist teachings to Western sensibilities with great skill and integrity.

The greatest privilege of all has been to apply the theories and tools for recovering resilience in my work with hundreds of clients, colleagues, workshop participants, and students who have rounded out my own learning about resilience with their openness and courage. Their stories are disguised or composited here to protect confidentiality. I owe them all a deep debt of gratitude.

I take full responsibility for any errors I have made in understanding the latest findings of neuroscience or in interpreting the thinking of the pioneers who are applying those findings to clinical psychology and mindfulness practice. Our interpretations of the emerging data and extrapolations of these findings to clinical applications are still filtered through our own subjective experience. Some of the other paradigms I draw on in *Bouncing Back* have hundreds, even thousands of years of evidence behind them to validate their efficacy. All of the tools and techniques used here are offered in the spirit of helping you discover for yourself what works best for you.

However, it is abundantly clear that we can learn to bounce back better by consciously rewiring our brain's learned patterns of coping. To do that most successfully and efficiently, we must know how to select the new experiences that will best do that rewiring. In the words of leading neuroscientist Richard Davidson, "Based upon everything we know about the brain in neuroscience, change is not only possible, but is actually the rule rather than the exception. It's really just a question of which influences we're going to choose for our brain."

In *Bouncing Back*, I present two powerful processes of brain functioning: *conditioning*, which determines how our learning of resilience is encoded in the neural circuitry of our brains in the first place; and *neuroplasticity*, which determines how we can use new experiences to rewire those patterns. Using these processes, you can master what I call the five Cs of resilient coping:

1. *Calm:* You can stay calm in a crisis.
2. *Clarity:* You can see clearly what's happening as well as your internal response to what's happening; you can see what needs to happen next; and you can see possibilities from different perspectives that will enhance your ability to respond flexibly.
3. *Connection:* You can reach out for help as needed; you can learn from others how to be resilient; and you can connect to resources that greatly expand your options.
4. *Competence:* You can call on skills and competencies that you have learned through previous experience (or that you learn through *Bouncing Back*) to act quickly and effectively.
5. *Courage:* You can strengthen your faith to persevere in your actions until you come to resolution or acceptance of the difficulty.

Bouncing Back helps you develop these five Cs of coping by teaching you how to rewire old patterns of response in your brain that derail resilience and how to wire in new and better coping skills. It shows how you can apply the latest discoveries of modern neuroscience to your everyday struggles to become more resilient.

In part 1, you will learn how the brain develops its strategies for coping in the first place, and how our earliest experiences in responding to stressors shape the functioning of the brain's CEO of resilience — the prefrontal cortex. Do you need to know how your brain works to skillfully navigate your daily life? No, no more than you need to know what's under the hood of your car in order to drive to work, or how the Internet works to check your email. But if you want to *change* how you manage your daily life, then knowing how your brain works, and how you can change how it works, will help you develop a sense of competence and mastery that in turn will engender a sense of confidence about rewiring your brain to become more resilient.

In part 2, you will also learn self-directed neuroplasticity — tools and techniques to harness the capacities of your brain to change and strengthen itself in lasting ways. The tools are drawn from two of the most powerful paradigms of brain change known to science: mindfulness, from the 2,500-year-old Buddhist contemplative tradition, and empathy, from the 150-year-old practice of Western relational psychology.

With the findings of modern neuroscience to guide the integrated application of tools from these two paradigms, you won't have to spend years either meditating in a cave or reclining on an analyst's couch to learn how to effect immediate and permanent changes in your coping strategies. You'll learn how to use an integration of these tools in ways that make it safe, efficient, and effective to tinker with, even wrestle with, the brain. You can become resilient again, creating options and choosing wisely, even during catastrophes.

The brain rewires itself by focusing attention on new experiences and encoding in its neural circuitry the learning from those experiences. And it does that most quickly through interactions with other people. Parts 3–7 lead you through a series of experiential exercises you can do on your own, with a partner, or in a small group that steadily build skills in *relational* intelligence, *somatic* (body-based) intelligence, *emotional* intelligence, *reflection and choosing options*, and the deep wisdom of *simply being*. These exercises strengthen the functioning of the prefrontal cortex and then use that platform both to rewire old coping strategies that don't work so well anymore and to learn new ones that work better. Following the exercises, I briefly explain the neuroscience underlying them, showing how you are rewiring your brain for resilience as you go along.

In my twenty years of clinical practice, over and over again I have seen people rewire their own brains, making lasting changes for the better in their capacities to respond to the storms and struggles of their lives. The well-researched tools and techniques presented here have been further refined by my own longtime practice and teaching of meditation, my personal journey through the ups and downs of life, and my study of the neuroscience of human development and self-transformation, all of which help guide me in suggesting which tools work well and why.

Many current models of self-help and personal growth and many modalities of coaching and therapy *presume* that individuals already have resilient brain functioning. *Bouncing Back* takes the time and practice to develop or rebuild that functioning. Part 8 examines what resilience in the brain makes possible: finding more meaning and fulfillment, creativity and productivity, connection and belonging, ease and well-being, and compassion to skillfully navigate your life and engage with a widening world. We rediscover the urgent need of the human mind to re-envision ourselves and the world, and the boundless depths of the human heart and soul to care.

I encourage you to try all the experiential exercises as you proceed through the book, as practical experiments in rewiring your brain. Because every brain is conditioned differently, everyone's experience using these exercises will be different. I suggest you do them at your own pace. It will be helpful to do the exercises in the order presented to progress steadily toward more complex skills. It will be useful to engage in these experiments with curiosity and openness rather than following fixed rules and expecting a guaranteed outcome. As you reflect on the learning your brain is encoding from each exercise, you will notice that you are rewiring your brain as you go along. As you learn to rewire your brain from the level of the neurons up, you will experience the joy of recovering a resilience that will last a lifetime.

PART ONE

HOW THE BRAIN DEVELOPS RESILIENCE – OR DOESN'T

CHAPTER ONE

How the Brain's Strategies of Resilience Become Wired In

What lies behind us and what lies before us are tiny matters compared to what lies within us.

— RALPH WALDO EMERSON

MY NEXT-DOOR NEIGHBOR has a big, affectionate, 125-pound malamute named Barney and an eight-year-old granddaughter who adores him. One day, as Samantha was arriving to visit, I watched her run up to Barney to give him a hug. Barney responded exuberantly, licking her face profusely. He was simply greeting her with affection, but Samantha clearly wasn't prepared for such rough-and-tumble love: she burst into tears.

As I witnessed Samantha's distress, I immediately felt a sympathetic response in my own body, as you may have felt in yours — a rush of "Oh, no!" I went to comfort Samantha with a hug and a quick wipe of her face with my sweatshirt. Then I held a bewildered Barney at bay while Samantha's mom came outside for a more thorough wash-down with a wet washcloth and clean towel.

With her mom's soothing words of "There, there," Samantha quickly calmed down, wiped a tear from her cheek, then took her mom's hand and walked over to Barney to start again. Her mom showed her how to hold her hand out and let Barney lick that first.

After that, they both patted the top of Barney's head, then Samantha slowly moved toward Barney and gave him a hug. His tail wagged exuberantly, but there was no more face washing.

As you may have noticed, Samantha learned several resilient coping strategies from her mom in this encounter with Barney. She learned that receiving support from others could help her calm down, and she learned how to approach the big dog in a confident, competent way that didn't overexcite him. Her brain immediately encoded those lessons in her neural circuits for future reference.

Resilience, like all innate capacities in the brain, develops as the brain processes or learns from experience and translates or encodes that learning into its neural circuitry. Because resilience is all about surviving and thriving, our brains begin to learn and encode lessons about coping strategies that keep us alive and safe from the very beginning of brain development. Some responses to "safe" and "dangerous" even begin in utero.

In this chapter we will examine how learning from experience is translated or encoded in our brains through the interaction of two powerful mechanisms of brain functioning. The first is *conditioning*: broadly speaking, how the brain learns and stabilizes our conditioned patterns of response through repeated experience. The second is *neuroplasticity*: how the brain remains flexible in order to change that encoding, learning or unlearning patterns of response, growing new neurons, and connecting them in new circuits. Conditioning and neuroplasticity work together as the brain develops and matures. Much of this work occurs in the prefrontal cortex of the brain. I call this structure of executive functioning in the brain the CEO of resilience because it guides the encoding process and integrates the work of other brain structures that use both conditioning and neuroplasticity to help us learn from our experiences in the first place and rewire that learning later if need be.

When our conditioning goes well, especially early in our lives, we build a solid neural foundation for resilience in the brain. The "rules" encoded in our neural circuitry allow us to respond skillfully and adaptively to the outer hiccups and hurricanes of our lives that trigger agitation or distress within. The brain structures that perform the encoding are stable, yet flexible enough to learn new coping strategies. They buffer us against the effects of external stressors and traumas later in life. And that's true for many of us, much of the time.

However, our conditioning — the wiring of our neural circuitry as we learn from experience — sometimes goes awry. When this happens, we can find ourselves stuck in negative, dysfunctional response patterns that leave us feeling ineffective and miserable and more vulnerable to stressors and traumas. We may refrain from pushing back to assert our needs, watching someone else get the promotion we worked hard for. We may avoid opening the envelope from an insurance company or doctor, afraid of bad news, only to discover a month later that the enclosed letter was no big deal. When encoded early enough in our development, these patterns can even derail the maturation of the brain itself. Chapter 2 explores how and why such glitches in our learning may arise.

With an understanding of how our brains develop, we can forgive ourselves for finding it hard to rewire those early coping strategies if they failed to become fully established, leaving us floundering in a "neural swamp," or if they became rigid, leaving us stuck in "neural cement." When we know how to choose specific experiences to deliberately rewire our brains for better coping, we can fully recover our capacities for resilience and even strengthen the brain structures themselves that encode the new strategies. Neuroscientists have proved irrefutably that you *can* teach an old dog new tricks; you can even heal the dog — or the brain — when necessary. Although the initial wiring of our brains is based on early experience, we know that later experiences, especially healthy relational ones, can undo or overwrite that early learning to help us to cope differently and more resiliently with anything, anything at all.

The Neurobiological Basis for Resilience

The human brain is a social-learning organ. Throughout our lives, it develops and matures most efficiently in interactions with other human brains. In fact, initially the brain develops *only* in interactions with other human brains. It relies on interactions with other brains to turn on the actual expression of our genes according to the developmental timetables that have evolved in small human groups over millions of years.

For example, a human infant typically recognizes the face of its own mother by three months of age and can say "Dada" and "Mama" (or the equivalent) for the correct gender of parent by ten months of age. Babies enjoy gazing at themselves in a mirror by twelve months of age and can string words together in phrases by eighteen months of age. They become interested in playing with other children by age two and can comprehend that someone else is thinking something different from their own thoughts, by age four. It's the social interactions of the child's brain with the brains of other people that nurture these neurological developments.

The rapidly growing field of epigenetics explores how non-genetic factors, such as environmental stimuli, can turn on the expression of parts of the genetic code. Research shows that contact with other people can catalyze or inhibit the expression of specific genes in humans. For example, a person may have a genetically inherited talent for music, but unless that talent is encouraged by people around her early on, those "musical genes" may not be expressed, and the talent will remain undeveloped. Interactions in the early environment stimulate more growth in brain volume between birth and three years of age than at any other stage of life. Those early years create the neural foundation for all subsequent development.

The prefrontal cortex develops on a longer timetable, approximately twenty-five years, stimulated by empathic relationships with other mature prefrontal cortices. Evolutionary psychologists now posit that it was the need for our ancestors to communicate with one another quickly, through body language and facial expressions, that catalyzed the emergence of empathy, language, and many other advances in human mental capacities. In other words, the increased brain volume and the strong executive functioning of the prefrontal cortex that we needed to become empathic and highly skilled communicators — discerning whether situations were safe or dangerous, whether other people were allies or enemies, making decisions based on those assessments, formulating a narrative of the experience and evaluating whether that worked or not, planning a future, and creating meaning — are what drove the evolution of the higher cortex of the human brain in the first place. It still does.

Secure Attachment: The Interpersonal Base of Resilience

We learn our earliest strategies of resilience in infancy, through interacting with parents, caregivers, and others close to us. The British psychoanalyst John Bowlby proposed sixty years ago that human babies are "programmed" by evolution to "seek physical proximity to a caregiver in times of perceived threat or danger." Neuropsychologists have repeatedly demonstrated that Bowlby's theory of attachment and the fear-attachment-exploration motivational system underlying it are valid and form the neurobiological basis of our earliest learning of resilience. Fear (like Samantha's startle reaction to Barney's licking her face) naturally drives us to seek reassurance and protection from someone older, wiser, stronger, and able to help. This behavior, wired in from birth, is lifelong. The successful soothing of the fear in an empathic and responsive relationship allows the child — or adult — to venture out and continue to follow the natural urges to play, explore, and create. This is resilient behavior based on what Bowlby called "secure attachment."

The parents' responses to the baby's initial attachment behaviors encode the earliest and most enduring internal working models or rules of coping in the human brain. You may recognize some of your own patterns of conditioning in the style of secure attachment described below, or in the three other universal styles described in chapter 2. In our quest to recover our resilience, understanding the results of this early conditioning is essential. The earliest strategies for resilience become stably encoded in our neural circuitry by twelve to eighteen months of age and have what the neuropsychologist Louis Cozolino calls "permanent psychological significance." They even affect the maturation of the developing brain itself. In rewiring our brains for resilience, we must take this early conditioning into account.

How Secure Attachment Leads to Stable and Flexible Coping

Bowlby and other attachment researchers have found that secure attachment is the relational style that is most effective in enabling the prefrontal cortex to mature and "teaches" the brain to be resilient, both stable and flexible. According to Pat Ogden, the developer of sensorimotor psychotherapy, "Secure attachment is the strongest inoculator you can have against future trauma."

When a parent repeatedly responds to a baby's smile with a smile in return, perhaps amplified by gentle holding, playful cooing, and empathic baby talk, the earliest processing of the baby's neural circuits is based on a sense of safety and trust. If a parent consistently responds readily and calmly to a baby's expressions of distress (by changing its diaper or with a feeding), the baby learns to soothe itself, and the baby's neural circuits begin to stabilize around the sense that "I am important. I matter. I am loved." The baby also learns that calls for help are answered and that solutions to problems exist. In other words, basic patterns of resilience are established. If a growing child sees that his efforts to communicate with a parent are valued and understood, even if the parent can't do what the child wants, right then or ever, the child's neural circuits stabilize around a trustworthy sense of his own competence and mastery.

Learning to communicate our needs and wants to others, mastering various strategies to get those needs met, trusting that we deserve to have those needs met, and delighting in our growing competencies to do so form our very first experiences of resilience. This resilience grows as we learn to bounce back from moments of fear, anger, grief, and shame. We learn strategies for reaching out to people for help and protection. As our neural circuits mature and integrate, the feelings of trust, being loved, and becoming competent generate a sense of inner security. They create neural patterns of response flexibility that become the brain's template for resilience for the rest of our lives. The maturation of the developing prefrontal cortex serves as a scaffolding for further healthy self-development, self-regulation, and self-confidence and further learning about resilient coping.

As we grow older, our brains learn to navigate an increasingly complex world, primarily through interactions with other resilient people: teachers, coaches, older siblings, peers, partners, mentors, therapists, and role models from life, history, and literature. Over our lifetime, it is through interactions with other people that we learn how to handle disappointment, how to stop gossip and backbiting at the office, how to pull a team of people together to stop the building of a toxic waste dump in our neighborhood, or how to think outside the box when it comes to helping a child overcome a speech impediment. Research indicates that even as adults, our brain's preferred method of learning resilience continues to be through interacting with resilient people around us, through dialogue and shared work and play. An ancient Chinese proverb reminds us: A single conversation with a wise man is better than ten years of study.

A secure base of neural stability and flexibility helps you remain open to new learning. You can easily harness the brain's neuroplasticity to change old patterns of response and to strengthen the prefrontal cortex, which coordinates the encoding of those responses. Confident in your ability to respond effectively, you can take advantage of new possibilities. Your innate capacity for resilience continues to develop fully.

How the Brain Learns Habits of Behavior

Focusing our attention on any experience stimulates cells called neurons in various parts of the brain to fire; this firing extends from the brain into the nerves in the rest of the body. The experience may be an external event, like Barney's licking Samantha's face, or an internal response to the event, like Samantha's reaction of upset. When neurons fire in response to experience, they send electrical and chemical messages to other neurons across the gaps that separate them (the synapses), at times creating synaptic connections with more than five thousand other neurons at once. This neural messaging and synaptic connecting reinforce pathways in the brain. The reactions of people around us then activate another response within us, like Samantha's calming down in response to her mom's soothing touch. (If her mother had acted differently, for example by raising her voice, Samantha could have experienced another fear response instead.)

These bursts of neural messaging and connecting (processing the sense that a person or situation is safe or dangerous) may last only milliseconds. But as an experience is repeated, the thousands of neurons that fired together and created the neural network of the initial response tend to fire together again, strengthening that network and preparing the brain to respond in the same way when it next encounters a similar situation.

The neuroscientist Donald Hebb coined the phrase "Neurons that fire together wire together." It describes how repeated experiences and repeated neural firings cause neurons to strengthen the connections between them. These strengthened synaptic connections wire the meaning of an experience into more and more stable circuitry and more enduring patterns of response. How we respond to an event — this situation was safe or dangerous; this is what I did to cope with that situation; that coping worked well or poorly — becomes a stable, enduring pattern of response.

As synaptic connections become stronger and more stable over time, they begin to link up in neural pathways. When circuits are stable, the strength of the neural networks of associated memories and meanings makes it very likely that we will respond to the same or similar experiences in ways that we have already responded before. For example, Samantha's early experience of overcoming fear by receiving comfort from her mother may be reinforced by later experiences in which other people provide comfort or protection. Over time, simply the memory of such comfort may be enough to soothe her in frightening situations. And eventually, the memory of such support may be enough to prevent the fear response from occurring at all. This encoding of experiences and responses into stable, enduring neural patterns is what neuroscientists call *conditioning*.

Conditioning creates automatic habits of behavior by encoding the neural firing patterns of repeated responses to experience, stabilizing the neural circuitry of that learning, and storing those patterns of response in implicit (unconscious) memory. When you repeat a pattern of behavior often enough, eventually you don't have to focus your attention on it anymore: the neural circuits underlying that behavior have stabilized in your brain, enabling you to respond to a similar situation automatically.

Creating habits of behavior through conditioning is your brain's way of being efficient. Without conditioning, you'd have to relearn how to tie your shoes every morning and figure out which siblings or colleagues were trustworthy all over again every day. You'd never have the time or mental bandwidth to enjoy the fruits of being human — never be able, for example, to teach your kids to think about people besides themselves, create a business plan, or write short stories.

We can deliberately use conditioning to create positive habits of resilience. For example, when the car won't start in the morning, prior conditioning determines whether you panic or have the presence of mind to call upon available resources. Perhaps you've already created a good relationship with a neighbor who can jumpstart the car, or you have an AAA membership so that you can call a professional. Maybe there's money in the sock drawer for a cab to take you to work, or maybe you know you can use your credit card to rent a car. In the three to five seconds it takes your brain to remember the resources available and choose the best plan, you have evoked that conditioned safety net of resilience.

This conditioning is, in part, how the prefrontal cortex of the brain develops the five Cs of coping. If we have learned from our experiences with others how to *calm* down our nervous system, we can remain levelheaded in a crisis. If we have learned how to reflect on and make sense of our experience, we can maintain *clarity* in evaluating our experience and possibilities of response. If we have learned to trust ourselves in relationships with others, we can *connect with resources*, both internal and external, that expand our options for coping. If we have learned specific skills and become *competent* at them through past experience (or the experiential exercises in this book), we can draw on those competencies now and in the future. If we have found the *courage* to persevere in coping with life experiences before, we can call upon that courage to help us persevere now.

The stabilization that comes from conditioning is a natural process in the brain; it is also neutral. Just as the same soil can grow strawberries or poison oak, the mechanisms of conditioning can create good habits or bad habits. Our response to feelings of anger, for example, can be positive or negative. We can learn to channel anger into effective action for a good cause, or we can shoot ourselves in the foot when our anger habitually causes us to act abusively toward other people.

Sometimes we realize that our learned and conditioned patterns of response to experience are less than fully resilient. We see that stable can mean "stuck." We may find ourselves blowing our top at the least provocation or slinking away from the dinner table when our spouse reminds us we've forgotten to do something as promised — yet again. If we have been dependent on someone else to handle our affairs, we may have no clue whatsoever what to do when we've lost our home to a fire or mortgage foreclosure. In order to cope with change, we have to change how we cope. No matter what the external trigger, it's our internal response, based on our neural wiring, that's important for resilience. Often we can't change the external stressors. But we can definitely do something about our internal conditioned responses to those stressors. Through the techniques of new conditioning, deconditioning, and reconditioning that I present in part 2, we can learn to rewire previous patterns of response that are less than resilient, or even dysfunctional. The capacity to rewire exists because of the brain's other powerful mechanism of functioning: our innate neuroplasticity.

How Patterns Can Be Rewired

If conditioning is the process that encodes stable patterns in our neural circuitry, *neuroplasticity* is the mechanism that works to alter them, to rewire learned responses to stressors. Technically, neuroplasticity is the lifelong capacity of the brain to create new neurons (brain cells) and connections among neurons (neural pathways and circuits). As mentioned earlier, focusing attention on an experience stimulates the neurons related to that experience to fire. This works for internal experiences, too. When you focus attention on the conditioned pattern you want to rewire, you activate the neural networks of that pattern and cause the neurons to fire again. When you know how to harness the neuroplasticity of your brain in that moment, you can alter the pattern.

When we flare in resentment when someone cuts in front of us at the gas station, for example, we can choose instead to rewire our coping strategies to let go of the resentment. We might make allowances because we can remember a time when we were in such a hurry that we did the same thing. Instead of putting off calling the plumber to fix the leaking showerhead, we can train ourselves to take action as soon as we see the leak. Because of neuroplasticity, we can always create new pathways and circuits that are more resilient and effective in responding to the challenges in our lives.

All mental activity creates neural structure. Using neuroplasticity to strengthen brain structure is like working out at the gym to build up our muscles. (Of course, the structures of the brain aren't actually muscles; they're densely networked circuits and pathways of neurons. But strengthening the capacities of these neurons to communicate with one another, and to integrate the information being processed into new responses, is comparable to working out to strengthen our muscles.)

As Norman Doidge says in *The Brain That Changes Itself*, "If you want to lift a hundred pounds, you don't expect to succeed the first time. You start with a lighter weight and work up little by little. You actually fail to lift a hundred pounds, every day, until the day you succeed. But it is in the days when you are exerting yourself that the growth is occurring." Once you've increased the "lifting capacity" of your brain structure through self-directed neuroplasticity, you can alter any stable (even stuck) patterns of coping that aren't working. You can recover your resilience.

Conditioning and neuroplasticity are mechanisms powerful enough not only to shape the brain's software — our learned habits — but also to shape its hardware — the structures coordinated by the prefrontal cortex. To learn how to skillfully use these tools to recover our resilience, and to better understand how that shaping and strengthening happen, let's "take a peek under the hood" of the brain.

Getting to Know the Brain That Does the Wiring and Rewiring

The adult brain weighs only about three pounds, but it consumes 25 percent of the energy used by the body every day. It uses that energy to process more than fifty experiences per second. There are approximately one hundred billion neurons in the average adult brain, with additional billions of neural cells extending throughout the body. Each neuron is capable of communicating with 5,000–7,000 other neurons. The number of possible connections among neurons at any given instant is greater than the number of atoms in the known universe. The complexity of the human brain creating its neural networks, including the multitudes of its schemas, or models, of how the world works (our patterns of resilience), is staggering.

The brain learns to be resilient from both the bottom (the lower brain) up and the top (the cortex) down. The lower brain is our evolutionary inheritance from our reptilian and mammalian ancestors. Located in the "downstairs" of the brain, from the base of the skull to the midbrain, the fast-track lower brain reacts to events rapidly (in milliseconds) and automatically (requiring no conscious effort). The higher brain — located in the "upstairs" of the human cortex — evolved later through our primate ancestors and operates consciously, reflectively, and on a slow track (requiring seconds or longer).

The Lower Brain: Fast Track and Unconscious

The lower brain controls our hard-wired responses to any stressor. In evolutionary terms, these were our earliest survival strategies. (See figure 1 and table 1.) Our initial perceptions of and reactions to safety or danger are always processed first by the limbic system (the five structures of the midbrain), especially by the amygdala, our brain's 24/7 alarm center, located just below the orbitofrontal area of the prefrontal cortex. This tiny structure constantly scans signals from the environment (filtered by the thalamus) and assesses them for safety or danger — assigning them an initial appraisal of good or bad. The amygdala, like all structures of the lower brain, operates entirely without conscious awareness and draws on its own *implicit* memories — those stored outside our awareness — to distinguish between safe situations ("good") and potentially dangerous ones ("bad") that require an immediate reaction.

Signals from the body that a situation is safe are also processed by the vagus nerve in the brain stem: the "vagal brake" keeps the nervous system calm and relaxed. But when the amygdala evaluates a person or situation as dangerous, within milliseconds it sends electrical and chemical signals along neural pathways to the prefrontal cortex. The signal "Do something!" is our first automatic survival response. It involves an immediate reaching out for connection and help and further assessment of danger. This is the neurobiological

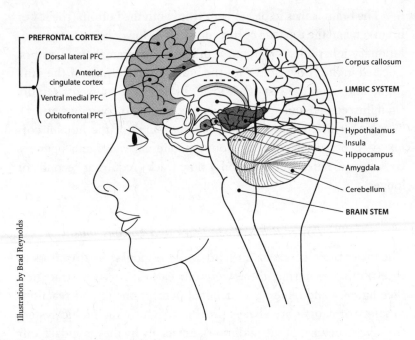

PREFRONTAL CORTEX
Dorsal lateral PFC
Anterior cingulate cortex
Ventral medial PFC
Orbitofrontal PFC

Corpus callosum

LIMBIC SYSTEM
Thalamus
Hypothalamus
Insula
Hippocampus
Amygdala

Cerebellum

BRAIN STEM

Illustration by Brad Reynolds

Figure 1. Key structures of the brain.

process behind the drive to seek connection and reassurance when we experience fear.

If no one responds to our reaching out for help, or if someone responds in a way that alarms us further, the amygdala sends a rapid cascade of chemical signals through the hypothalamus-pituitary-adrenal (HPA) axis to the *autonomic nervous system*, which regulates the muscles and organs of our body, also outside our awareness. This signal says, "Do something else": either rev up into fight-flight-freeze mode or shut down, going into submit-collapse mode, which is our secondary automatic survival response. (One branch of the vagus nerve can also directly trigger a collapse response of fainting.) The lower brain operates so fast that its signals can trigger the survival responses of fight-flight-freeze or submit-collapse even before the prefrontal cortex has a chance to direct actions to reach out and connect to others. These instinctive survival responses are

Table 1. Resonance Circuit of the Social Brain

Lower Brain	Higher Brain
Unconscious but fast	Conscious but slow
Brain stem: regulation of automatic body functions related to survival responses	Cerebral cortex: organization of sensory, motor, and conscious experiences; processing of learned interactions with the world
Limbic system: initial processing of emotions, learning, memory, approach-avoid responses	Frontal lobes: regulation of motor behaviors, language, executive functioning, decision making, abstract reasoning, and directed attention
Amygdala: initial appraisal, meaning making, emotional processing of "safe" and "dangerous," storing of learning in implicit memory, decision making based on past experience	Prefrontal cortex: executive center, master integrator (see table 2 for functions)
Thalamus: relay station for sense perceptions	Anterior cingulate cortex: focusing attention; sensing pain; coordinating thoughts, feelings, and body's responses to feelings; noticing errors
Hypothalamus: release of neurotransmitters and hormones related to body's equilibrium	Insula: sensing what's happening in body; conduit between limbic system and cortex; aids reflection on emotional experience
Hippocampus: retrieval of memories from the past; encoding of experience into explicit memory; "time stamping" of memories	Mirror neurons (not shown): distributed throughout the brain; comprehension of another's intentional behavior

what we default to when other, conscious strategies haven't been learned or are temporarily unavailable. This is why it's so essential to strengthen the prefrontal cortex to recover our resilience. A strong, mature prefrontal cortex can regulate the revving up or shutting down response of the nervous system and quell the fear response of the amygdala.

The Higher Brain: Slow Track and Conscious

The frontal lobes of the cerebral cortex, or the higher human brain (see figure 2), perform conscious processing and the functions of reasoning, reflection, language, and empathy. The structures in the

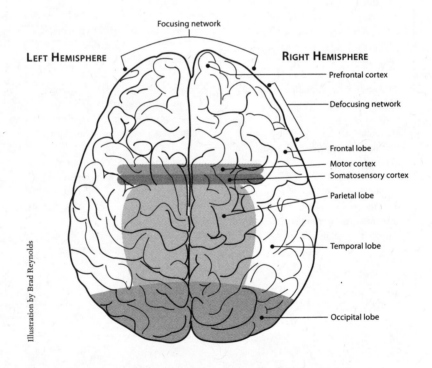

Figure 2. Key structures of the higher brain. (Structures identified in Right Hemisphere also exist in Left Hemisphere.)

frontal lobes enable us to identify and choose among options and develop new coping strategies.

The prefrontal cortex, located in the lower part of the frontal lobes, can be thought of as the executive center of the brain. It integrates information coming from the lower brain with input from the higher brain. (See table 2.) As a result of its integrative capacities, the prefrontal cortex can regulate the survival responses from the lower brain. It coordinates information from two different memory systems: implicit memory, which is outside our awareness, and explicit memory, which is within our awareness. This capacity is essential for rewiring the patterns of our earliest conditioning.

The prefrontal cortex manages the surges of our body-based emotions through conscious reflection and wise discernment, which allows us to retain energy and passion for coping and thriving while preventing us from being constantly panicked by floods of emotions or paralyzed by shutting down against the emotional flood.

The prefrontal cortex also makes possible the processes of attunement (tuning into the feelings of others), empathy (making sense of the feelings of others), and self-awareness (making sense of ourselves and our story), which enable us to efficiently rewire our brains. This rewiring is what increases our capacities for response flexibility, the neurobiological platform of resilience.

All of these executive, top-down functions are integrated by the prefrontal cortex, primarily by coordinating the functioning of the right and left hemispheres of the brain. The higher brain has two hemispheres that respond differently to experience: the right hemisphere, which is primarily associated with feelings and emotional responses, and the left hemisphere, which is associated with more rational and logical processing. The prefrontal cortex coordinates the processing of these two hemispheres, a function that is essential to encoding new and more resilient patterns of coping.

Both the right and left hemispheres perceive, process, and respond to life events consciously — with awareness. Both encode learning into explicit memory. However, they do so very differently. (See table 3.)

Table 2. Functions and Structures of the Prefrontal Cortex

Functions	Integrative Pathways
Regulating body; recovering from a stress response	Coordinating processing of lower brain and higher brain; integrating bodily sensations and emotions with thoughts, reflections, and conscious decisions
Quelling fear response of the amygdala	Integrating right hemisphere (felt sense of feelings and social-emotional self) with left hemisphere (logic and rational thought and verbal narrative of self)
Managing emotions; modulating extreme emotions	Integrating implicit (unconscious) with explicit (conscious) memories; retrieving dissociated or compartmentalized trauma memories
Attunement: tuning into another person's feelings and perspectives (or our own); sensing even without words what action is appropriate	Integrating awareness of past, present, and future; creating a continuity of self
Empathy: the thinking, feeling, imagining, and discerning that make sense of what's happening in ourselves or in another	Integrating ego states, or "parts" or voices of the personal self into a whole self
Insight and self-knowing; developing a coherent narrative of self	Managing interpersonal experience, the resonant influence of one human brain on another
Response flexibility: the ability to pause, step back, reflect, shift perspectives, create options, and choose wisely	Managing states of consciousness: the flow between doing and being, focus and spaciousness, self and nonself
Intuition: inner wisdom, different from logic; felt rather than thought	
Morality: behaviors based on empathy for the common good	

Table 2. Functions and Structures of the Prefrontal Cortex (*continued*)
Subareas of the Prefrontal Cortex
Orbitofrontal: coordinates appraisals of lower brain and higher brain; integrates information from external and internal worlds; helps regulate emotions, motivation and reward, empathy with others
Ventral medial: processes judgments about people and actions to take; ponders meaning and assesses alternatives
Dorsal lateral: working memory; play space to reshape memories

The dynamic integration of these functions and pathways supports resilience and well-being.

The many structures of the right hemisphere process experience received through our senses (such as visual images and sensations of motion) and our emotions, as well as through our relationships with others. The fusiform gyrus, a small structure in the right hemisphere, recognizes faces, interprets the emotional meaning of another person's facial expressions, and helps us regulate our own alarm by connecting to the resources of safe others. The right hemisphere processes our experiences holistically: for example, we recognize someone's face all at once rather than adding up individual perceptions of the eyes, nose, lips, and other features to make a whole. It processes any situation as a gestalt, the big picture, automatically. Because of its extensive neural connections with the limbic system in the lower brain — the source of our most primitive emotions — the right hemisphere is sometimes referred to as our "emotional brain." It is the seat of the sense of self — who we know ourselves to be in relation to the world — and the seat of our common humanity.

In contrast, the left hemisphere processes experience logically (for example, by identifying cause and effect), linearly (by

Table 3. Right and Left Hemisphere Structures and Functions

Left Hemisphere	Right Hemisphere
Verbal processing: language, speech, symbols	Nonverbal processing: visual images, body movements, emotions, experiences in relationship
Linear processing (one bit of data after another in sequence)	Holistic processing (seeing the big picture)
Logical, rational processing: abstract reasoning and analysis, cause and effect	Emotional processing, including processing of facial expressions in fusiform gyrus
	Sense of social and emotional self

Corpus callosum: links the processing of the two hemispheres (integrated by the prefrontal cortex)

Lobes of the Cerebral Cortex (see figure 2)

Occipital: visual processing

Parietal: touch, sensory perception, orienting in time and space

Temporal: auditory processing, language and memory

Somatosensory and motor: information about the body, movement

Frontal: concentration, organization, planning, reasoning, judgment, decision making, creativity, abstract thinking, emotional processing, relating to others evaluating one piece of data after another in sequence), and through language. (The verbal processing and speech centers are located on the left side of the brain.) The left hemisphere matures in the developing brain significantly later than the right and so it has fewer neural connections with the limbic system than the "emotional" right does. The left hemisphere has been dubbed the rational side of the brain: its massive powers of analysis, judgment, and planning are what have made science and civilization possible.

That nature evolved the two hemispheres so differently in effect doubles the volume of neural real estate we can use to assess, reflect on, and solve our problems. The right and left hemispheres are linked by a small band of integrative fibers called the corpus callosum. This brain structure tends to be thicker in women than in men, perhaps explaining why women sometimes process their emotions more easily than men do.

In addition to integrating the right hemisphere's felt sense of our emotions with the left hemisphere's rational assessment of them, the prefrontal cortex integrates the various facets or "parts" that make up the personal self, creating a coherent narrative of our self and a continuity of self across time. It integrates the past and the present with anticipations for the future — what we can do about the next unknown. It also integrates the focused states of "doing" with the defocused states of "being."

Three more structures enable the prefrontal cortex to coordinate the mechanisms of conditioning and neuroplasticity. The hippocampus, located next to the amygdala and technically part of the limbic system, functions as part of the cortex. It translates experiences and learning from implicit into explicit memory. The hippocampus greatly increases our capacities to make wise, conscious choices by allowing us to draw on explicit memories of what has worked previously in order to guide us in coping resiliently now.

The hippocampus doesn't become fully functional until about 2½ years of age, which is why we have "childhood amnesia" — little or no recollection of our earliest childhood. Body-based emotional memories, however, still operate implicitly — below the radar — lifelong. I discuss how significantly these early implicit memories affect our resilience in chapter 2.

The anterior cingulate cortex is adjacent to and functions almost as a part of the prefrontal cortex. It allows the brain to focus attention. The anterior cingulate also functions as a sort of switching station between the right and left hemispheres, enabling integration of our thoughts and our feelings.

Tucked behind the prefrontal cortex is the insula, a body of cortical tissue that folds down into the limbic system. The insula serves as a vital conduit between the higher and lower brains; it allows us to know consciously our body's responses to internal or external signals.

The insula also helps us interpret the meaning of other people's behavior through mirror neurons. These neurons fire in various parts of the cortex when we observe another person's actions, and they help us learn new behaviors by imitating others. They also help us comprehend the intentions of other people's behavior when we see them act in a particular way. For instance, when we see someone across a room lifting her hand, mirror neurons help us discern whether she is waving to attract attention or reaching up to get something off a shelf.

The discovery of mirror neurons by neuroscientists is a good example of extrapolation from scientific data to clinical applications. Neuropsychologists have hypothesized that mirror neurons also allow us to feel and comprehend the emotions of another person and could be the neurological basis of empathy. As we observe another person's nonverbal communication, neurons are firing in our brains, mirroring what we're seeing and sending the signal of that mirroring to the insula so that we feel in our own bodies what the other person is feeling in theirs. The insula then sends these emotional signals to the prefrontal cortex to be interpreted.

Three Circuits of Self-Directed Neuroplasticity

The prefrontal cortex integrates the functioning of all the brain structures you have learned about in this chapter, processing our experiences through what I call three circuits of self-directed neuroplasticity. The first is an *interpersonal resonance circuit*. This resonance circuit allows us to use interactions between our brain and another (resilient) human brain to strengthen the prefrontal cortex and to learn better strategies for coping. You will learn to use this resonance circuit in chapter 4.

The second circuit is what I call a *focusing network*; it is the basis of two of the three processes of brain change you learn to use in chapter 6. The focusing network uses mostly the structures in the midline of the brain — the brain stem, the amygdala, the hippocampus, the anterior cingulate cortex, the insula, and the prefrontal cortex itself. We can think of the prefrontal cortex using these midline (or *medial*) structures to focus attention on a specific experience, encode strategies of coping into the neural circuitry, and pull together the sense of self — our personal history, personality, and identity and our sense of how we operate in the world. The focusing network is purposeful and self-referencing. The processes of new conditioning and reconditioning (discussed in chapter 6) rewire the coping strategies encoded by this network.

I call the third circuit a *defocusing network*. It incorporates the functioning of structures on the sides of the cortex (a lateral circuit), level with and above the ears, to orient us in time and space. When our attention is drawn away from an intense focus on immediate events, as in a daydream or reverie, the neural circuitry in our brain can relax. The brain is free to create new associations among the networks of old encoded responses. This defocusing network, operating especially in the right hemisphere, is the basis of the deconditioning discussed in chapter 6, which allows us to unlearn and then rewire the strategies encoded by the focusing network.

These brain structures and networks function together to

support our capacities of resilience. Here's a simple example of how it happens. I can startle as quickly as anybody when I see a spider in the bathtub. My fear response is a reflex hard-wired into my lower brain, operating to keep me alive when I suddenly encounter a potentially dangerous situation. However, my higher brain has spent years learning about spiders, and I know that the spiders in my bathtub are almost certainly harmless. I also know that they can't crawl up the slippery side of the tub to attack me, and I've learned that spiders are, in fact, beneficial allies in my garden, eating all kinds of bugs. The startle reflex to the threat of the spider in my tub is now tempered by reflection from my higher brain.

I can also choose how I respond to my startle. Killing the spider would get rid of the threat right away. But I know that I will feel better about myself if, rather than squashing it and flushing it down the drain, I scoop it up with a cup and a stiff piece of paper and take it out to my garden. (In this situation, I'm a much bigger threat to the spider than it is to me.) I have trained myself to keep a plastic cup and old greeting card on the shelf in the bathroom for just such purposes.

My response in this situation illustrates the value of strengthening the capacities of the prefrontal cortex to rewire the brain to employ the five Cs of coping. I remain *calm*. I can see *clearly* that the spider is not a threat. I've become *competent* at dealing with this situation. I am *connected* to resources: I have my "spider transport" handy. All of this knowledge and conditioning helps me feel *courageous* rather than frightened when I next encounter a spider in the tub.

Pulling It All Together

In this chapter, you have been introduced to several key points about resilience and your brain.

- Capacities for resilience — bouncing back when you're thrown off center — are evolutionarily hard-wired into your brain, part of your birthright for coping with the stresses inherent in being alive and human.

- Interactions with others — such as experiencing empathic, responsive parenting — instill a sense of safety and trust, a sense of importance and being loved, and a sense of competence and mastery that become your brain's first templates of resilience and serve as lifelong buffers from stress and trauma.

- That sense of security supports healthy self-development, self-regulation, self-confidence, and the maturing of the prefrontal cortex of the brain. The prefrontal cortex coordinates other brain structures and circuits to use conditioning and neuroplasticity to learn and stabilize patterns of resilience and to unlearn or rewire them later when necessary.

In the next chapter, you will learn some of the common ways in which the early learning of resilience can go awry, as it does in all of us more than we would like, and how, when that happens, you can use the strengthening of the prefrontal cortex and the brain's innate neuroplasticity to get your resilience back on track.

CHAPTER TWO

How the Wiring In of Resilience Can Go Awry

All the world is full of suffering. It is also full of overcoming.

— Helen Keller

As our brains develop, it is all too easy for the learning of resilient coping strategies to go awry, causing us to encode responses and behaviors that are unproductive or even harmful. We may have learned to respond to thwarted plans by threatening people rather than negotiating. We may pretend to not see bullying on the playground as long as our kid isn't involved, rather than taking up the cause of safety and supervision at recess with the school administration. We may hang up the phone in irritation when the customer service representative puts us on hold again, leaving our business unfinished, rather than proactively asking to talk to a supervisor directly. This chapter examines five possible glitches in the ways our brains process experience that can derail the development of our resilience, and then it looks at how we can use neuroplasticity to restore our resilience.

1. Problems in Learning Strategies of Resilience from Others

Chapter 1 shows how a secure attachment between a growing child and his or her parents supports the development of resilience and enhances the maturation of the brain's prefrontal cortex. John Bowlby and other attachment researchers also identified three other styles of attachment that are less successful in developing resilience and may even derail it. Portions of these may resonate with your own experience. If they do, remember that these are not permanent conditions. In later chapters of this book you will learn how to strengthen the functioning of the prefrontal cortex and rewire these patterns to recover your resilience.

Insecure-Avoidant Attachment Leads to Coping That Is Stable but Not Always Flexible

When a parent is indifferent or distant, paying scant attention to the complex (and sometimes overwhelming) inner life of a baby and missing or ignoring the baby's attempts to connect, the baby's neural circuits begin to encode a feeling that "I'm not important. I don't matter. How foolish of me to ask for attention." As these circuits are reinforced through repetition, that feeling can solidify into a kind of rigid self-reliance: "Knock, knock — nobody home; I guess it's all up to me."

If a parent is dismissive, rejecting, or downright critical, the baby toddling toward childhood begins to internalize the message "I'm bad, not good enough, not worthy." The hurt, shame, and loneliness of such experiences can be too much to bear, and the neural circuits conditioned by these experiences begin a defensive process of walling off or shutting down against emotions or connections with people. With that rigid walling off, the prefrontal cortex doesn't develop its full range of neural flexibility. This pattern is known as insecure-avoidant attachment.

These strategies for protection may serve the child's short-term need to cope, but they take a toll. A child who has experienced this style of early conditioning learns to avoid many emotional experiences as potentially painful. She may fear interacting with people and withdraw. It is better to feel nothing at all than to feel so much pain; it is better to be alone than to risk being repeatedly hurt. In this emotional environment, it becomes harder and harder for the prefrontal cortex and related structures to take in new experiences and develop new strategies. In extreme cases, the neural circuitry can become like a neural cement: patterns of response become more and more rigid rather than remaining fluid and receptive to change, and the capacity to adapt is lost.

Adults who have learned to cope by shutting down their emotions and narrowing their range of relational experiences can nonetheless be phenomenally successful in this world. There is a value in learning to rely on oneself, to be able to forge ahead without asking for help or needing guidance. Such individuals can develop a great aptitude for focusing on the nuts and bolts of a complex external world rather than navigating a messy inner swamp. The lone ranger can deal.

But researchers have documented that the insecure-avoidant style of coping can lead to a compulsive self-reliance, a continual minimizing and devaluing of other people. As we grow older, this style can also cause a deep discomfort with a person's own feelings or those of others, even when these individuals want to open their hearts and feel concern and compassion. The old, conditioned patterns of coping can lead to real fears of intimacy, vulnerability, and dependency, and a marked inability to learn anything new. If it becomes rigid enough, this coping style precludes learning how to feel and to relate to others well.

Insecure-Anxious Attachment Leads to Coping That Is Flexible but Not Always Stable

When a parent is consistently inconsistent, sometimes attentive and loving and at other times harsh or punitive, sometimes overinvolved and at other times off in their own world, the child doesn't know which end is up or what's coming next. She develops an excessive focus on the parent just to survive and may become one of the compulsive caregivers our society actually relies on to keep itself going. In consequence, she cannot focus sufficiently on her growing self, and many important neural circuits remain underdeveloped and unintegrated in her brain. The prefrontal cortex doesn't stabilize fully.

A person who has experienced this style of early conditioning can experience a sense of inner quicksand. Patterns of coping remain in the chaos of a neural swamp rather than solidifying into stable circuits. Adults who never felt secure with a parent or sure of themselves are painfully subject to abandonment fears and can be hypervigilant about loss of connection. The capacity for resilience can be too easily derailed to become passivity, an anxious preoccupation of what others think of them, or a sense of victimhood.

Disorganized Attachment Leads to Coping That Is Neither Stable nor Flexible

This is the style least likely to occur, but inevitably derailing of resilience when it does. A history of unresolved trauma or abuse in a parent can cause episodes of dissociation or "checking out" — a momentary neural disintegration. When this happens to a parent, the child may develop the sense that the parent has disappeared, triggering an implicit sense of threat to his or her own survival. When a parent abuses a child, whether just once or continually, the child experiences the parent as a source of fear and pain rather than as the child's one guaranteed safe haven. In either case, the child may want to run to the parent for soothing and protection, but she finds that doing so is way too scary.

In this environment, the child's developing neural integration can be stalled. The prefrontal cortex is at risk of not developing its capacities to integrate multiple functions of the brain. The child may still be able to learn more functional coping mechanisms from people other than the parent. She may reach out to other people for help, care for others as a way to get help, or become brilliantly, if rigidly, self-reliant, not needing any help. Or she, like the parent, may experience episodes of helplessness, paralysis, dissociation, and fragmentation — collapsing rather than coping. We wouldn't be able to function as adults if our brains were this disorganized much of the time. But the vulnerability to falling into even momentary disorganization puts the possibility of being reliably resilient at risk.

How Early Attachment Conditions Our Resilience

The first two and a half years of life are crucial to the development of the prefrontal cortex. The brain is not only learning strategies of resilience but also developing its own ability to create such strategies. When the functioning of the prefrontal cortex itself is compromised, it becomes much more difficult to unlearn ineffective coping strategies and replace them with better ones.

Neuroscientists and developmental psychologists have demonstrated repeatedly that these four general styles of attachment and coping remain stable over a lifetime — reliably so 85 percent of the time. Unless new experiences cause a rewiring of the old circuits, the patterns of coping we learn as toddlers become our default responses to life's perils and pitfalls. "As the twig is bent, so grows the tree" holds true for the nature of our brain functioning as well as for nature itself.

For example, we may have learned that if we didn't do what our parents wanted us to do, they wouldn't like it (or us!) and they would react with anger, indifference, or scorn. In consequence, we may later find ourselves too easily complying with other people's wishes or demands, to the detriment of our own well-being, without realizing which implicit habits or rules in our brains are driving this response. If, as children, we learned to believe from other people that we were not good enough in some way, that core belief will very likely operate unconsciously for the rest of our lives, *unless we learn how to change it.*

Fortunately for those of us who didn't experience optimal conditioning early on, we can learn new skills and strategies of coping and develop "earned" secure attachment from new experiences with other people. We can learn resilience through relationships with people who are more resilient than we are. We can harness the neuroplasticity of our brains to rewire the patterns of our previous conditioning. We can even rebuild the brain structures needed to do that rewiring. All of this you will learn to do in part 2.

2. Problems in the Self-Reinforcing of Conditioned Habits

A powerful and efficient outcome of the brain's mechanism of conditioning is that once we have learned ways of responding to a certain event or stressor, the patterns of response become deeply ingrained in our neural circuitry; we don't have to think about them anymore. For example, we may sometimes have trouble remembering the person's name when we recognize a friend of a friend at a local school board meeting. If we have conditioned ourselves to reach out for a handshake with a friendly "Hi, I'm so and so; please tell me your name again," we can engage with them using a skillful habit rather than saying nothing or ignoring the person out of embarrassment.

As we learned in chapter 1, conditioning is neither good nor bad in itself: it is simply one way that the brain learns. Conditioning becomes a problem when it reinforces unhelpful patterns of response, ingraining them into our neural circuitry, where they can become extremely difficult to budge. If we habitually get anxious before taking a test or speaking in public, for example, this anxiety tends to get worse over time, not better. If we have had difficulty making major decisions in the past — whether to join the military or apply to graduate school, to buy a home or sell the home that's been in the family for three generations — chances are we'll have difficulty making the next big decision as well. If we witnessed both of our parents frequently handling conflict by walking out the door in tight-lipped anger, chances are that under enough stress, walking out the door in tight-lipped anger will be our default method for handling conflict, too.

Just as traces of rain that wash down a hillside will eventually create gullies in the earth, the reinforcement of these neural pathways can make it very hard to respond to a new experience differently and to create new grooves or pathways in our circuitry. Once we are stuck in a less-than-resilient pattern, our conditioning makes it difficult to get unstuck and learn anything new, even when we're trying very, very hard.

Negative patterns, learned early or late, may become self-reinforcing: the patterns themselves act as filters that preclude or distort new learning. We find ourselves in a habit of procrastination, of perennial indecisiveness, of disappearing when we hear, "Honey, we need to talk," or throwing a tantrum when other people disappear on us.

When our strategies for coping become too rigid and constricted, remain too chaotic and unstable, or even fall into paralysis and collapse, they become maladaptive and defensive. We get stuck. We can't forgive someone for stealing our girlfriend or getting the promotion we knew we deserved — fifteen years ago. We insist on "my way or the highway" even when that way leads to divorce or dismissal. We find it impossible to speak up for ourselves at the dinner table or a company lunch; we find it just as impossible to take an assertiveness workshop that might help us do so.

When we're stuck, our capacities for flexible response contract. We begin to suffer from either inner rigidity (neural cement) or inner chaos (neural swamp) when faced with outer dilemmas and disasters. When we bounce three checks in a row, we yell about the stupidity of the bank rather than taking thirty minutes to balance the checkbook. A friend suggests a camping weekend, but we get overwhelmed by the online search for the perfect campground and wind up staying home.

Getting stuck in self-reinforcing, defensive coping patterns can have tragic consequences. Our neighbors managed to rebuild their home six months after the tornado destroyed it, but we haven't been able to find our way through the insurance maze after three years. Our sister-in-law is unthinkingly passing on to her teenage daughter the same alcoholic binge-rage patterns she learned from her own mother.

To recover our resilience and unlearn these bad habits means using tools to harness our brain's neuroplasticity to completely rewire these entrenched negative coping strategies. Chapter 6 and part 2 show you how to do this safely, efficiently, and permanently.

3. When Bad Habits Become Buried in Implicit Memory

As human beings we pride ourselves, and rightfully so, on the phenomenal capacities of our higher, "thinking" brain to learn from past experience, sort through complex issues, and resolve current problems. We recall previous coping strategies that were processed consciously and stored in our explicit memory; we intentionally reflect on our options and deliberately choose the best strategy for the current circumstances.

However, we may be giving too much credit to the higher brain for these responses. Neuroscientists have discovered that about 80 percent of the neural instructions for behavior are recorded in implicit memory, outside our conscious awareness. Driving home from work on automatic pilot while thinking about something completely different is an example of operating on implicit memory.

Implicit neural activation is a powerful influence on our behaviors. For example, if you are bitten by a dog at six years of age, you will probably store a conscious memory of the event itself, as well as how you and your parents coped with it. You can consciously retrieve that memory and remember what you learned from the experience. Later, when you encounter another dog that scares you, you know why, and you can consciously choose how to respond.

If, however, you are bitten by a dog at six *months* of age, your brain has not yet developed the capacity to process that event or store the memory explicitly. Neither the memory of the dog biting you, nor the knowledge of how you and your parents coped — resiliently or not — is available to your conscious memory. But the memory is still stored implicitly in the form of body sensations and emotions and may affect the way you cope with other dogs later. Whenever you encounter another dog, dangerous or not, the implicit memory may automatically make you feel scared, but you may not understand why. (Of course, the later dog may in fact be dangerous, but often we feel fear because of a past implicit memory rather than because it is warranted in the current situation.)

Even when we are old enough to process experiences explicitly, many are forgotten; but they remain stored in our implicit memory and affect our choices and behaviors in ways we aren't aware of. My client Margaret went into a tailspin one night when Daniel, the guy she had been dating, didn't call her when he said he would. When she put in an urgent call to me, I thought it was understandable to be disappointed, worried, and upset, but Margaret's agitation suggested something deeper was going on. As we talked her reaction through, I asked Margaret when she had ever felt that same kind of panic in her past. She immediately remembered two incidents that happened when she was five years old. Twice her dad had promised to pick her up from kindergarten and failed to show up. She had been left alone, with no teachers around, too young to get home by herself, helpless and afraid. Daniel's failing to call when he said he would was enough to bring up all the feelings of helplessness and abandonment encoded in her neural circuitry by her dad's failure to keep his promise. Margaret's stress response was entirely tied to her past.

To recondition this unresolved trauma memory, I asked Margaret to imagine that both times her dad had forgotten to pick her up, she had walked back into the school and asked her teacher to call her dad. In this imagined rewrite, her dad arrived to pick her up within five minutes. Pairing the old memory of helplessness with the new sense of being empowered, taking action to get the help and response she needed, rewired Margaret's neural circuitry. She could remember the previous events with more equanimity and feel more resourceful. And her current experience with Daniel was no longer linked to her previous trauma. The next day she was able to talk things through with him calmly and get their relationship back on track.

Implicit memories have no time stamp. All the body sensations, emotions, and even views and beliefs about ourselves and our capacities encoded from the past event are vividly present, with *no* awareness that what we're experiencing right now is a memory. Because it feels so real, it must be happening now.

Researchers know that the coping styles we learn from attachment behaviors stabilize in our neural circuitry by eighteen months of age and continue to operate well into adulthood. Since the hippocampus doesn't fully mature until we're about two and a half years old, our default coping strategies are already deeply embedded in our implicit memory by the time the hippocampus begins to translate raw experience into explicit memories. Thus our earliest strategies of resilience are encoded in our brain's neural circuitry before we have any conscious choice about them or conscious awareness of them.

These automatic ways of coping then continue to operate, becoming the internal working model for the ways we respond to all the hiccups and hurricanes of our lives. We can react in milliseconds to any perception of safety or threat precisely as we have learned in our attachment relationships, with no sense whatsoever that our behavior is deriving from a memory, or any awareness of where that original learning came from. Unless we alter our patterns of coping using the practices described in part 2, these strategies tend to remain our default reactions well into adulthood.

At the same time that the hippocampus is maturing enough to convert raw experiences into explicitly encoded neural networks, the left hemisphere of the cortex is maturing enough to put words to those experiences. At age two to three, we develop the capacities to process our experiences both consciously and verbally, thus enormously expanding our options for learning and resilience.

These new capacities of conscious reflection and articulation overlie the previously encoded, unconscious coping strategies that remain more oriented toward survival and continue to operate lifelong. They help us consciously learn new patterns of resilience that can be more oriented toward thriving:

- remembering the fourteen times we've already resolved an argument with a brother-in-law and trusting we can do so again;

- spending the first week after losing a job repeating like a mantra, "I'm not alone; I'm not the only one; others have been through this; someone can help," and then contacting ten friends who might help us find a new job;
- watching films like *The King's Speech* that remind us of the power of perseverance and deep friendship to overcome adversity.

Even so, the implicit memory glitch remains. Learning resilience through conscious effort still rests on the foundation of our earliest, unconscious conditioning. Most of the time, when our early conditioning is resilient and serves us well, we're blithely unaware of that scaffolding. And even when there are occasional wobbles in the foundation, our intentional work with implicit memories later in life can take us a long way toward overcoming our early, unhelpful learned responses. But in times of threat or danger, our brains may automatically respond in the patterns we learned first.

It's humbling to realize the power of our implicit memories: *anything* we learn or come to believe later in life, about ourselves, about others, or about how the world works, can be overridden or hijacked by our earliest learning. And it often is. We can experience that response from implicit memory with such force and vividness that we have no sense whatsoever that we're experiencing an emotional flashback to our earliest ways of coping rather than something that is happening now. (Part 2 shows you how to skillfully rewire those implicit memories.)

4. The Negativity Bias of the Brain

Our early ancestors survived on the savannah for millions of years because our lower brain evolved to react almost instantaneously to threat or danger. It is better that our reflexes cause us to jump out of the way of a snake that turns out to be a stick than to mistake a snake for a stick, step on it, get bitten, and die. Survive first, thrive later: that's the motto of the lower brain. The well-documented tendency of our lower brain to encode negative, fear-based memories more readily into our unconscious memory than positive ones is referred to as *negativity bias.*

As we've seen, the lower brain operates from the first moments of life, while the higher brain, with its capacities to reflect and discern options, takes several years to mature. Within the higher brain, the right hemisphere matures earlier than the left hemisphere and consequently has more densely networked connections with the lower brain than does the left. This means that the right hemisphere has evolved to focus far more attention on experiences that trigger the more primitive emotions of fear, anger, or shame related to our survival than feelings of delight, carrying forward the negativity bias of the lower brain. We might wish philosophically that this were not the case, but this is, for better or worse, how our brains develop; this is how we as a species have survived.

Our early conditioning influences the strength of this negativity bias. If we learn adaptive ways of coping with fear and other negative feelings early on, we can respond to a threat by calming and soothing ourselves. We are more likely to pause in a moment of anger and reflect on the most constructive response in the situation. We can respond to potential shaming by connecting to resources that remind us that we are loved and cherished. Our responses stabilize in the direction of the five Cs of coping. If, however, our conditioning simply reinforces the body's survival responses of fight-flight-freeze or submit-collapse, we become less resilient and more vulnerable to experiences of terror, rage, self-loathing, pessimism, and depression. Part 2 examines ways to harness the brain's neuroplasticity to overcome this negativity bias.

5. When Bad Things Happen to Good People

Most of us have learned strategies that enable us to cope adequately with the everyday ups and downs and stressors of our lives, either from our conditioning early on (a blessing) or from the school of hard knocks later (a triumph). Learning to cope with adversity through bitter experience can, in fact, be a good thing. Triumph over trouble builds character. As Eleanor Roosevelt said, "You gain strength, courage, and confidence by every experience by which you really stop to look fear in the face. You are able to say to yourself, 'I lived through this horror. I can take the next thing that comes along.'" If we do cope well with seemingly adverse events, if we deploy our five Cs of coping, if we come to terms with what has happened, then we are not traumatized. We deal, and we can move on.

Trauma is different. Trauma, by definition, is the overwhelming of our capacities to cope. We often use the word *trauma* to describe experiences that can temporarily overwhelm some people: visiting the dentist, flying on an airplane, failing an exam, being sued, causing a fender bender. More serious examples — being assaulted, losing a home or a family member in a natural disaster, watching a buddy die in combat, crushing a child or a dog under the wheels of our car — are experiences that could overwhelm *anyone's* capacities to cope. It's whether we can cope or not that determines whether an event is called trauma, not the event itself.

When we can't consciously come to terms with a potentially traumatizing event — by acknowledging, "That happened in the past, but I'm okay now" — then our brain protects us from further overwhelm by isolating the memories of the event in a "trauma capsule" buried in implicit memory, no longer connected with the brain's conscious processing of the experience or with other memories or learning that could help us cope.

Once a trauma memory has become dissociated and placed into a trauma capsule, any new event can be unconsciously linked with that implicit memory. Sudden braking in a car can trigger implicit memories of an earlier car accident. A banging door can trigger implicit memories of Daddy's coming home drunk. A bounced check can trigger implicit memories of the family running out of money to pay the bills. So our loss of resilience is not so much locked into any particular external event as it is caused by the meaning our brain attributes to that event and our response to that perceived meaning. This encapsulated memory — of body sensations, emotions, beliefs, and meanings — can make us vulnerable to losing our resilience in the face of stress and trauma later. We now know that even responses to trauma that have been deeply buried in our implicit-only memory can be rewired. Recovering that resilience involves not avoiding the storms of life but learning to be at peace within ourselves in the midst of those storms.

Traumas, if left unresolved, however, can damage the hardware of the brain itself. Traumatizing experiences — a rape or abortion with no one to turn to for help and support afterward, an emergency leg amputation as a result of a car accident, losing someone you tried to rescue in a flood to the rapid current flowing downstream — can have a devastating effect on brain functioning. Trauma floods the brain with the stress hormone cortisol. Cortisol gets us moving quickly to save our lives, but it also kills brain cells in the hippocampus. When we lose too many brain cells in the hippocampus, we can no longer learn from our experience. This damage compromises our ability to recover from the trauma. If repeated trauma happens at the age when the hippocampus is just developing, the floods of cortisol can derail the maturing of the very structure we need to organize our experience into conscious memories that we can learn from later. Damage to the hippocampus can also delay or inhibit the maturation of the prefrontal cortex. Even in these circumstances, however, the neuroplasticity of the brain makes it possible to recover from the damage of repeated trauma. You learn how to rebuild the structures of the hippocampus and the prefrontal cortex in part 2.

No Blame in This Game:
Repairing Our Less-than-Optimal Conditioning

Glitches in how our brains learn from experience can derail our resilience and make it hard to cope with everything we need to cope with. The inevitable reality of human conditioning is that while most of us experienced good-enough conditioning early in life, at least some of the time, all of us experienced less-than-optimal conditioning as well. The natural capacities of our brains to remain open and flexible — to learn to respond in wholesome ways to both inner and outer experience — can get derailed in one way or another, which can have negative and even tragic consequences. The misery we are heirs to as human beings is not the result of our true essence but is the product of our inescapable conditioning. We can lose touch with our capacities for flexibility and resilience and thus compromise our well-being. We can become reactive and miserable.

Researchers have shown us that no one — not the Dalai Lama, not the president of the United States, not the most beloved child — is exempt from this process. Less-than-optimal conditioning is the human condition. Does that need to be a permanent problem? No. Modern brain science gives us more evidence every day that we can harness the brain's innate neuroplasticity to change its functioning and even its structure. We have every reason to be *en-courage-d* when it comes to recovering our resilience.

It's important, as we learn how to recover our resilience, not to dwell on shame or blame about how and why our resilience went awry. Instead, as the new positive psychology movement is teaching us, we can use the power of new conditioning to install and sustain positive patterns of resilience and coping. We can use the practice of mindfulness — nonjudgmental awareness and acceptance — to reverse depression, the practice of gratitude to heal from grief, and the practice of shifting perspectives to create options. And that's precisely what this book aims to teach you to do.

Neuroplasticity has always existed in our brains, even though our understanding of it is relatively recent. It has been at work for millions of years, using new experiences in life to generate the complex neural pathways that underpin all learning, all individual development, all personal growth and self-transformation. Neuroplasticity has also generated the densely networked brain structures and the interactions between them that underlie the advancement of all human cultures.

Only in the past twenty years have advances in brain-imaging technology allowed scientists to probe the mysteries of the brain in action. We know now that our brains can create new brain structures to recover from traumatic brain injury and psychological trauma. Thanks to this new understanding of neuroplasticity, we know that the brain itself is inherently resilient: capable of responding flexibly, adaptively to trauma, stress, and plain old everyday life.

Our brains can recondition and rewire themselves on their own over time. If we leave this process to chance, however, the recovery of resilience may be very haphazard, slow, and uncertain. Unless we deliberately choose to learn how to work with the gift of our neuroplasticity, how well our brains respond to adversity might even get worse over time. We all know folks whose lives, hammered by unrelenting stress and trauma, have gone downhill. No matter what conditions we currently face in our lives, neuroscience is increasingly teaching us which tools and techniques we can use to best harness the brain's innate neuroplasticity to fully recover our innate capacities of resilience. These are the tools and techniques that help people move from overwhelm, confusion, negativity, anxiety, depression and trauma, through resourcing and neural programming, toward a mature and stable resilience. We can learn how to live our lives with equanimity, energy, and a sense of well-being.

Pulling It All Together

Yes, our innate capacities for resilience are vulnerable to being derailed by evolutionary realities.

- Our earliest strategies for resilience are developed in interactions with other brains. Depending on how those early interactions go, we may encode coping strategies that are unstable (a neural swamp) or inflexible (neural cement).
- Repeated experiences reinforce the conditioning of these patterns in the human brain: we create good or bad habits of coping that, if reinforced without awareness, become harder and harder to change.

- The brain's innate negativity bias helps us survive as individuals and as a species, but it can skew our response to stressors toward the negative as we grow older.
- Trauma overwhelms our coping strategies and can even overwhelm our capacities to recover.

Here's the good news:

- Although early experiences do much of the initial wiring of our brains, later experiences, especially healthy relational ones, can rewire our brains to allow us to cope differently and more resiliently.
- The changes we make in our behaviors can last because we're creating new brain structures and circuits to support them. Even learning how to rewire our brains rewires our brains as we go along.
- New experiences can strengthen the functioning of the prefrontal cortex itself. The more skillful the prefrontal cortex is — the more easily it integrates information from other parts of the brain to help us make wise decisions — the more resilient we can become.

By applying the tools and techniques offered in the next several chapters, you can accelerate your own process of recovering resilience and effect changes that are both immediate and permanent. You can create a solid neural platform for thriving.

PART TWO

HARNESSING THE BRAIN'S NEUROPLASTICITY TO RECOVER YOUR RESILIENCE

CHAPTER THREE

Using Mindfulness to Foster Self-Awareness and Flexible Responses

It is not the strongest of the species that survives, nor the most intelligent that survives. It is the one that is the most adaptive to change.

— CHARLES DARWIN

A CLIENT I'D BEEN SEEING for several months came in one day beaming with success. Ellen had often suffered from anxiety in dealing with computers and other new technologies. She had grown up with typewriters and rotary phones, not laptops and cell phones. Several times she had arrived for a session in tears of frustration after a disaster at work, not being able to figure out how to do something on her computer that most eight-year-olds could handle. We'd been working on finding people who could teach her what she needed to know and on developing her trust in herself to learn and master the necessary skills.

In this session, she reported a huge breakthrough. "Yesterday my computer crashed, and instead of going into shock, I found myself saying, 'Oh, that's a big problem to solve.' I almost laughed, it was so out of character for me to be okay with something like that."

Ellen was describing an important, definable moment of developing a new way of coping. Because she had sought the help of people who could teach her the computer skills she needed, and because she had seen her situation clearly and hadn't panicked, Ellen was able to take the steps that would resolve the problem, delighting in her trust in herself to do so.

Like Ellen, when we realize we need to change the way we're coping with life's dramas and traumas, we can harness the power of neuroplasticity in our brain to create those changes. But we need to learn how.

Two Essential Catalysts for Self-Directed Brain Change

Harnessing neuroplasticity — what Jeffrey Schwartz, a neuropsychiatrist at UCLA, calls "self-directed neuroplasticity" — is essentially about choosing. All mental activity creates new neural structure. Any experience rewires the brain in some way. When we want to direct that rewiring — for example, when we want to rewire specifically for resilience — it's necessary to carefully choose the new experiences that will help create that new neural structure and rewire old pathways effectively, efficiently, and safely.

Using self-directed neuroplasticity means focusing attention on specific new experiences or on old patterns that we want to rewire. When we focus attention on old patterns, we activate, or "light up," the specific networks of neurons where those patterns are stored. In directing how those neurons fire and rewire, we want to avoid reinforcing negative patterns. We don't want to retraumatize ourselves or etch the grooves of a dysfunctional or traumatic pattern any deeper.

Two practices of choosing new experiences that science shows to be powerful catalysts in rewiring our brain are *mindfulness* and *empathy*. These practices are drawn from two very different paradigms: mindfulness from the 2,500-year-old Buddhist contemplative tradition, and empathy from 150 years of Western relational psychology. But both offer well-proven tools to reduce suffering in ourselves and others and to cope wisely with unwelcome changes.

Mindfulness — the steady, nonjudgmental awareness and acceptance of experience — leads to self-awareness and to shifts in our perspectives that allow us to see clearly what's happening and how we are reacting, to respond to triggers and traumas with far more open-mindedness, and to face the process of necessary change with far more flexibility and tolerance. These capacities are all hallmarks of emerging resilience. Empathy — a wholesome practice of connection and acceptance — expands our awareness of resources we can draw on, both within ourselves and from others. This is another hallmark of emerging resilience.

Research is increasingly showing that practices of mindfulness and empathy are among the most powerful agents of brain change known to science. Both can catalyze brain change and guide it in a positive direction. Both strengthen the functioning of the prefrontal cortex to rewire old patterns. Both can safely and efficiently process carefully chosen new experiences to maximize that rewiring in the brain and sustain the desired changes over time. When we can see a situation clearly and accept compassionately what we are seeing, we can rewire old patterns without harm to ourselves. Mindfulness and empathy create a safe mental environment for the three major processes of self-directed neuroplasticity you will use to do that rewiring.

Neuroscience is also increasingly validating the effectiveness — even the necessity — of integrating the two practices of mindfulness and empathy. *Mindful empathy* is our single most important tool for strengthening the functioning of the prefrontal cortex. That strengthening in itself leads to more integrated functioning in the brain. Using experiential exercises to develop mindful empathy in this chapter and the next is the first step toward harnessing your neuroplasticity to recover your resilience.

Seeing Clearly with Mindfulness

Although a number of different skills can be grouped under the umbrella of mindfulness, in essence, being mindful simply means paying attention to the experience of the moment, whether inner or outer, with an acceptance or friendliness toward the experience and without judgment or ill will. Rather than acting as a cognitive analysis of experience, mindfulness operates in the brain as an embodied inquiry into the true nature of whatever we are experiencing.

The practice of mindfulness — training the brain to focus its attention and to strengthen conscious awareness — allows us to see our conditioned patterns of response clearly so that we can get unstuck from them when we need to. Mindfulness trains the brain to become astutely aware of our experiences in the moment and of our responses to those experiences, even of our enduring patterns of response (resilient or not), and entire styles and strategies of coping and their effectiveness.

With mindfulness, we begin to notice that all experience unfolds moment by moment. We notice our how breathing changes: inhalation, exhalation, quick or slow, deep or shallow. Our mood changes over longer periods. Maybe I felt hunky-dory two hours ago, but now the job of fixing a leaky faucet has turned into a major and expensive replumbing of the entire house, and I'm starting to feel deeply worried and unsure of what to do. Or maybe this morning I was so annoyed with my nephew that I wanted to ship him off to Australia, but now, watching him build an airport out of Lego blocks, I can't even remember what the fuss was about.

As we mindfully focus on our experiences in the moment, we realize that it is in the nature of all experience to change: this too shall pass. That insight into the impermanence of all experience helps us to begin to unpack what's actually happening, to see clearly all the elements contributing to the situation and understand how they, too, are changing, no matter how inescapable or compelling the experience feels to us in the moment. Mindful awareness — observing and reflecting — allows us to *step back from the experience of the moment and observe it from a larger field of awareness that is not any of those experiences*, that is larger than any of those patterns. With that awareness, we can begin to see different possibilities for responding.

Seeing things from this awareness, we're present and engaged, noticing and curious, but we're not embedded or trapped in the experience. This moment of pause helps us discern new perspectives and options that weren't visible to us before. Ellen experienced this new awareness when she was able to step back from the computer crash and consider options she wouldn't have seen in her previous state of panic and frustration.

With mindful attention we can choose a different, more effective and more wholesome response. We learn to respond flexibly, and flexibility is the essence of resilience.

Mindfulness of Breathing Builds Neural Structure

We can begin cultivating this mindfulness by focusing our attention on one specific object of awareness — in Eastern wisdom traditions, usually the breath. Research has shown that even this introductory level of mindfulness practice can increase the cell volume of the anterior cingulate cortex (the brain structure that focuses our attention) and other associated brain structures. That makes sense; the more we use any structures of the cortex, the more they can grow new cells. Studies show that violinists who have mastered rapid fingering in the left hand have greater cell volume in the area of the motor cortex responsible for that dexterity. Taxi drivers in London, who are required to memorize the city's many circuitous streets and alleyways and then use that information day after day, show a measurable increase in the volume of the area of the brain responsible for directional orientation. In the same way that working out our muscles at the gym actually builds them, focusing our attention strengthens the structures that our brain uses to focus that attention. This helps us see clearly what's going on and then see our choices about what to do about what's going on.

Research also shows that mindfulness practices, even at this introductory level, increase the volume of the insula and improve its function of *interoception* — awareness of what's going on in the body. Better interoception strengthens our capacities for self-attunement, self-awareness, and self-empathy: it helps us track how physically comfortable, how emotionally nourished, and how relationally supported we feel. This in turn enhances the confidence in ourselves that increases resilience. We can strengthen the structures in the brain that help us become more present, engaged, and confident in our lives, simply by paying attention to our breathing. Here is a simple exercise to start out with.

Exercise 1: Cultivating Mindfulness of the Breath

1. Find a time and place where you can sit or lie down undisturbed. Find a comfortable posture: relaxed yet alert. Allow your eyes to gently close or rest open in a soft gaze. If mindfulness practice is new to you, you can begin to experience what it means to focus your attention by first being aware of the wall in front of you, then of the wall behind you, then of the walls on either side of you. Then focus your attention on your throat, and then on your breath. This simply demonstrates that you can direct your own attention.

2. Bring your awareness to your breath flowing gently in and out of your body, gradually noticing changes in the rhythm, the intensity, and the sound of your breathing. Notice your belly rising and falling with each breath. You may feel your breath moving throughout your entire body — your whole body breathing.

3. As you focus on your breathing, allow yourself to notice that you are aware not only of the breath itself — the object or noun or thing of your awareness — and the breathing itself — the process or verb or the unfolding of experience moment to moment that you are observing — but also that you can be aware of the fact that you are focusing your attention: you can be aware of the steadiness of the awareness itself. You are aware of the experience of the moment but not embedded in it.

4. You may notice that your attention occasionally wanders as you focus on your breathing. No problem. Noticing this wandering is part of the process of "waking up" to awareness. If it happens, bring your attention back to your breathing. Practice noticing your breath until you can remain focused on the breath for one full minute. You are training your attention to remain steady. Even one minute of practice begins to change your brain.

How Mindfulness Steadies Awareness

As we practice becoming mindful of various objects — the breath, a pain in the knee, a memory of a cousin, a worry about aging — we become aware of awareness itself. We notice, and we notice that we are noticing. With practice in mindfulness, our awareness steadies. We can readily notice when we're "awake" and when we're not, when we're present and engaged and when we're not. This awareness of being aware helps us feel safe while we begin to notice patterns through our mindfulness. As James Baraz, the cofounder of Spirit Rock Meditation Center in the San Francisco Bay Area, points out, "That which is aware of fear is not itself afraid" — or sad, angry, or overwhelmed. Once we can perceive difficult patterns without anxiety, we can work to rewire them. No matter what experience is arising in the mind, when we remain steady in awareness, we're not upset or retraumatized.

There was no way my client Steve could resolve his massive credit card debt until he could look squarely at his spending and even more directly at his need to bolster his sense of self-worth through his spending. But before he could even begin to look at and recognize those patterns, he had to develop enough awareness through his mindfulness practice to tolerate looking at all: to see the consequences of his behaviors and sit with the feelings of fear, disappointment, and shame that arose in the process. As Steve steadied his awareness, he was able to step back from his experiences. Viewing them mindfully, he could begin to discover new options.

Being mindful allows us to recognize any feeling *as* a feeling, any thought *as* a thought, any cascade of emotions *as* a cascade, any pattern of thoughts *as* a pattern. We become aware of entire processes of mind or states of mind as simply that — processes and states of mind. We recognize any beliefs or "truths" *as* beliefs we believe to be true. We become aware of entire belief systems, views, identities — as no more and no less than belief systems, views, and identities. These may include stories we've told ourselves since we were five, or twelve, or since we got married or divorced, or since we became a CPA and wished we had become a welder instead. All the while we remain anchored in the awareness that is noticing and observing these phenomena (anything that can be observed by the mind) *as* phenomena, distinguishing between what is actually happening in the present moment and what is merely a pattern from the past.

Research data from neuroscience are just beginning to illuminate what happens in the brain during mindfulness practice as we focus on increasingly complex objects of awareness:

- We strengthen the insula. Focusing our awareness on body sensations, impulses, and movements — such as an itch, an ache, a tightness in a muscle — builds our capacity to become similarly and resiliently aware of big surges of rage, grief, terror.
- We train the brain to notice and be aware before events and our responses get out of hand. We can attune to our experiences and can classify them as pleasant, unpleasant, or neutral, and no more. We learn to recognize and limit our initial reactions to thoughts like "I like this; I want more" or "I don't like this; go away" or "Huh? Did something just happen?" rather than spiraling into major reactivity.
- We become aware of patterns that some Buddhist practitioners would lump together as "mental contents" and that

Western psychologists would thoroughly unpack as emotions, thought processes, states of mind, states of being, identities, and belief systems. Examples of "contents" include guilt, judgment about the guilt, and solutions to the guilt to stop the judgment. Thought processes include imagining, describing, analyzing, planning, and evaluating. States of mind might include feeling grumpy, sleepy, discouraged, curious, and complaining. When we become aware of these patterns, we greatly increase our choices and flexibility in responding to them, thus increasing our resilience.

Guy Armstrong, a senior teacher at Spirit Rock Meditation Center in the San Francisco Bay Area, tells of a time when he was having great difficulty settling into a long, silent meditation retreat. Restless and agitated, he could finally notice and name what he was experiencing: "Oh, despair!" As soon as he could name the despair, he was no longer embedded in it; he could observe it and begin to let it be, let it naturally unfold, and then let it go. Any time we can notice and name the experience of the moment, we have re-engaged our prefrontal cortex. In Guy's case, noticing and naming allowed him to reflect and come to resolution without feeling caught or trapped.

This level of awareness helps us clearly see patterns in our thinking that might make us less resilient, as Ellen could notice her panic at technical snafus and begin to work with it skillfully. For example, we might react to a tickle in the throat by assuming that a cold is coming on, which might mean missing work, which might mean losing our job, which might turn into a financial disaster for the family. These dreaded outcomes are not always inevitable or even knowable, and jumping to conclusions about them makes us less resilient. When we can become aware of patterns of thinking that lead us in the direction of less resilience, we can begin to identify choice points where we might actually be able to discern and choose alternative options.

Exercise 2: Steadying Awareness as What We Observe Becomes More Complex

1. Sit comfortably; come to a peaceful sense of engaged stillness in your body, feeling present, relaxed, yet alert. You may wish to focus your attention on your breathing at first. This helps you quiet the chatter in your mind, concentrating on just this moment, just this breath. Gradually, spontaneously become aware of the awareness that is aware of your breathing. As that awareness steadies, you can let go of the focus on your breath and anchor your awareness in the awareness itself.

2. This bare, open awareness, not anchored in any particular object, is often compared to a vast sky, open and spacious. Memories, plans, and complaints float through like clouds, not disturbing the unchanging sky itself. A Zen teaching says that when our minds contract — with anxieties or complaints — it's like looking at the sky through a pipe. If you find yourself getting caught up this way in a thought, story, or emotion, return your awareness to your breathing. Becoming present to the moment will clear your mind and help it open up again to spacious awareness.

3. Once your awareness is anchored in awareness itself, you can notice events and sensations: the sound of a door opening or closing and that sound falling away into silence again. You can notice a burp, a cough, or a sneeze erupting in your body and then falling away into stillness again. Anchored in awareness, you can notice boredom, impatience, or restlessness arising. You can notice and name states of mind, states of being, or belief systems you have been wrestling with for years. Without your moving to fix them or push them away, these states, too, will pass away again into a spacious, peaceful awareness.

4. When you are ready, bring your attention back to the present moment, becoming aware of how you are sitting, how you are breathing.

5. Take a moment to reflect on your experience of steadying your awareness. Note any changes in your capacity to focus your attention. Take in that you are developing a skill essential to seeing clearly, which is essential to responding flexibly, which is essential to resilience.

With practice, we can more naturally anchor our awareness in awareness, and then, when challenges arise, we are prepared to see clearly what's happening and how to cope with it well.

How Mindfulness Dissolves the "Stuff" of Self

One of the most important focuses of our awareness for recovering resilience is the self: the constellation of thoughts, feelings, and behaviors we come to identify as "me" or "I." This "I" is seen in traditional mindfulness practice as ever changing, ever unfolding, not a fixed or permanent entity but simply one of the many objects (however fascinating they may be at the personal level) that are categorized in Buddhist psychology as "mental contents."

With steady practice, mindfulness begins to penetrate the "substance" of our personal self, much as modern physics has been able to understand the substance of any material object. We now know that there is far more space between atoms, and particles of atoms, than there is "stuff," or matter. There is a vast spaciousness in the densest of matter, paralleling the vast spaciousness between the stars in the galaxies.

Similarly, the practice of mindfulness allows us to experience a spaciousness between the thoughts, judgments, and reactivities of the self and to experience the possibility of flow. As the functioning of our brain shifts from an intentional focus on stuff to a receptive awareness of the space between the stuff, we begin to experience a flow among the many parts that make up what we identify as the self. Instead of the self as a noun, an object with defined perimeters, we begin to see it as a verb, a process of continual change.

With a more fluid understanding of the self, we relax into an experience of openness, clarity, and calm. With practice in mindfulness, this can happen within a breath or two. Even though we have penetrated through the layers of "stuff" to the space that holds the stuff, a kind of emptiness or nothingness, the subjective experience is often more of an all-embracing awareness of everything, a sense of fullness. This new object of our awareness — *nonself* — is called *true nature* in the Buddhist tradition or *presence* or *essence* in other traditions. It is a universal phenomenon of being human, no matter how much our conditioning might obscure it

This true nature feels like home. We feel centered, balanced, at peace, whole, and complete. The qualities that people have identified as the expressions of this true nature — trust, equanimity, energy, integrity, and generosity, to name a few — are the qualities we come to recognize as constituting the *true self*.

While the patterns of neural firing that generate this subjective experience of true nature have not yet been fully mapped by neuroscientists, the experience itself has been verified by millions of individual practitioners over thousands of years.

Neuroscientists *have* begun to identify pathways and circuits in the brain that could explain the shift from focused attention to spacious openness, from self to nonself. The circuit of focused attention is the focusing network described in chapter 1. The associated brain structures, especially the prefrontal cortex, pull the sense of self together — our history, personality, and identity. We know this stable (yet flexible!) and coherent sense of self is essential to resilience.

A second circuit involved in this shift from self to nonself that we, and science, may be less familiar with is the defocusing network (see chapter 1). The defocusing network allows the brain to link neurons together in a less stable, more fluid way, creating a mental "play space" where ideas, sensations, and memories are likely to connect with each other in new, unfamiliar ways. In this mental space, the "facts" and "rules" of who we are and how we operate are relaxed. The defocusing network operates mainly on the right side of the brain. The processing of the right hemisphere allows us to perceive the world in a more holistic, big-picture way and develops our deep, intuitive knowing. The prefrontal cortex is engaged in this lateral network also, though less actively.

The defocusing circuit operates when we are daydreaming or in reverie. We can consciously use it to let ourselves relax into a more open, spacious awareness. (It helps to be trusting and curious.) As we do so, the sense of self that we have so carefully crafted over the years and the strategies that we have developed to stay safe and strong in the world begin to ebb away, and we come into an experience of simply *being* that feels vast and timeless. This defocusing network is the basis of the deconditioning we use to unlearn and then rewire the strategies encoded by the focusing network.

To switch between these two networks of self and nonself requires a mature prefrontal cortex. This is what allows us to be self-aware: to accomplish the developmental task of forming a functional personal self and remaining aware of that self and, at the same time, to feel safe enough to let go of that self and enter a more spacious consciousness. The more flexible neural receptivity of the defocusing network allows us to rewire different patterns constituting the personal self. Learning to use *both* networks gives us more choices in rewiring our brains to increase resilience.

Because all mental activity sculpts neural structure in some way, any effort we put into deepening our awareness of any objects of mindfulness will in turn strengthen the prefrontal cortex, increasing our capacity for self-awareness, self-reflection, and self-knowing. In this sense, paying attention to the self, knowing it honestly, without distortion or camouflage, is not self-indulgent. It is an awareness of self that still leads to the awareness of being aware. And that awareness is foundational to resilience.

Mindfulness: A Cornerstone of Resilience

As practices of mindfulness — awareness and acceptance — have come to the West from the ancient Buddhist and Hindu traditions in Asia, they have become secularized. Mindfulness is being integrated into tools of self-reflection in psychotherapy, attention training in public schools, and stress-reduction and pain-management programs in hospitals. It is being taught to business and law students as a tool for enhancing concentration. But we should remember that mindfulness is more than just a tool to "train the mind to change the brain to change the mind for the better." (I first heard that phrase from my colleague Rick Hanson; he would agree with the reminder, too.) For the past 2,500 years, mindfulness has been taught as a reliable path to the awakening that leads to the "sure release" from suffering and teaches us the ultimate resilience: trust in our capacity to wisely and compassionately meet whatever comes our way.

With enough mindfulness practice, we arrive at our own embodied understanding of the wisdom teachings about conditioning and getting stuck in patterns. We perceive the universality of suffering, the natural arising of compassion in the face of suffering, the direct experience of the interconnectedness of all beings and the interrelatedness of all events, and the nothingness of all phenomena — pleasant, unpleasant, or neutral. To paraphrase my colleague Andy Dreitcer, we learn to "take it all seriously and hold it all lightly." Because the teachings themselves point to experiences of deep resilience that we can all partake of with enough practice, and because focused attention on repeated experiences of resilience does create brain change, mindfulness practice is a cornerstone of any program to rewire our brains toward resilience.

Mindful Awareness and Western Psychology

Western psychology has developed an equally useful counterpart to mindfulness in its practice of reflective investigation. As we will see next, mindfulness and the "observing ego" work together to strengthen the prefrontal cortex and help us develop resilience.

When Sue arrived for her regular therapy session one evening, she was agitated and upset. Her son's bicycle had been stolen two days before, the washer-dryer had gone on the blink, and her car needed new brakes. As a single parent, Sue had budgeted barely enough to cover seeing me each week. Now, with these unexpected expenses, she felt she had to stop therapy, now.

I asked Sue to slow down, to pause for a moment, to breathe deeply, to feel my presence with her in the room. I asked her to let in my care and concern and to borrow my trust, if need be, so that we could find a way through this.

Then I asked Sue to step back a bit from her feelings in the moment and to put on her "observer" hat. This would help her reflect on the situation, to be curious but not embedded in the anxiety. We began to pay attention to sensations in her body: the queasiness in her stomach, the tightness in her throat, the feeling of a steel fist in her chest.

After a time of sitting quietly with those physical sensations, not trying to figure them out, make them go away, or jump to any conclusions because of them, I asked, "Do these sensations have any images or words that go with them, Sue?" She immediately responded, "There's no way out. We're doomed."

Knowing something of Sue's history from previous sessions, I asked, "Whose voice is that? Who has ever said 'We're doomed' before?"

Sue reflected a moment, then looked up. "That was me when I was ten. My dad lost his job, and my mom was sick. My parents saw no way out but for me to quit my piano lessons just weeks before an important recital. That's when I felt the doom."

I knew that Sue was at a critical point in her therapy, ready to make a significant breakthrough. This would not be the time for her to quit. And we were working on this very issue as part of her therapy. But to continue had to be her decision.

I encouraged Sue to explore the hurt, disappointment, and anger of the ten-year-old who had felt so blocked in dealing with her parents' fears and financial distress. Together we looked at the belief system that had formed itself back then and had remained out of her awareness for the next twenty years: the conviction that there was no way out of financial catastrophes except to quit anything that seemed nonessential.

With that implicit belief system brought into conscious awareness, Sue could begin to mindfully assess whether what was true then needed to be true now. She began to remember other times when she and her children had gotten through impossible-seeming financial crunches.

With her fears regulated and with a sense of calm and clarity gained from her observer role, Sue began to look for other options in her current dilemma. Instead of abandoning therapy at a critical point, she negotiated a payment schedule with me and thought through ways to shift household funds around to resolve the current cash crunch. In the process, she recovered a sense of competence and resilience and learned ways to manage stress that were appropriate to the adult that she was.

Reflective investigation, as Sue and I practiced it, leads to what psychologists call "witness awareness" or the "observing ego." The word *ego* here does not carry the colloquial meanings of "conceited" or "self-absorbed": quite the opposite. It refers to the healthy functioning of the executive center of the brain — the prefrontal cortex. The observing ego allows us to notice our experience, tune into the felt sense of it as we do when we practice mindfulness, and also step back from our experience a bit and reflect on it nonjudgmentally and objectively. We can investigate what's true and what's not true about what we're noticing, what works and what doesn't work in what we're observing.

A key to investigating what is and isn't working is to ask ourselves the question, "What story am I believing right now?" By *story* I mean those personal narratives we create about who we are or who we think we are. Our perception of a current crisis can be skewed or filtered by previous beliefs that were shaped by previous conditioning. To respond flexibly, we need to be able to objectively see through those beliefs, no matter how compellingly true they may seem or how familiar they are.

Exercise 3: Using Reflection by the Observing Ego to Formulate Wise Choices

1. Identify a particular problem in your life that seems unresolvable or remains unsolved to date, such as a car insurance claim from a long-ago accident that hasn't been resolved, a conflict with a divorcing spouse who is refusing to cooperate in scheduled mediation sessions, or an overload at work because management hasn't yet replaced the coworker who left two months ago.

2. Put on your "observer" hat and reflect on the problem. Become aware of whatever you're experiencing — thoughts, feelings, body sensations — without becoming hijacked by them. Come into a mode of objective observation: I notice I'm thinking this; I notice I'm assuming that; I realize I forgot to ask about this; I don't even want to think about that.

3. As you observe your own process of trying to solve the problem, ask yourself, "What story am I believing now?" about yourself, about the situation, about others in the situation. Asking the question doesn't necessarily lead to an immediate answer, but it could lead to new observations and new questions. It's meant to help us develop the capacity to look again, to see new perspectives, new options, without triggering more agitation about the problem.

4. Reflect on what you've noticed about your patterns of thinking, feeling, coping, and relating. Note that you are doing an exercise to strengthen your prefrontal cortex to do its job of observing patterns and becoming more self-aware, which will allow you to create options to respond more flexibly.

The work of the observing ego is very similar to that of the "evenly hovering attention" of Sigmund Freud and the "unconditional positive regard" of Carl Rogers in Western psychology. The observing ego pays attention to the meaning of the mental contents, finding value in the unfolding personal story, even as it allows us to step back from our experience and observe it nonjudgmentally (as mindfulness also does).

When we choose to do brain-changing practices like mindfulness or observation-reflection, we set in motion the process of changing the brain itself. When the strengthened prefrontal cortex is functioning in its observing ego mode, paying attention to all the details of our subjective experiences while also letting them go (as mindfulness does), the process of reflective inquiry penetrates through all the layers of previous conditioning. With enough practice, we come to experience a deep intuitive knowing of our inner worth, the sense of a vital and essential goodness, which lies underneath all the patterns and strategies we have learned.

For millennia, spiritual traditions around the world have taught that every individual has an essential worth and goodness, that human beings are "nobly born," that "the kingdom of God is within you."

Spiritual activist and lecturer Marianne Williamson expressed it this way:

> We ask ourselves, who am I to be brilliant,
> gorgeous, talented, and fabulous?
> Actually, who are you not to be?
> You are a child of God.

Western psychology is catching up to that view of the soul or mind. (The ancient Greek word *psyche* means both "soul" and "mind.") The traditional medical model of the human brain, or mind or self, has emphasized illness. But by taking a more neutral view of genetically encoded biological mechanisms that can be shaped by conditions and experiences (conditioning), clinical practitioners are now arriving at the view that the natural development of the brain leads to complexity and integration of capacities that enhance well-being and wholeness. When the deep, inner reflection of mindfulness or the observing ego brings us to an awareness of this birthright of well-being and wholeness, we have recovered a key component of our resilience.

Pulling It All Together

In this chapter you have learned some of the conditions needed to create reliable, lasting brain change. Because of our brain's innate neuroplasticity, we can choose which new experiences we want to use to rewire our brains for resilience; we can become skillful at self-directed neuroplasticity.

- Mindfulness — steady, nonjudgmental awareness and acceptance of experience — is one of the most powerful tools for brain change known to science. By strengthening the functioning of the prefrontal cortex and related structures, mindfulness leads to the self-awareness and shifts in perspective that allow the brain to remain flexible in its response to triggers and trauma, more easily rewiring itself for resilience.

- Mindfulness allows us to perceive directly that it is the nature of all experience to change, including the constellations of thoughts, feelings, and behaviors we have come to identify as "me" or "I." With practice, we can loosen our grip on the "stuff" of our "self" and relax directly into an open, spacious experience of our true self and the wisdom of our true nature, allowing our patterns of self to be more easily rewired.

- The reflective investigation of mindfulness practice dovetails easily with the conscious examination of the observing ego of Western psychology, helping the brain integrate a sense of genuine wholeness that is key to resilience.

CHAPTER FOUR

Using Empathy to Create Connections and Self-Acceptance

The roots of resilience are to be found in the felt sense of existing in the heart and mind of an empathic, attuned, self-possessed other.

— DIANA FOSHA

WHILE MINDFULNESS and observation-reflection create the self-awareness and expanded brain capacities that allow us to create the changes in our behaviors critical to resilience, the other essential catalyst for brain change — empathy — requires skillfully interacting with other people to generate the connection and self-acceptance we also need for resilience.

Chapter 1 shows that the early learning of resilient coping strategies and the development of the prefrontal cortex itself rely on the empathy developed through experiences of secure attachment. Research shows that five elements of that empathy are essential for maturing the prefrontal cortex in the first place and for continuing to strengthen it throughout our lives:

1. *Resonance:* picking up the "vibe" of other people
2. *Attunement:* feeling your way into another person's experience and "feeling felt" by them

3. *Empathy* (as one part of the larger umbrella of empathy): making sense of your experience or another's, conveying a shared understanding of the meaning of the experience, and sensing that any experience is completely understood and accepted

4. *Compassion:* literally "feeling with," keeping the heart open and caring in the face of struggle or suffering

5. *Acceptance:* coming to terms with what is or has been, so that you can cope going forward

The power of neuroplasticity is such that even if our earliest conditioning did not lead to secure attachment, we can use new experiences in relationships with others now to strengthen the functioning of the prefrontal cortex and expand the capacities for trust, connection, and self-acceptance that lead to more resilience.

Empathy uses the resonance circuit described in chapter 1 to catalyze powerful changes in your brain and the create safe conditions for doing so. This chapter includes experiential exercises to develop each of the five elements of empathy, which will strengthen the prefrontal cortex so that it can more easily rewire your strategies for coping. That better-functioning prefrontal cortex in turn reinforces a sense of innate worth and competence that fuels your resilience.

Resonance

All human beings are hard-wired to reverberate, instantaneously and without any conscious processing, to the emotions and actions of people around them. This process of basic sensory perception and instant communication, especially of signals of safety or serious danger, is called *resonance*. Some form of this capacity is essential for all living organisms, from single-celled protozoa to flatworms and sea anemones, frogs and eagles, squirrels and chimps, and us and our neighbors.

The prefrontal cortex uses resonance to relate to other human beings. We reflexively read the body-based signals that constantly flow between us and others. Resonance helps explain why we yawn when we see somebody else yawn; why we flinch and say "Ouch!" when we see someone else get hurt; and why we spontaneously say "Oh!" when the baby says "Oh!" Resonance is the basis of the emotional contagion that can bring us into a shared emotional state: it is at work when anger sweeps through a soccer crowd, when an entire concert audience jumps to its feet in applause, and when anxiety about failing health or a failing marriage gets passed on, unconsciously, to a child.

We can misread these signals, of course. When we walk into a meeting or a party, depending on how our early conditioning might have nurtured or distorted this capacity, we may see safety where there is truly danger or perceive danger or hostility where there is none. But the capacity to use resonance skillfully is hard-wired and completely recoverable. Though resonance itself always operates completely outside awareness, we can learn to be mindfully aware of its workings. We can sense a "vibe" and learn to know whether it is coming from someone else or from inside ourselves. As we recover our capacity to use resonance skillfully, we simultaneously strengthen the capacities of the prefrontal cortex to relate, feel, and cope resiliently.

Frank Ostaseski, the founding director of the Zen Hospice Project in San Francisco, taught a valuable lesson about resonance in a workshop I attended on compassionate caregiving. Every Friday afternoon, Joe, a hospice volunteer, visited Nathan, who was dying of complications from AIDS. One particular afternoon, Nathan's partner, Dan, and his sister and brother-in-law were already visiting; two friends from work were in the room as well. The room was full of laughter and chatter. Joe felt superfluous, but he decided to take a seat at the foot of the bed and simply hold Nathan's feet. As he silently did so, the chatter in the room began to subside. Within a few moments, everyone in the room relaxed into a gentle, quiet stillness. Nathan later told Joe that those moments of silent presence, compassionate touch, and resonant togetherness were the most healing experiences of the entire week. The people closest to him in his life were quietly present with him; he had relaxed into more peacefulness in his ailing body. Nathan had found a place of calm that resonated out to include everyone in the room.

Exercise 1: Bringing Resonance to Consciousness

1. Ask a friend to say out loud to you, seven times, variations of "No!" and really mean it.
2. Next, ask the friend to say seven different variations of "Yes!" with equal conviction.
3. Notice the differences in your own body sensations as you hear "No!" and "Yes!" As you become more aware of how experiences resonate within you, you become better able to choose experiences that help you feel more open, more engaged, more flexible, and more resilient.

Attunement

Attunement is the capacity to pay attention and consciously tune in to an inner experience, our own or another person's. It is the element of empathy that moves the processing of experience from the lower brain, the primitive emotional processing centers of the limbic system, through the insula and mirror neurons, into the cortex. Attunement strengthens the capacity of the prefrontal cortex to read the meaning of our own or other people's emotional signals, starting with basic assessments of safe, dangerous, or neutral (similar to the hedonic tone of pleasant, unpleasant, or neutral) all the way to detecting fine emotional nuances.

Although attunement involves the conscious processing of the prefrontal cortex, we read the emotions of others mostly through the nonverbal signals of facial expressions, body language, and tone of voice. These signals are processed by the right hemisphere of the cortex. According to A. Mehrabian in *Silent Messages*, 55 percent of all emotional meaning is conveyed through facial expressions and body language; another 38 percent is communicated through tone and rhythm of voice; only 7 percent is communicated through words. Many neuropsychologists hypothesize that mirror neurons are the means by which the brain registers and comprehends the emotions of another person. As we observe another person's facial expressions and body language, neurons in the brain are mirroring and processing those signals in a way that makes it feel as if they are being generated in our own bodies. The insula then sends the information about those sensations to our prefrontal cortex to be deciphered. This may very well be the neurological basis of attunement.

As I imagine the story of Joe and Nathan continuing, the next time Joe visited Nathan, he saw instantly from the look on Dan's face that things had taken a turn for the worse. Without even hearing the change in prognosis, from the drop in his own stomach and the thickening in his throat, Joe began to feel in his body the grief in the room. Attunement speeds up our capacity to know what's happening and to respond to what's needed, even before we have time to formulate the experience in words.

Exercise 2: Bringing Attunement to Consciousness

1. At a large, busy public place — in line at a movie theater or at an airport, at a football game, or in a department store — spend a minute or so noticing the facial expressions and body language of ten different people. Notice your inner sense of what the other person might be feeling, based on what you're feeling in your body.

2. Reflect on your experience of tuning into other people's emotional states and using your own body sensations to decipher the meaning of what you are observing. Take in that your practice of attunement is strengthening the functioning of your prefrontal cortex and rebuilding the entire resonance circuit for more accurate emotional communication and connection between you and other people.

Attunement adds awareness to emotional resonance: we intentionally and consciously tune into our subjective experience or another's, and we know that we are doing so. This mindful awareness allows us to name the emotional states we are perceiving, as Joe could do in my imagined scenario when he named for himself the grief he felt from Dan, as Guy Armstrong did when he could name his despair during meditation. The ability to notice and name emotional experience enhances the capacity for empathy and deepens the resources of connection that you will use to rewire your previous patterns of relating.

Empathy

Empathy works through the prefrontal cortex and related structures on both sides of the brain to move beyond noticing and naming emotional experience, ours or that of another, to generating a cognitive understanding of that experience: to be aware of why somebody (including us) might be feeling the way they do. This process makes sense of the experience, present or past. Empathy generates meaning out of our experiences and our reactions to our experiences. We can get caught in very powerful stories about what is happening or has happened before, positive or negative — and frequently do. We saw how Margaret began to spin a story about Daniel's failure to call her when he said he would, based on her childhood experience when her father failed to pick her up after school. We may carry a belief that we were the sole cause of our parents' divorce or the sole cause of our fledgling business going under. Using mindful empathy to come to clarity and make sense of how we came to be who we are, or how others came to be who they are, is essential if we are to begin to be resilient.

The subjective experience of empathy — of being seen and understood, or of understanding ourselves — is one of the primary catalysts for rewiring our brain's encoded messages about ourselves, our connections, our competence, our vulnerability, and our courage. This is what happened for Dan as Joe sensed something had changed.

Nathan lay silently in his bed at the hospice as Dan told Joe the results of the latest lab tests. They showed that the medications being used to support Nathan's vital organs were no longer working. Nathan's system was rapidly shutting down. Rather than the months they had expected to share, they now had a week at the most.

Joe could feel Dan's sadness and grief spilling into the room. As he tried to offer some words of comfort, though, Dan jumped to his feet and began venting his anger and frustration at — everything. Pacing back and forth in the tiny room, he yelled at the unfairness of what was happening. He raged at the "system" for not having found a cure for AIDS yet. He went off on the general ignorance seven years earlier that had left Nathan vulnerable to contracting the disease.

Seeing Dan in this distress, Joe shifted gears. He let Dan know that his anger made sense, given the shock of the turn of events. Joe let Dan know that he completely understood the struggle to understand, accept, and cope with the new reality.

As Joe spoke, calmly and engagingly, Dan began to settle down. He could feel and accept Joe's empathy; he knew that Joe really understood. Dan sat down again in his chair, placed his head in his hands, and let himself begin to grieve. Joe's empathy for Dan's anger and grief allowed Dan to become present again to the realities he and Nathan would be facing in the coming days.

The English novelist Dinah Craik expressed the healing power of empathy this way:

> Oh, the comfort,
> The inexpressible comfort
> Of feeling safe with a person.
> Having neither to weigh out thoughts
> Nor words,
> But pouring them all right out, just as they are,

Chaff and grain together;
Certain that a faithful hand
Will take them and sift them;
Keeping what is worth keeping and,
With the breath of kindness,
Blow the rest away.

Empathy is based in relationships with other people. The emotional truth and the meaning of one person's experience have to resonate with the other person. The attunement has to be accurate; the empathic process has to verify that understanding — a "moment of meeting" — has indeed occurred, as it had between Joe and Dan.

Self-empathy entails understanding what is happening within ourselves, what has happened in the past and how that is affecting us now, or how something affected us in the past. It also entails understanding who we sense ourselves to be now or who we have believed ourselves to be in the past. In order to mature toward well-being, our current self must understand and be accepting of all the earlier parts of the self that were conditioned by previous experiences. True understanding and compassionate self-acceptance are especially necessary when there are parts of ourselves that are still caught in negative stories about what has happened to us — parts that still feel invisible, misunderstood, not accepted, or a failure.

When we or others relate to these wounded parts of ourselves with empathy, that empathy makes it safe to allow any residual emotional pain connected with them to arise. We can stay connected with our experience in the moment, which is what will allow us to rewire any less-than-resilient strategies that developed from that wounding. Without the safety of mindful empathy, we can become disconnected from these experiences or parts of ourselves. We may lose touch with our feelings if we have negative judgments about reexperiencing them or sense danger about revisiting old pain. We may lose touch with the vital wisdom from the very foundations of the resonance circuit. We may lose touch with our inner resources, such as memories of times when we have coped well before or the faith that if we ask for help, people will respond. This neural disintegration makes it harder to reconnect with our own experiences and cope effectively. Ample research shows that blocked or underdeveloped empathy or self-empathy markedly derails resilience.

Exercise 3: Cultivating Empathy and Self-Empathy

1. Identify a behavior you've observed in someone, a behavior that you don't like very much, at least in the moment. Maybe the driver in the lane next to you is yelling at another driver who just cut him off on the freeway. Your spouse put off paying the credit card bill, and now he's racking up late fees and jeopardizing your credit rating. Your best friend arrives fifteen minutes late to pick up his son from soccer practice and picks a fight with the coach to cover his chagrin.

2. Notice your own reaction to this behavior, including any opinions or judgments that may have been buried in your implicit memory and are now coming to consciousness. Notice, then set your own reaction to the side for the moment.

3. Begin to be curious (you're activating your prefrontal cortex here) about what might be going on in that other person to cause him to act that way. Already stressed? Swamped with things to attend to? Feeling a lack of experience, lack of skill, or low self-esteem?

4. Remember a time when you have acted similarly. For example, I occasionally yell at a driver who cuts me off on the freeway. Then I remember times when I've inadvertently done the same thing. I can understand and forgive the other driver if I put myself in his shoes and can understand and forgive myself.

5. Remember that any behavior — in ourselves or others — is rooted in learned, conditioned responses that served some survival purpose for us originally. Knowing this, we can

extend some understanding, compassion, and forgiveness to the other person now.

6. If possible, communicate your empathic understanding of the other person's experience to him (maybe not the driver on the freeway, but to your spouse or your friend) to make sure that your understanding is accurate and that your empathy "lands," or registers with the other person. For you, experiencing and communicating empathy strengthen your prefrontal cortex and thus your ability to respond flexibly and resiliently. For the other person, feeling that empathy may help him recognize and rewire his own encoded patterns and become receptive to changing his behavior.

Empathy requires a capacity that psychologists call *theory of mind*: the ability both to know what someone else is feeling and thinking and to recognize that their thoughts and feelings could be different from our own in the same moment. Joe could feel Dan's grief through attunement; he could feel his own grief, too, through self-attunement. Just as important, Joe could sense Dan's anger, understand it, and convey that understanding without feeling angry himself. The capacity of theory of mind allowed Joe to distinguish his own experience from Dan's. That awareness made it possible for him to be fully present to Dan's experience without being hijacked by it. By being "affected but not infected," he could remain helpful to Dan.

As you use the tools in this chapter to strengthen the functioning of your prefrontal cortex, you will also be rewiring your brain to expand your capacity of theory of mind, enabling you to respond more effectively to others.

Compassion

As your empathy allows you to understand your responses and those of others to perils and predicaments, you can naturally begin to experience compassion for the full spectrum of those responses. As compassion keeps the mind and heart open in times of confusion, suffering and sorrow, we can remain engaged with what needs addressing right in front of us. When your son Johnny bursts into the kitchen wailing because the boy next door pushed him off his bike, you comfort Johnny, cleaning up his skinned knee and soothing the mix of fear, hurt, and anger surging through him, but you try to have empathy and compassion for the other boy, too. What was going on in him that caused him to behave in such a belligerent way? When you hear that a friend who has lost primary custody of his children in a divorce settlement is refusing to pick up the kids after school, you meet him over coffee to talk and try to understand — and have compassion for — the fear, hurt, and anger that are causing him to withdraw.

We all learn how to react to the slings and arrows of outrageous fortune in different ways. We can have compassion for the suffering that is part and parcel of being human and for the suffering that we sometimes cause by our own reactions to that suffering. Compassion and self-compassion are necessary antidotes to messages from less-than-optimal conditioning that have told us it's selfish, or weak, to stop and say, "This is tough; this hurts."

The power of compassion came into play when Joe visited Nathan a few days later. Nathan was sleeping, and Dan was sitting in a chair nearby, slumped in grief and worry. Joe took one of Nathan's hands in his and placed the other hand in Dan's hand. Nathan stirred slightly as Dan began weeping. After a few moments, Nathan woke up, heard Dan crying, and asked Joe, "What did you say to him?" Joe replied, "I didn't say anything. I just sat with him. I helped him cry."

Joe's compassion helped Dan safely acknowledge and express his own grief. When we can give and receive compassion, we are cultivating a stance of approaching experience rather than avoiding it. This "approach" stance creates more flexibility in the brain that makes it easier to find resolutions to our problems or to come to terms with what cannot be resolved. Researchers have found that self-compassion is even more effective in recovering our resilience than self-esteem.

Exercise 4: Cultivating Self-Compassion

1. Recall a moment when it was relatively easy for you to feel compassion for someone else's heartache or sorrow. You saw your neighbor struggling to carry bags of groceries up the driveway with a recently broken ankle. Your cousin lost her luggage two airports back before she arrived at your house for a weekend visit. Your eight-year-old collapsed in tears after she was late for an after-school meet-up and the school bus took off for the class picnic without her. Your cat sprained her hip jumping down from a high kitchen counter and has limped around the house for three days.

2. Imagine this person or pet sitting in front of you or per-haps sitting in your lap. Notice any warmth, concern, and goodwill arising in your own heart as you sit together. Feel the empathy, compassion, and love flowing from your body, from your heart to hers.

3. When the feelings of empathy, compassion and love are steady enough, shift gears a bit and remember a time when you were facing a difficult situation of your own. However big or small it was, let yourself experience that pain again for a moment.

4. Return to the feelings of warmth, concern, and goodwill for the person or pet you are with now. Without changing anything, simply redirect this flow of empathy, compassion, and love for her toward yourself. Let yourself receive your own care and concern, your own empathy and com-passion for your own pain, for whatever has happened, whatever you've done or failed to do, at any age or level of your psyche that needs to receive it. You may express

this feeling toward yourself in words: "May this suffering pass.... May things resolve for me.... May I feel less upset over time."

5. Let yourself take in the feeling of being understood and nurtured. Let your own heart relax into a more peaceful sense of understanding, compassion, and forgiveness. Let this compassion settle in your body and help to rewire your sense of yourself in this very moment.

6. Reflect on your experience of this exercise. Notice any new sense of openness or approach to your own experiences. Notice whether this approach stance opens up possibilities for change and resolution of difficulties that have concerned or hurt you before.

As you cultivate an approach stance toward experience, you are increasing your brain's capacity for flexible response, thus creating the conditions for more resilience.

Self-Acceptance

The curious paradox is that when I accept
myself just as I am, then I can change.

— CARL ROGERS

Neuroscientists haven't fully mapped the function of self-acceptance in the brain yet, partly because *self* is such a complex construct. What we call the human personality encompasses identities, roles, views, and beliefs that evolve over time, including patterns of coping and defensiveness. But neuropsychiatrists do know that self-acceptance is a crucial element in the capacity of the prefrontal cortex to construct a coherent narrative of the self, and we also know that coherence is essential to resilience.

Acceptance involves no blame or shame: it allows us to honor and accept an entire event and integrate it into our sense of our self. We can do so by creating a narrative of the event with the following components:

1. This is what happened.
2. This is what I did to survive it (understandable, even brilliant).
3. This has been the cost (compassion makes it safe enough to even look at that).
4. This is what I have learned (a new narrative of self that allows us to live with, even be proud of, ourselves).
5. This is how I can respond to life now (be resilient going forward).

William James, a pioneer of American psychology, wrote of the role of acceptance in recovering resilience over 100 years ago: "Be willing to have it so. Acceptance of what has happened is the first step to overcoming the consequences of any misfortune."

We use both mindfulness and empathy to recognize, allow, tolerate, accept, and finally embrace and honor who we are exactly as we are, and what is or has been exactly as it is or has been.

The last time Joe visited Nathan and Dan, he found that Nathan was trying to come to terms with all the events in his life that had led up to this passage from life to beyond. He was recognizing and accepting the choices he had made and the patterns of conditioning that had shaped those choices, positive and negative. Nathan acknowledged mistakes and misjudgments; he was also experiencing pride in wise choices he had made and coping strategies that had worked well. He paraphrased something he had heard on the radio the day before: "Life is not a journey to the grave with the intention of arriving safely in a pretty and well-preserved body, but rather an opportunity to skid in broadside, thoroughly used up and totally worn out, and loudly proclaiming, 'Wow, what a ride!'" Nathan was sharing his "What a ride!" moments with Dan and Joe, coming to an acceptance of himself that was allowing him to meet his situation openly and resiliently.

Exercise 5: Cultivating Self-Acceptance

1. You can begin to accept aspects of yourself that you have previously found unacceptable by pairing a negative message or belief with the embracing stance of self-acceptance. For example:

   "Even though I feel lost and confused right now, I deeply and completely love and accept myself."

   "Even though my finances are a mess and I'm in real trouble, I deeply and completely love and accept myself."

   "Even though I feel as if it's all my fault that my wife left, I deeply and completely love and accept myself."

2. If both the awareness and acceptance seem like too much of a stretch, head yourself in the right direction with a modified phrase like "I'm willing to consider trying to deeply and completely love and accept myself." Let yourself notice that even if you deeply believe the negative statement about yourself to be true, the deep love and acceptance of yourself can simultaneously be true as well.

The negative statement may change over time, or it may not change for a long time. But your relationship to it can change very quickly. Acceptance and integration of this aspect of yourself can increase, allowing you to experience more wholeness of self.

The five elements of empathy, based in the neurobiology of the resonance circuit in the brain, develop and strengthen the functioning of the prefrontal cortex from the very first moments of our brain's development and continue to do so all our lives. The prefrontal cortex can integrate the "feeling" of our experience (largely processed by the right hemisphere) with the making sense of it to ourselves and then articulating it to others (largely processed by the left hemisphere).

As you learn tools to strengthen your capacities for resonance, attunement, empathy, compassion, and acceptance, you are skill-fully harnessing the innate neuroplasticity in your brain that will strengthen the brain itself to perform those functions. As you prac-tice skills of both mindfulness and empathy — observing your expe-rience and connecting to others through the sharing of experience — you are enhancing your brain's capacities to rewire for resilience.

Wiser Self and True Nature

In both Western psychology and Buddhist philosophy, practices of self-awareness, self-reflection, self-compassion, and self-acceptance lead to the subjective sense of well-being that I've referred to as our true nature or wiser self. The mature functioning of the prefrontal cortex allows us to recognize this sense of wiser self and use it to guide our responses to life's stressors.

There are many ways to develop a relationship with this wiser self. One is through imagination. The wiser self can be seen as an imaginary guide who embodies all the positive qualities — such as wisdom, courage, resilience, and patience — that you see yourself growing into. It is a figure who embodies your highest aspirations and has succeeded in achieving all your dreams and ambitions: a wellspring of resilience, equanimity, and well-being. The wiser self is someone who truly cares for you, is understanding and nurtur-ing, strong, capable and helpful, willing and able to help you on your journey. Your wiser self could be someone you know — a role model, mentor, or benefactor, or it could be a composite of the qualities of several people. However we constitute it, we can pose a particular problem or question to this wiser self and then listen for the answer, which comes from our own intuitive wisdom.

Exercise 6: Cultivating the Wiser Self

1. Find a comfortable position to sit quietly. Allow your eyes to gently close. Breathe deeply a few times into your belly

and allow your awareness to come more deeply into your body. Allow yourself to breathe comfortably. Become aware of relaxing into a gentle field of well-being.

2. Imagine that you are standing on a beach where the land and water meet. Imagine the details of the scene and your presence there in vivid detail. When you are ready, imagine yourself rising up into the air, floating up above the beach, and traveling across the water to land on another beach in another land. This is the home of your wiser self.

3. Imagine the dwelling of your wiser self: a home, cabin, garden, or any setting that seems fitting. Picture yourself walking toward the entrance. Notice how your wiser self greets you. Does she (or he) come out to meet you? Does she invite you in? Does she shake hands, bow, or hug you? Notice how old your wiser self is, how she is dressed, how she moves.

4. Imagine yourself sitting and talking with your wiser self. Notice her presence, her energy, and how it affects you. Ask your wiser self how she came to be who she is. Ask what helped her most along the way. What did she have to let go of to become who she is? Can she share examples of when and how she triumphed over adversity? You may choose to ask her about a particular problem or challenge facing you now. Notice what advice your wiser self offers that you can take with you. Listen carefully to all she has to tell you.

5. Imagine what it would be like to embody your wiser self. Invite her to become part of you. Notice how it feels to inhabit your wiser self from the inside out and to experience your wiser self within you. When you are ready, imagine your wiser self becoming separate from you again.

6. Imagine that your wiser self offers you a gift — an object, a symbol, a word or phrase — to remind you of her. Receive this object into your hand and place it somewhere in your

clothing for safekeeping. Your wiser self will let you know her name; remember it well.

7. As you prepare to leave, take a few gentle breaths to anchor this connection with your wiser self. Know that you can evoke this experience of encountering her any time you choose. Imagine thanking her for the time you have spent together; imagine saying good-bye. Walk back to the place where you landed, then imagine yourself floating back across the water to return to the beach where you started. Gradually become aware of your surroundings and, when you are ready, slowly open your eyes.

8. You may wish to write down your experience with your wiser self to help integrate it into your conscious memory and to use it any time you need guidance from within about how to be more resilient. As with any use of imagination to access our deep intuitive knowing, the more you practice encountering your wiser self, the more reliably you will be able to embody her wisdom as you respond to the challenges and difficulties of your life.

Imaginative exercises such as this one actually change the neural circuitry of our brains, creating new, positive habits of mind that become genuine resources in coping with anything, anything at all.

Integrating Mindfulness and Empathy

Practices of empathy and mindfulness involve skills drawn from two very different paradigms that understand the self or nonself differently, that transform or transcend the self differently, that alleviate suffering differently by strengthening or by letting go of the self. Yet both are shown by neuroscience to steadily strengthen the functioning of the prefrontal cortex. Both use embodied reflection and empathy to access the most deeply embedded patterns of the brain and hold them in conscious, compassionate awareness. Both of them use new experiences, and conscious investigation of those experiences, to catalyze the rewiring of old patterns. The validation of the efficacy of these practices to catalyze significant and productive brain change is fueling the emerging integration of Eastern mindfulness into Western psychology.

Practitioners of each paradigm are coming to understand that neither one of these paradigms alone is sufficient to rewire our brains for improved resilience. Both are necessary to fully develop the prefrontal cortex and allow it to do its job of rewiring our brain to be more integrated and flexible within itself.

The Buddhist tradition considers wisdom and compassion to be the two wings of the dharma (teachings); some Western psychologists think of the observing ego and a healing, empathic relationship as two legs with which to walk the journey of life. So mindfulness and relational empathy are not just complementary paradigms: they are completely collaborative. The synergy of these two practices is what I call mindful empathy. Mindful empathy can safely and effectively contain and catalyze the powerful processes of brain change.

As you employ the tools of mindful empathy to self-direct the rewiring of your own brain, you will also come to master the five Cs of coping: to be calm, to see with clarity, to connect with resources, to become competent, to be courageous. In the story of Joe, Dan, and Nathan, we see Nathan finding calm in the midst of his struggles, coming to see clearly the choices he has made in his life, connecting to resources like Joe, competently thinking through his choices, courageously coming to terms with his dying, and coming into resilience and peace.

Pulling It All Together

Empathy is a powerful tool of brain change and one that helps create a safe environment in which to undertake that change. Practices of resonance, attunement, empathy, compassion, and self-acceptance activate the resonance circuit in the brain, which strengthens the prefrontal cortex, enabling it to rewire strategies for coping with people and life events.

- *Resonance* allows us to pick up the "vibe" of other people.
- *Attunement* allows us to feel our way into another person's experience and feel their awareness of ours in turn.
- *Empathy* helps us share an understanding of an experience, ours or another's.
- *Compassion* allows us to stay open and engaged with experience so that the brain can rewire itself, even when that experience is difficult.
- *Self-acceptance* allows us to come to terms with experience, learn from it, and create new patterns of response.

Together, mindfulness and empathy allow us to experience the true nature or wiser self that can guide our actions. A synergy of mindfulness and empathy strengthens the functioning of the prefrontal cortex to rewire our brains for both stability and flexibility.

CHAPTER FIVE

Five Additional Practices That Accelerate Brain Change

The difference between try and triumph is a little "umph."

— AUTHOR UNKNOWN

THERE ARE FIVE additional experiential practices that work synergistically with mindful empathy to guide and safely accelerate any process of brain change: cultivating presence, intention, perseverance, refuges, and resources. Here I describe some of the neuroscience that explains why these additional practices add a crucial momentum to the major practices of mindful empathy described in the previous two chapters. Each of these practices safely speeds up the processes of brain change we learn to use in the next chapter, allowing us to rewire our brain for resilience sooner rather than later.

Presence

To be present is far from trivial. It may be the hardest work in the world. And forget about the "may be." It is the hardest work in the world — at least to sustain presence. And the most important. When you do drop into presence...you know it

instantly, feel at home instantly. And being home, you can
let loose, let go, rest in your being, rest in awareness,
in presence itself, in your own good company.

— JON KABAT-ZINN

The brain learns and rewires itself best when it is calm and relaxed, yet engaged and alert. Becoming present means "showing up," coming out of absentmindedness or distraction, out of denial or dissociation, into a mindful awareness of being here, now, in this body, and then gently sustaining this state of simply being as we rewire the brain's conditioned patterns of coping.

Through the practice of mindful empathy, it's possible to come into an embodied sense of presence in just a breath or two. Presence can be a momentary refuge or respite from worries and concerns: we can relax and simply breathe and be. Presence is also the gateway to neural receptivity: the brain takes a breather from doing and creates the mental play space that allows it to explore something new. Presence allows us to calmly engage with our experience in order to choose what patterns we want to rewire, and how.

Exercise 1: Coming into Presence

1. Start where you are. Orient to your environment, noticing features of your external world: the shape of the furniture in the room, the color of the art on the walls, the sound of a door opening or closing.
2. Shift your attention to your internal world, noticing and naming states of mind, feelings, and thoughts as they come to your awareness: annoyance at forgetting to answer your cousin's email, anticipation of a company barbecue this weekend.
3. Let your awareness drop below those conscious events to a deep inner awareness of being here, in the present

moment. Eyes closed or softly open, focus attention on body sensations — your feet on the floor, your back against the chair — and become aware of your awareness.

4. Shift your attention to your breathing, gently in and out. Become aware of your awareness of your breathing. As this awareness of awareness of your experience in the present moment deepens, the mind quiets and the chatter stops. You can drop into a sense of being here, now, in this moment — into a steady sense of simple presence. This moment...this breath...here..and now. This present moment ...this present breath...this precious moment...this precious breath...

5. Let your awareness come to rest in a steady inner peace of being rather than doing. Stay in this sense of steady presence as long as you can, even if it's only for a few seconds at first: it's delicious. A sense of spaciousness, a stillness, or a sweetness is a reliable marker that you're present. Take a moment to notice any shifts in your consciousness as you come to that stillness, that quiet of mind, that allows you to access and listen deeply to the wisdom of your own true nature.

The practice of presence and the trust in the deep inner wisdom that arises from it can bring a new sense of assurance in your capacity for wise, resilient action.

Intention

And the day came when the risk to remain tight in a bud was more painful than the risk it took to blossom.

— ANAÏS NIN

As chapter 1 shows, focused attention causes neurons in the brain to fire; repeated focusing on the same object or experience causes repeated neural firings; and repeated neural firings create a new and stable neural structure. When we focus our attention on cultivating a particular pattern of behavior, a character trait, or attitude or lens for filtering our experience, we incline the mind toward that objective. We notice more readily the desired trait or behavior, register it more fully in our consciousness, and direct mental activity toward it. For instance, when we formulate an intention to become more mindful, more self-accepting, and more flexible as support for becoming more resilient, the repeated focus on that intention begins to build new brain structure and circuitry that support us in achieving the intention. The brain is primed to make us more likely to act in ways that will actually manifest that particular intention. We turn a neural goat path into a freeway.

Researchers have found that, more than half the time, it's the need to get out of an attitude or circumstance that is causing us suffering or pain gets us moving on a new course of action. The sincere intention to develop resilience and well-being can fuel a determination to persevere in rewiring the brain for more resilience.

There is one caveat to keep in mind when thinking about intentions. Adopting the stance that we *should* cultivate a particular behavior or trait sets us up for potential failure, whereas taking the attitude that we *can* cultivate it sets us up for learning. When my client Nigel wanted to overcome his fear of public speaking, he found venues where he could speak in front of a group if he chose to, but he didn't ever have to. He resisted the temptation to feel that he *should* speak. The possibility of speaking without pressure to perform allowed him to build his success slowly, at his own pace, but steadily. The skillful setting of an intention is based on creating options and possibilities, not forcing ourselves into particular defined behaviors. Moving from "must" to "trust" of ourselves encourages learning and more quickly rewires our brain for flexibility and resilience.

When my client Sean was going through a particularly tough time, waking up every morning in a bit of existential panic, I suggested he set the intention to not get out of bed until he could bring his mind and body to a state of calm. Sean began noticing the state he was in when he first woke up and practiced coming into the state of presence described in exercise 1. A few weeks later, when he came in to report his progress, Sean acknowledged that he had to practice self-empathy and self-compassion, too. At first, his body and brain needed more than an hour to come to the state of ease and equilibrium from which he wanted to launch his day. But within two weeks, he was able to arrive at that state of calm in forty minutes; soon he was able to reduce the time to twenty minutes, then five minutes, then the space of just a few breaths. What a grand day it was when he woke up *in* that state of calm.

Because setting an intention, and following through with deliberate behaviors to fulfill that intention, sculpts neural structure in the brain, we need to choose our intentions carefully. To recover resilience, we can incline the mind in specific ways: "May I learn to stay grounded in my body when my sister-in-law picks a fight with me." "May I be patient with myself as I learn to stay grounded." "May I remember to breathe when I get startled or upset." "May I pause and reflect before impulsively fixing somebody." "May I focus on what's right in the moment at least as often as I do on what's wrong." "May I have compassion for myself when I forget all of the above." A simple yet powerful way to practice setting intentions is to set the intention to *notice.*

Exercise 2: Setting Intention

Every morning for the next week, set the intention to notice what you notice first thing as you say hello to your child, partner, or pet; as you step outside your home; as you smell your morning coffee; as you taste the flavors of your sandwich at lunch.

Noticing strengthens your mindfulness practice. Noticing your noticing strengthens your awareness. Setting an

> intention, and then noticing yourself carry out that intention, strengthens your confidence and your capacity to create new patterns of response to experiences. You are strengthening a neural mechanism that underlies all resilience.

Perseverance

How long should you try? Until.

— JIM ROHN

Recovering resilience in the face of challenges and changes can be difficult and painful work. Perseverance in our efforts to harness neuroplasticity is the sine qua non of rewiring our brains. By persevering in the use of new tools and techniques, we are stabilizing the new neural circuitry so that it can serve as a reliable platform of resilient behaviors, not easily overridden by the pulls of the past.

Scientists differ in their assessment of how many times a pattern of neural firing must be repeated to be reliably encoded in the brain. Some data indicate seventeen times; another study concluded fifty-six. But even if we don't know exactly how long we must practice a habit to stabilize the new brain structure, we do know that a few moments of practice many times a day is more effective than an hour once a week. Frequent and regular repetition creates steady neural firing and rewiring and accelerates the process. We also know that a stance of willingness — focusing on possibilities — is more effective than a stance of willpower — focusing on performance. It almost doesn't matter at first how small the increment of change is. What's important is that we choose practices that catalyze positive change and that we persevere.

A reporter interviewing Thomas Edison asked him how he felt about failing two thousand times before he discovered how to harness electricity in a lightbulb. Edison is said to have replied, "My dear young man, I did not fail. I did invent the lightbulb. It was simply a 2,000-step process."

Exercise 3: Strengthening Perseverance

1. Set an intention to implement a practice that will rewire your brain in a way that feels important to you, such as one of the following

    (a) to cultivate an attitude you value, like gratitude;

    (b) to see circumstances from a new perspective rather than responding automatically with preconceived notions;

    (c) to respond to an ongoing stressor with a new behavior, breaking the cascade of automatic reactions and deliberately choosing something new.

2. Create a cue to remind yourself of your intention. There are various ways to do this:

    (a) put a sticky note on your computer reminding you to notice events in the day to be grateful for;

    (b) shift gears by counting to three before you answer the phone or the doorbell to give yourself time to become present and able to respond with a more open frame of mind;

    (c) use a common action, like plugging in the coffeemaker or turning the key in the car's ignition, as a cue to remember your intention for the day.

3. Identify behaviors that help manifest that intention and experiment with implementing them. Some examples include

    (a) expressing your appreciation to your partner for five generous things he or she did that day;

    (b) putting yourself in the shoes of the person on the phone or at the door and trying to see the interaction between the two of you from the other person's point of view;

    (c) when encountering disappointments, mistakes, or dysfunction, asking "What's right with this wrong?" as part of framing a skillful response to the stressor.

4. Repeat the behavior for a week, then another, then a month. You can experiment with expanding the behavior as you learn what works to manifest your intention. Here are some ways to do this:

(a) express your appreciation to your child, your sister-in-law, your coworkers, and the grocery store clerk for any generous behaviors on their part;

(b) shift your perspective, maybe by acknowledging the sincere motivation of your brother George when he surprised you by weeding your backyard for your birthday, even though he unknowingly pulled up all the daffodils along with the weeds;

(c) Keeping in mind that the Chinese written character for the word *crisis* is made up of the characters meaning *danger* and *opportunity*, find an opportunity in at least three crises this month.

5. Notice what changes in your brain as you persevere in your practice.

I once had a client who, after practicing for weeks to stay open-minded rather than cursing when she watched the evening news, told me she had bounded down the stairs in excitement one day, saying, "I'm growing new neurons!" The courage to persevere in rewiring our brains toward the five Cs of coping is supported when we see that our intentional rewiring is working: we see ourselves getting over the hump and establishing behaviors that are new or different from before. When we see that we are learning, changing, and growing, we keep going.

Refuges

We do not believe in ourselves until someone reveals that deep inside us there is something valuable, worth listening to,

worthy of our trust, sacred to our touch. Once we believe
in ourselves, we can risk curiosity, wonder, spontaneous
delight or any experience that reveals the human spirit.

— E. E. CUMMINGS

Modern neuroscience confirms what we can experience on our own: safety and trust are the wellsprings of resilience, exploration, and growth. They are also essential to healthy brain development and to rewiring our brains at any age. In the earliest periods of development, a frightened child seeks safety, protection, and comfort from a parent; when soothed, he bounces up to go off and explore again. The brain is open to learning again. The same holds true all our lives. Experiencing anything within a context that helps us feel safe also helps us remain resilient and responsive. I spent all forty-five of the shaking, rocking minutes of the 1989 earthquake and its aftershocks in San Francisco huddled under a big conference table with six coworkers, all of us holding hands, offering one another reassurance, as the earth rippled underneath us. That refuge of companionship allowed us to stay calm enough to see clearly what was happening and to connect with each other as resources. When the aftershocks stopped, we went home to find further refuge in friends and family and maintain our flexibility to respond as we began to deal with the damage to homes and possessions and took steps to rebuild.

Refuge simply means a safe, supportive place to be when we are fragile or confused, a safe place to cry or rant as long as we need to, or somewhere to wait patiently until a course of action begins to emerge from the chaos. We all need refuges, safe havens, and sanctuaries, not to escape from the current demons and dreads but in order to regroup, to pull ourselves together, to "resettle our molecules," as my friend Phyllis Kirson would say. The calm we find in those refuges helps us return to calm inside; from there, our brain can recover its capacities to see clearly and to cope in new and better ways.

We find refuge in trustworthy relationships, in the sacred spaces of home or nature, in meditative activities (which can include any activity done meditatively, like washing the dishes or gardening). We find refuge in the vitality of our own bodies, in the juiciness of our emotions, in the clarity of our consciousness, in the wisdom of our true nature. We learn to create a quiet space, a leisure of time, a retreat from the *Sturm und Drang* of daily living to do what I like to call REST — *relax* and *enter* into *safety* and *trust*. In this refuge, we replenish ourselves. We help our nervous systems return to, or remain in, the state of physiological calm and equanimity called the "window of tolerance" that allows us to cope with anything without resorting to our primitive survival responses.

The following sections and exercises illustrate ways to find simple refuges in people, places, and practices that can help you return to the process of harnessing your neuroplasticity to learn even more resilient ways of coping.

Finding Refuge in People

We may seek refuge among good friends, people we can trust to not judge or disdain us when we become emotionally unglued or our thinking becomes unhinged: people who can simply be with us until we regroup and are ready to face the world again. We saw how Joe was this kind of refuge for Dan. These are people whose own stability and calm we can borrow until we can regain our own. They may be on our short list of "go-to" people whom we can call at 2 AM, trusting that we will be held in what the psychologist Carl Rogers calls "unconditional positive regard," that they will reassure us that we are (or will be) okay, even though our world is crashing around us. Or we may find refuge in other people who simply happen to be there when a crisis arises, as my colleagues and I turned to one another during the earthquake.

If you don't have a lot of people in your life at the moment who can offer a refuge, don't be discouraged. You can create a genuinely effective circle of support in your imagination. This circle can include people you trust and feel supported by, or it may be made up of imaginary people you would like to meet. Your circle may include a spiritual figure like Jesus or the Dalai Lama. It may include your own wiser self. Visualizing ourselves as encircled by real or imaginary friends who "have our back" can greatly enhance our ease and resilience as we face an unknown or frightening situation.

I experienced the power of calling on support in my imagination almost a decade ago, when I chose to have LASIK eye surgery to correct lifelong nearsightedness and astigmatism. The operation was risky, so I went into it with understandable anxiety. I had asked friends to think of me that day, at the time I was actually in surgery, so that I would feel supported and not alone during the procedure. I had to remain conscious during the operation, and focusing my eyes on the light above me so that the laser could track exactly where to reshape the cornea to give me 20/20 vision. While lying on the gurney, as still as I could, I thought of all my friends thinking of me; I took in the love and caring that I knew were being sent my way.

About ten minutes into the operation, quite suddenly, I lost all sense of anxiety. Instead I was flooded with an overpowering sense of love and belonging. There was nothing to be afraid of, nothing at all. I remained in that state of serenity for the remainder of the surgery (which was completely successful).

Imagined experiences can be nearly as powerful as actual events for creating new brain circuitry. Neuroscientists have discovered that the same neurons fire in our visual cortex when we imagine seeing a banana as when we see one for real. When you use the power of your imagination to repeatedly visualize people supporting you, you are installing a pattern of coping in your neural circuitry that you can use as a refuge in times of difficulty or challenge.

Exercise 4: Creating a Circle of Support

1. Identify a specific situation for which you would like support, such as going to a supervisor to discuss a complaint or a raise, preparing for an audit by the IRS, telling your

brother and sister-in-law you won't be joining them for Thanksgiving this year, or confronting your teenage son about drug paraphernalia stashed in his bedroom closet.

2. Take thirty seconds to identify several people you would like to have, in your imagination, by your side in this situation. Imagine them fully present, fully supportive. You're not alone. Practice evoking this sense of refuge again and again until it becomes a natural habit of your brain that you can call on any time you need it.

Evoking refuges and resources in the imagination can feel as real to the brain as having them physically present. The possibilities of using imagination to rewire our brains can stretch toward the infinite. The next time you face an unexpected challenge or crisis, notice any increased sense of inner safety as you evoke your circle of support to help you act resiliently.

Finding Refuge in Places

The Peace of Wild Things

When despair for the world grows in me
and I wake in the night at the least sound
in fear of what my life and my children's lives may be,
I go and lie down where the wood drake
rests in his beauty on the water, and the great heron feeds.
I come into the peace of wild things
who do not tax their lives with forethought
of grief. I come into the presence of still water.
And I feel above me the day-blind stars
waiting with their light. For a time
I rest in the grace of the world, and am free.
— WENDELL BERRY

We all need a safe place we can retreat to when the going gets rough — wilderness or a garden, a church or temple, our car or office, a friend's home or our own snug bed — to reconnect with our wisest, most resilient self. When a place has repeatedly been used as a refuge, by ourselves or by many other people, the physical place itself reverberates with a feeling of welcome and safety. We can sense its energy and feel ourselves calm down when we enter it.

Anywhere can be a safe place of refuge if it is "ego-syntonic" — if it suits our temperament, conditioning, and life circumstances. It may be a favorite tree in a park or a rock by the ocean to sit on while we search for the way through a current dilemma. Every time we go to our safe place, we deepen our sense of being held by a compassion larger than our own small world; we can come to terms with our losses and difficulties more quickly and resiliently.

My friend Dale lost most of his retirement savings in the financial downturn of 2008. Understandably distraught, he went to his safe place, a particular bench in a city park overlooking a small lagoon. When he showed up afterward at my front door, he said simply, in his Texas drawl, "That was the most peaceful half hour I have ever spent in my entire life." Going to his safe place didn't solve Dale's financial problems, but it did help him recover a relaxed flexibility in his brain so that he could remember his own capacities to deal with difficulties and begin the work of doing so. The following exercise is a guided visualization that will help you cultivate a sense of refuge in a safe place, one that you can evoke in your imagination any time you need to.

Exercise 5: Creating a Safe Place

1. Sit comfortably and quietly. When you are ready, imagine that you are standing in front of a gate. Imagine in rich detail how tall the gate is, how wide, how thick, what it's made of, what color it is. Make this gate as real as you can in your mind's eye.

2. Then imagine yourself opening the gate and walking through. When you are on the other side, visualize what lies ahead: a path, a hallway, a trail, or a street that will lead you to a place that is very special, just for you. This is your safe place.

3. Begin to walk along the path. As you walk, notice whatever you are seeing, hearing, or smelling, or anything you are simply noticing.

4. After a while, you come to a place that you know is your safe place. It may be a meadow, a cottage, a special room in a house, a beach, a garden courtyard, or anywhere that is a special place for you. Allow yourself to walk up to your safe place and enter.

5. Take time to look around: notice all the things that help you feel safe and comfortable here. Relax and enjoy being here; feel the sense of confidence and inner strength your safe place gives you.

6. If you choose to, find a place to sit down. Add anything you want to this space to help you feel safer and more at ease. Remove anything you don't want. You can change anything you want. Then simply relax, feeling at ease, enjoying your safe place.

7. When it's time to leave, imagine standing up, leaving the safe place the same way you came in, walking back along the same path or walkway you took to get here, eventually passing through the gate, turning around, and closing it. Your safe place is on the other side, but you know you can return any time you need to.

8. Practice evoking this safe place in ordinary, nonstressful moments so that it is available to you when the flak hits the fan. Recognize that you are using your brain's neuroplasticity to create a new and reliable resource of coping.

Finding Refuge in Contemplative Practice

One day I was meditating in my office on a break, but I had left the phone ringer on, and when the phone rang, I answered it. My doctor was calling to say there was an abnormality in my most recent mammogram; would I schedule an appointment to come in and have another X-ray? My anxiety went right through the roof. All the stories about friends' courses of cancer treatment started rushing through my head. But because I had been meditating and had come into a state of calm awareness before the phone rang, I could clearly see my own anxiety go through the roof, see clearly that it was going through the roof, schedule the appointment for the second mammogram (which turned out to be normal), and return to my meditating, now with a different object of awareness but still held in awareness, aware of being aware.

The Buddhist tradition emphasizes the importance of taking refuge in the practices that lead to wisdom. Practices such as meditation, yoga, and centering prayer deepen mindful empathy, the compassionate capacity to hold whatever curveballs life throws at us and take us further on the process of recovering resilience.

Exercise 6: Choosing a Practice

A path of practice is an established collection of teachings and tools that have been demonstrated over time and in different cultures and circumstances to be useful guides to developing skillful behaviors and the conscious awareness and compassion that sustain those behaviors.

1. Many practices are available in our modern Western world. The key to finding one that works for you is to approach practices from a variety of traditions with openness, curiosity, a sense of exploration and experiment, and willingness to "see for yourself," as the Buddha taught.

2. Resonance — tuning into what feels right for you — is key to choosing a practice that will accelerate your process of brain change.

3. It's helpful to try only one practice at a time rather than diffuse your energy by flitting from one practice to another. It is also important to give any potential practice a fair try. The focus and discipline involved in sticking with a practice allow your brain to rewire more deeply. Discernment and dedication will help you settle into a practice that can sustain your process of change over the long haul.

4. You may find it helpful to identify role models — people who seem to have the qualities of resilience you want to develop for yourself — and ask them what practices have helped them. Notice which communities of practice most resonate with you, the you that you are becoming.

All of these refuges — people, places, and practices — provide the conditions of safety and trust that make it easier to bounce back from trouble or trauma, to cope resourcefully and resiliently. And they create the conditions your brain needs to most reliably rewire itself.

Resources

Sometimes I go about in pity for myself, and
all the while a great wind is bearing me across the sky.

— OJIBWA SAYING

Resources are the safety net of resilience. Connecting to resources — seeking support that will either alleviate a difficulty in concrete, practical ways or that will nourish and replenish us so that we can persevere in trying to resolve it — is one of the five Cs of coping. Resources bring strength and energy to our endeavors at the very moment we need them, shoring up our courage rather than letting us fall into depletion or despair. Resources keep us steady and balanced so that even in crisis, we can try to rewire our brains in a more resilient direction. It is important to cultivate multiple layers of resources, so that if one safety net fails we can rely on another. As you build your resource bank, remember that resources are interchangeable: a lack of one kind of resource can be compensated for by an abundance of another.

Material Objects as Resources

Prepare for emergencies, big or small, by keeping helpful objects at hand such as a granola bar stashed in the glove compartment in case the fatigue of a busy day starts to set in while we're stuck in traffic; safety pins kept in a desk drawer in case a shirt button falls off ten minutes before a meeting; extra blankets stored under the bed in case a power failure means no heat for three days. They are a form of "saving for a rainy day" that is part of our intention to create more well-being in our lives.

Exercise 7: Creating Material Resources

1. Identify one potential emergency that you could be better prepared for with a little forethought: for example, a power failure that knocks out your refrigerator.
2. Create at least one material resource to prepare for that emergency, like storing bottles of water in the freezer to help keep food cold in the refrigerator when the power goes out. This preparation will make you more resilient and may save you a great deal of time and frustration later.

Seeing yourself take action to strengthen your safety nets of resilience helps develop competence, another of the five Cs of coping. Registering that increasing sense of competence in your sense of self helps strengthen your overall resilience.

People as Resources

People who serve as role models offer wisdom from their own experience, giving us keys to crack the code of how to live resiliently, whether we are observing them, talking with them, or evoking their presence in our imagination. From them we learn competencies and values to guide our actions, sometimes through direct instruction and practical suggestions, sometimes by the "contagion" of coping: the resonance from spending time with a resilient role model can call forth the same capacities for resilience in us. And because our brains can encode new patterns of coping directly from interacting with other resilient brains, identifying people as resources greatly accelerates our own brain change.

I learned the power of people as resources when I began seeing clients in graduate school, putting in the hours of clinical practice required for becoming a licensed psychotherapist. My emerging resilience was being tested every day by the chaos and confusion of my clients' lives, but never more so than one afternoon when a client called to say that her teenage daughter had committed suicide the night before.

Nothing in my training or my life experience up to that point had equipped me to know how to stay fully resilient in that moment. I managed to schedule a time to see her that night, but I was in a state of shock — not a calm presence, certainly not yet the stalwart, skillful clinician my client needed to help her through such bewildering, devastating loss and grief.

I told my supervisor at the clinic what had happened. With two teenage daughters of her own, she wobbled a bit, too. She went to see the clinic director, who, a bit more removed and a lot more experienced, was rock solid in knowing how to handle the situation. She was able to steady my supervisor and suggest many things to do that would be helpful to me and my client. With her own equilibrium restored, my supervisor could be clear and empathic with me about how I could best support my client. I felt her steadiness, recovered my own, learned some essential skills for handling such situations, and was able to be quite helpful to my client that night.

The resources we connect to by reaching out to others can greatly accelerate the rewiring of our coping strategies. My client Doug grew up in a family that was both dysfunctionally disconnected within itself and isolated from other families. He had never even attended a birthday party until his first year of community college, and no one had ever thrown a birthday party for him. As he approached his twenty-first birthday, he decided to throw a party for himself. For Doug, this event was as significant a marker of becoming a competent adult as knowing how to buy a car or rent his own apartment.

He approached a guy he had met through pick-up basketball games who seemed to know how to get people together for social occasions. Doug's request for advice turned into a three-week mentoring project: Neil helped Doug identify whom to invite, what sort of event to host, and when to hold it, and coached him on the details — obtaining the food and drinks and planning activities and rituals that Doug had only glimpsed from afar. Doug had a great time celebrating his twenty-first birthday, resourced by people who could help him figure out how to make his way in the world in this particular way. And he learned the value of finding a role model to help him crack the code and rewire his own brain.

Exercise 8: Discovering People as Resources

1. Identify one skill or capacity of resilience you would like to develop.
2. Identify one person you could have a conversation with — a friend, a coworker, a neighbor, a therapist — to learn that skill. Or ask these same people whom they would

recommend as a role model. You can even select a role model whom you may never have a direct conversation with but from whom you can learn by observation and listening. This conversation could even be a dialogue with the intuitive wisdom of your wiser self.

3. Initiate the conversation between yourself and your role model. (If this step seems challenging, you can even identify a role model who can help you learn how to initiate conversations.) Or initiate a period of observation of your role model, learning from watching and listening.

4. Notice what you're learning from your role model about the chosen skill. Also notice what you are learning about learning from people as a resource.

Spirituality as a Resource

One summer night, out on a flat headland, all but surrounded by the waters of the bay, the horizons were remote and distant rims on the edge of space. Millions of stars blazed in darkness, and on the far shore a few lights burned in cottages. Otherwise there was no reminder of human life. My companion and I were alone with the stars: the misty river of the Milky Way flowing across the sky, the patterns of the constellations standing out bright and clear, a blazing planet low on the horizon. It occurred to me that if this were a sight that could be seen only once in a century, this little headland would be thronged with spectators. But it can be seen many scores of night in any year, and so the lights burned in the cottages and the inhabitants probably gave not a thought to the beauty overhead; and because they could see it almost any night, perhaps they never will.

— RACHEL CARSON

I love this reminder from Rachel Carson, the noted conservationist and author of *Silent Spring*. Moments of awe — noticing for even one moment the beauty, harmony, and miraculousness of the life around us and the life within us — remind us of the wonder that anything exists at all. They connect us to the (re)source of all of existence. Neurologically, in moments like these, we are entering the "being" mode of brain processing that allows us to see the big picture and loosen our grip on our accustomed ways of perceiving reality. In this mode it is much easier for our brains to rewire our patterns of coping.

One workshop participant shared one of her favorite ways of opening herself to this resource. Any time Molly noticed sunlight sparkling on water — in a drop of water on a leaf, in the flashing diamonds of ripples on a small lake — she was transported into spacious awareness. Both the physical beauty of that scene (processed by the defocusing consciousness) and her awareness of the facts of the physics — that the sparkle of sunlight had just traveled 93 million miles in eight seconds to reflect off the leaf or lake onto the retina of her eye — (processed by the focusing network of the brain) left her in awe of the mystery of it all. The deep knowing that she, too, was part of that web of existence became another resource for Molly.

Exercise 9: Connecting to Spiritual Resources

1. Take a moment to follow the poet William Blake's advice

    > To see a world in a grain of sand,
    > And a heaven in a wildflower;
    > Hold infinity in the palm of your hand,
    > And eternity in an hour.

    It doesn't matter what object you focus your attention on: it could be the prism of colors of a drop of car oil on your driveway, the bubbles in an ice cube, the perfect arc of toenail on your child's foot.

2. Let your perceptions open to beauty and sense the mystery hidden in the ordinary. Let your consciousness become extraordinary for a moment. Notice any shifts in your sense of possibility as you do. An expanded sense of possibility fosters flexibility and increases your brain's capacity for resilience.

All of these resources — material, relational, and spiritual — provide the tools and support we need to cope with the unexpected, the unwanted, the apparently insurmountable. They keep us afloat in a sea of troubles. They allow us to continue to exercise choice in responding to life's travails, deciding how we want to manage how we respond and making it more likely that we will succeed.

To be resilient, we need both the safety of refuge and the courage provided by our resources. You may notice that the same person, place, or practice can function as both refuge and resource. That's not a problem. When we take refuge in a good night's sleep, we also create a resource for the next day. Virginia Woolf wrote of the need for a room of one's own — a refuge — and five hundred pounds a year — a resource — to support creative and resilient endeavors. If refuge and resource overlap, creating an integrated platform for resilience, that is just fine, even efficient.

Pulling It All Together

The five practices you have learned in this chapter — cultivation of presence, intention, perseverance, refuges, and resources — are all helpful in any process of personal growth and self-transformation.

- *Presence* — showing up and engaging with experience — is a gateway to neural receptivity that helps the brain more easily learn and rewire.

- *Intention* inclines the mind toward resilient behaviors and strengthens the neural circuitry that supports them.
- *Perseverance* creates new neural structure through repetition, making it easier for desired brain change to last.
- *Refuges* create the safety and trust that support brain change and growth.
- *Resources* generate the strength, energy, steadiness, and balance we need for adaptive coping.

These practices are essential for rewiring your brain for resilience. Along with mindful empathy, which helps you see clearly, the practice of presence brings you into a state of calm. When you connect to refuges and resources, you create more options for coping. When you set intentions to cultivate practical skills of resilience, and when you persevere in those intentions, you become more competent. All of these practices, and the reward of more resilient coping that comes from them, boost your courage to keep going. These practices are the foundation of the program of brain change presented in the next chapter: they help make the changes safe, efficient, and effective. You can look forward to immediate benefits from rewiring your brain for resilience.

CHAPTER SIX

Self-Directed Neuroplasticity

*To exist is to change; to change is to mature; to mature is to
go on creating one's self endlessly.*

— HENRI BERGSON

THE PRACTICES TAUGHT in the previous chapters help you establish
a safe and strong neural platform for rewiring conditioned patterns
encoded in your brain's circuitry. Over time, these practices steadily
strengthen the prefrontal cortex to do that rewiring and sustain the
changes you create in your brain circuitry.

The actual rewiring, and the establishment of new patterns of
coping, occurs through the three processes of brain change presented in this chapter: new conditioning, deconditioning, and reconditioning. All three processes can be used again and again as you
discover more old strategies that you want to replace with more
resilient ways of coping. These processes have a cumulative effect.
The more you rewire into your brain skillful, resilient patterns of
coping, the more competent your brain becomes at the task.

New conditioning creates new neural pathways in your brain.
You learn new, more adaptive coping strategies that will then lead
to greater resilience. We know that new experiences, and repeating
those experiences, cause neurons in your brain to fire in ways that

create and stabilize those neural pathways. To rewire your brain for resilience, you seek out new experiences that you know will encode these more adaptive coping strategies into your brain's circuitry and repeat them.

For example, if you want to create circuits in the brain that help you remain calm, you seek out and practice experiences of being calm, as my client Sean did with his intention to wake up in a state of calm. If you want to create the circuitry that supports your competence in negotiating with customer-care representatives on the phone, you seek opportunities to teach your brain through experiences of doing that well.

The neural patterns of resilience that result from new conditioning can, over time, become automatic habits of coping. With practice, these strategies can even completely override the old, less functional habits. New habits of coping can become so steady, so reliable that you behave resiliently without having to think about it anymore.

Deconditioning creates the receptivity and flexibility in your neural circuitry that reopens your brain to learning and change, enabling it to unlearn old, less effective coping strategies. Deconditioning uses the awareness and acceptance that come from a compassionate mindfulness practice to shift the processing of your brain to the diffuse, "soft" focus of the defocusing network. The defocusing network generates a neural flexibility, allowing you to alter even patterns learned unconsciously and deeply embedded. Deconditioning creates a new mental "play space" in your brain, making it far easier to wire in the new strategies as you choose to.

Reconditioning helps you rewire the neural circuitry of an existing strategy by pairing that strategy with a new, more effective one. When the strategies are paired in your conscious awareness, the simultaneous firing of neurons encoding both strategies allows them to deconsolidate (fall apart), then reconsolidate (rewire) *together* a fraction of a second later. The neural firing pattern of the new strategy can supersede the old, often rewiring it completely, immediately, and permanently.

All three processes of self-directed neuroplasticity, like any conditioning in the brain, are neutral. They will encode either more resilient or less resilient patterns. They will more reliably encode better strategies for resilience when supported by the synergy of mindfulness and empathy — awareness of the process and compassionate acceptance of any responses that the process evokes. These processes have a global impact on brain functioning. They will help you recover many innate capacities in the brain in addition to resilience, such as motivation, equanimity, self-expression, creativity, and altruism. Resilience itself is a capacity that allows us to recover many others.

New Conditioning

New conditioning occurs through intentional learning from experience. By selecting experiences that can teach us new, more adaptive coping strategies, we deliberately create new neural connections — new pathways and circuits of resilience in the brain. We must be careful in our choices for that new learning. Rather than encoding more facts — cramming more data into the storage locker of memory — *learning* here means training the brain to respond in new and more effective ways to the challenges of our lives. We learn to take a moment to breathe, count to ten, focus on "what's right with what's wrong," and regroup. We learn to listen to our wise mind amid the other voices of our "inner committee." We learn how to ask for help in ways that people actually hear and respond to; we learn to receive and benefit from the help offered. As we expand our brain's capacity to link the new strategies that come from these experiences into new patterns, we are learning to be more resilient. And the more we practice new conditioning, the more we are strengthening those structures in the brain that do that conditioning and help us learn.

When my client Bill learned to use new conditioning to override one particular old pattern, he was able to create a more loving connection with his partner, Sharon. Bill grew up feeling disappointed in his dad, who was never a reliable provider for the family. Bill's way of handling his disappointment was with relentless criticism of his dad, which extended to anyone else who disappointed him. When Bill recognized how automatically and relentlessly critical he became whenever he felt disappointed by his partner, Sharon — maybe twenty times a day — he realized he had to do something to change.

When he came in for his appointment, we worked on new conditioning to change his response. Each time Bill noticed criticism beginning to flare, he was to be aware of what was happening in his body and brain and compassionately accept that it was happening. The inner tightening and clutching he felt when he became critical were a cue for him to pause and be aware. Then he would say to himself the words "Be kind!"

This process broke the old, automatic circuit of complaining and criticizing, creating a choice point. Bill could then begin to open up to empathy, compassion, and acceptance for himself and for Sharon. With enough good intention and diligent work, the process also opened up the possibility for them to find a better way through their difficulties.

New conditioned patterns and new habits of behavior can override our earlier conditioning, especially in realms of feeling, dealing, and relating to others. We redefine the self in relationship to triggering events and create a new reference point for coping. And as we develop and reinforce these new patterns for coping, we grow into our more competent and courageous adult selves.

Although Bill was able to put the new conditioning into effect immediately, it took six months before it became automatic. Eventually, he could drop into a sense of kindness whenever he chose to, and the old pattern of criticism or complaint was rarely triggered at all. The newly conditioned pattern — reacting to feeling critical with kindness — now lives side by side in Bill's brain's circuitry with the old pattern of being critical. Most of the time Bill can rely on it to override the older habit. The success of this new conditioning and the strengthening of the brain structures he needed to do it made it easier for Bill to make other changes. Integrating new conditioning with other old patterns became easier and easier to do.

Exercise 1: Creating a Better Choice through New Conditioning

1. Identify a habitual negative reaction — impatience, boredom, startle, temper, rejection — that you would like to use as a cue to practice rewiring your brain.
2. Identify the new response you would like to substitute: allowing, exploring something new, calming down, pausing to reflect, seeing the good.
3. Identify a positive code word or phrase you will use to break the circuit and cue yourself to change the channel in your brain: "Allow," "Explore," "It's okay," "Pause," "What's the good here?" The choice of words is up to you: what's important is to use the cue as soon as you identify the trigger, to prevent yourself from falling into your old, conditioned reaction. You may choose a word that already brings to mind a state of resilience or well-being if you have one: "Love," "Learn," "Breathe," "Slow down," or "Open." Practice saying your cue word to yourself while you're in that actual state so that your brain conditions itself to shift to that state when it registers the cue.
4. Each time the trigger arises, practice the new pattern of response: say your cue word and shift to the state you've chosen as the new experience (for example, a genuine kindness) as many times as you need to for the new pattern to become the new habit.
5. Notice as the old pattern fades away into the background and the new pattern becomes more automatic. You have conditioned new learning in your brain, and you have learned that you can do so. Take in the sense of success and mastery as you experience the actual rewiring in your brain.

Deconditioning

As part of his effort to change his old conditioning, Bill began to practice mindful empathy to open his awareness to the bigger picture of his relationship to Sharon. As he became more aware of the compassion and love in their relationship, he could relax and come into a deeper sense of inner peace and well-being. He felt a sense of his inner goodness, always accessible underneath all the learned patterns of coping, which brought him to a greater sense of Sharon's inner goodness, too. With this new awareness, the grip of the old patterns of reactivity began to loosen. From the receptivity generated by his deconditioning, Bill was able to view Sharon with more kindness.

Exercise 2: Entering a Mental Play Space through Deconditioning

This exercise helps you use awareness of experiences of goodness and well-being to defocus from the worries and concerns of the personal self and relax into a spacious mental play space where rewiring old patterns of coping becomes easier to do.

1. Sit or lie down comfortably. Breathe slowly and gently into your belly, in and out. Breathe in a sense of goodness, a sense of safety and well-being.

2. Gently bring into your awareness the people and things in your life you are grateful for. Savor the gratitude throughout your body. Remember moments when people have been kind to you, and when you have been kind to others. Savor the feeling of kindness throughout your body. Remember a moment of feeling loved and cherished by someone, then remember a moment of your loving and cherishing someone (or a beloved pet). Savor the feeling of love.

3. Let yourself claim your own goodness. Notice any feeling of ease and peacefulness as you relax into this state; know

that this state of spacious awareness and acceptance is the source of kindness, compassion, and goodwill. Trust that from here it becomes possible to change old patterns in whatever direction you choose.

Using mindfulness practice to shift to the defocusing network of the brain helps your brain become more trusting and receptive of new learning and new possibilities. The larger awareness can also help you let go of your previous conditioning. As you become more practiced at entering this defocused play space, you can apply this process of deconditioning to work past any trouble spot in your old patterns of conditioning, as discussed in part 2.

Reconditioning

Although new patterns of coping generally serve us well, they can be challenged when we are fatigued, stressed, or overwhelmed. When the brain switches into survival mode, it can easily revert to the default coping mechanisms tucked away in implicit memory. Even though we know better, we find ourselves reacting in old, less resilient ways: yelling, panicking, criticizing. If that old reactivity becomes dominant again, we can turn to the third process of brain change: reconditioning.

Bill returned to my office a year after our initial work together. Sharon had recently lost her job, and the financial strain was taking a toll on their relationship. Bill noticed that his old pattern of automatic criticism and judgment had resurfaced. His perception that Sharon was failing to be a good enough provider was triggering Bill's old patterns of disappointment with and criticism of his dad. This time we set out to use reconditioning to rewire the implicit memories underlying the habitual criticism.

Reconditioning depends on an intricate neural mechanism that neuroscientists have been able to detect with brain-imaging technology only in the past ten years. This research shows that neural networks that constitute any individual memory (or thought or belief) spontaneously fall apart (deconsolidate) and then reconsolidate again a fraction of a second later. This is the naturally occurring process by which memories, thoughts, or beliefs change over time: for example, it's why ten different people may remember the same car accident differently years later. It's the strength of our conditioning — the repetition of experiences that cause repeated neural firings, which strengthen neural connections that create entire circuits of memory — that keeps us from losing all our learning as a consequence of this falling apart and rewiring.

Neuroscientists can now demonstrate how, under the right circumstances, we can choose to harness that natural deconsolidation-reconsolidation process to intervene between the deconsolidation and reconsolidation phases and redirect the reconsolidation. This is how reconditioning happens.

When we deliberately focus our attention on a negative memory we want to resolve or dissolve, the focused attention causes the neurons constellating that memory to fire at every level — from implicit body-based and emotional memories to explicit cognitive thoughts. Neuropsychologists call that process "lighting up the network," making the old memory available for rewiring.

Using mindful empathy is a critical part of rewiring through reconditioning. It is essential to be able to observe the old experience rather than remaining embedded in it, which runs the risk of strengthening the old memory and retraumatizing us. In Bill's case, we began by establishing a strong state of mindful empathy to safely hold this powerful process of rewiring the brain.

Once I was sure that Bill could keep one foot mindfully, empathically, in the present while he evoked a memory from the past, I asked him to remember one specific moment of criticism of his dad that we could use to begin to recondition his brain. Bill remembered a time when he was eight years old and his dad had come home with news that he had been laid off from the factory — again. Bill's mom got upset and angry; Bill remembered that he had joined his mom in yelling at his dad and calling him a loser.

To light up the networks of that memory, I had Bill share as many details of his experience as he could: where he was standing when his dad came home, what he was feeling when his mom got upset, what he said to his dad, how he felt as he was yelling at his dad, how he felt afterward when his dad retreated to the garage, and how he was feeling now sharing this experience with me.

Once the memory we wanted to work on was lit up, I asked Bill to recall a more positive experience that directly countered the first memory: a happier moment with his dad, a moment of feeling kindness toward him. Bill remembered a time at about the same age when he and his dad played catch in the backyard. Neither one of them was very good at catching the ball, but they were laughing, goofing off, and having fun. Bill's eyes teared up as he remembered the simple joy of that afternoon. He had felt kindly then toward his dad and felt a surge of kindness toward him again as he shared that memory with me.

Once Bill had lit up both the memory of criticism and the memory of the kindness, we had the groundwork laid for reconditioning.

The key to reconditioning is holding any two contradictory experiences or memories in awareness at the same time, a state known as *simultaneous dual awareness*, and to intensify the focus on the positive memory while also remaining aware of the negative memory we have chosen to rewire. This simultaneous awareness requires practice. If it is challenging at first, you can begin by switching back and forth between the two memories, always refreshing and strengthening the positive memory so that it becomes stronger. Eventually there can be a simultaneous awareness of the two memories. This creates the simultaneous neural firing that allows the two memories to reconsolidate together in a new network.

As Bill's focused awareness strengthened the more positive memory of his dad, there came a moment when the firing of the networks that held that memory trumped the firing of the memory of criticism. Bill experienced this rewiring as an easing of the intensity of the emotions he had felt the day that he yelled as his dad: the memory no longer had the same emotional charge when he remembered it in session now. We repeated this reconditioning process several times. Finally Bill reported that the emotional charge connected with the negative memory had disappeared: it had gone "poof" in his brain. Once Bill rewired the implicit memory of criticizing his dad, the emotional charge that had unconsciously driven his behavior with Sharon was also simply no longer there. No longer so reactive to Sharon's job loss, Bill was able to work with Sharon to deal more productively with their financial situation.

Reconditioning doesn't change what happened before, but it changes our relationship to what happened before. It doesn't rewrite history, but it does rewire the brain. You can practice this technique with memories that are not emotionally fraught. Eventually you can use it to resolve truly traumatizing memories.

Exercise 3: Out with the Old, In with the New through Reconditioning

This exercise is modeled on Bill's experience of using a memory of a feeling of kindness to recondition memories of disappointment and critical feelings. You can use the exercise as written, if you wish; you can choose to recondition the pattern you worked with in the new conditioning exercise; or you can work with something completely different.

1. Settle yourself in an awareness of your own mindfulness and compassion for yourself.
2. Remember a moment when you felt a genuine kindness in your heart. If you are working on reconditioning a memory involving a specific person, it could be a feeling of kindness for that person, but it could also be for anyone else. Evoke the memory of that moment in as much detail as you can: when and where you experienced it, what you were

doing or saying, what the other person in this memory was doing or saying. Notice whether you can feel now the feelings you experienced in your body then. You're lighting up a resource of a very positive memory first, to stabilize the process of reconditioning.

3. Let the initial memory of kindness fade into the background. Now evoke the memory of a moment when you felt critical of the person you want to work with in this exercise. Evoke the memory of that moment in as much detail as you can: when and where you experienced feeling critical, what you did or said, what the other person did or said. Notice whether you can feel now the feelings you experienced in your body then. You're lighting up the network of this negative memory as completely as you can, safe in the container of mindful empathy.

4. Now imagine feeling kindness toward the person you want to work with in this exercise. This experience of kindness can be a memory or an imagined moment. Visualize this moment of kindness in as much detail as you can, imagining what you're saying or doing — as long as it directly counters the negative memory. Let the new experience of kindness become strong and steady in your awareness, feeling the kindness in your heart and in your body. You've now created a "neural sandwich" with the negative or traumatic memory sandwiched between the initial stabilizing memory of kindness and the countering memory of kindness you are using to do the rewiring.

5. Hold the negative memory and the new positive experience together in your awareness — simultaneously if possible (this capacity comes with practice), or switching back and forth between the two if necessary to get started. Refresh the new positive experience as needed to keep it steady and strong.

6. Eventually let go of the negative memory and focus your awareness only on the positive experience of kindness. Notice any shifts in sensations or feelings in your body; notice any shifts in your thoughts about yourself or the person you are practicing kindness with.

7. Recall the memory of the critical moment again; notice any decrease in the intensity or charge of this memory. Let it go again and return your awareness to the memory of the experience of kindness.

8. Repeat this process as many times as needed. Eventually the critical response will no longer be triggered at all or will simply feel like no big deal.

Reconditioning can be used to fully resolve trauma, whether the early attachment trauma described in chapter 2 or trauma experienced later in life. When using reconditioning in therapy with clients, I have witnessed them finish processing a trauma or phobia and say, literally, "Well, what was I so upset about?" The fact of the memory is there, but the feeling of the trauma is no longer encoded in the brain to trigger distress. When you are using reconditioning on your own, it's best to begin by practicing with simple negative experiences. If you want to resolve an actual trauma, you may choose to work with a therapist trained in one of the trauma therapies based on reconditioning, such as EMDR. As you rewire your brain, you will learn that post-traumatic growth can be immediate; moving beyond the trauma can be permanent.

Pulling It All Together

In this chapter you have begun to use the three processes of self-directed neuroplasticity that can be used to strengthen the prefrontal cortex and establish new patterns of coping.

- *New conditioning* creates new neural pathways in your brain; you can apply it by seeking out new experiences that you know will encode new, more adaptive coping strategies into your brain's circuitry.
- *Deconditioning* creates the receptivity and flexibility in your neural circuitry that reopen your brain to learning and change, making it easier to wire in new, more effective coping strategies.
- *Reconditioning* helps you rewire the neural circuitry of an existing strategy by pairing that strategy with a new, more effective one. It allows you to rewire old, default coping mechanisms buried in implicit memory.

As you become comfortable using the tools of self-directed neuroplasticity, you'll find that you begin, in the words of the German neuropsychologist Gerald Huther, to "use the brain so that the potentialities built into it become fully realized." As you replace your brain's old, conditioned patterns of coping with better ones, you will notice yourself naturally developing the five Cs of coping. In the face of stressors like challenging bullying at your child's school, you will remain *calm*. If your son's life is derailed by drugs, you will *see clearly* what steps need to be taken next. You'll immediately know and *connect* with the resources you need to bring a divorce to closure or rebuild a home after an earthquake or fire. You'll have a new flexibility in your brain to become *competent* in the skills you need to rework your finances. You'll have the neural receptivity to find the *courage* to face a friend's mortality, or your own.

As you learn to use these tools to direct desired changes in your brain, you'll develop a sense of mastery that gives you the confidence you need to tackle even bigger challenges.

PART THREE

RECOVERING RESILIENCE THROUGH RESONANT RELATIONSHIPS

CHAPTER SEVEN

How Bonding and Belonging Nourish Resilience

Love guards the heart from the abyss.

— WOLFGANG AMADEUS MOZART

RESONANT RELATIONSHIPS HELP US recognize our own deep inner goodness and feel competent and confident in the world. The film *The Blind Side* (2010) offers a good example of how people learn to be resilient through resonant relationships with others, even after trauma and neglect. This film is based on the true story of a homeless African American teenage boy adopted by a socially conscious family in Memphis, Tennessee. Leigh Anne Tuohy is portrayed as a fierce champion of her new son, Michael Oher, as he adjusts to life in a wealthy white family. Michael has never slept in his own room before; he has never even had his own bed. And he certainly hasn't had the nurturing experiences that would have helped a growing boy feel resiliently good about himself. Michael is isolated from others his age and failing in school.

The rich connection and parenting by Michael's new mom give him new experiences of himself and new ways of seeing himself. The father and younger brother pitch in, coaching, tutoring, and encouraging. Everyone's faith in Michael's potential, their reflecting his true self back to him, not only helps Michael learn to play football but also helps him earn good enough grades to be eligible to play on high school and college teams — and eventually to play as a pro in the National Football League. Connection — steady, loving connection — and others' seeing Michael for the resilient human being he is, help him recover a sense of his own innate goodness and fulfill his potential.

If your earliest experiences of attachment and bonding gave you a sense of security and a sense of yourself as a uniquely resilient human being, that's great news. Even before you had any conscious choice in the matter, your brain was able to develop a solid inner sense of safety and trust in those relationships. The reflection and encouragement from empathic, responsive people for your true self engendered a sense of trust within you as well. You learned what it felt like to be a healthy, secure "me" and knew the innate goodness of that "me." This belief in yourself as someone who belongs and matters is what allows your inner sense of self to "gel" and creates a platform of confidence that allows you to explore yourself and the world, developing all the competencies you need to realize your potential.

Even if you didn't get the full benefit of that trust, confidence, and resilience from your earliest experiences, it is possible to recover or develop those capacities now. The brain develops its hardware and software of resilience, for better or worse, through engaging with other brains. The prefrontal cortex matures — and is repaired — most rapidly through interactions with other mature prefrontal cortices. The most effective way to learn resilience is by interacting with other resilient human beings.

We learn the five Cs of coping from people who embody them. Michael learned to connect to resources — such as coaches, tutors, and agents — from his adoptive family. You might learn to see additional options in a situation from other people who can observe it from different perspectives. You might become more competent at negotiating with other people by carefully observing people who are skilled at negotiation. Certainly, as you spend time with people who are consistently calm or steadfastly courageous, you come to embody those qualities too.

When Past Relationships Make Us Skittish

Although relationships can be healthy, resonant, and conducive to positive brain change, they can sometimes be oppressively toxic and a cause of less-than-resilient functioning. Many people with experience of such relationships may be very wary indeed of relying on relationships with other people to gain resilience.

If we have been hurt, devalued, betrayed, or exploited, especially by people close to us, the people we wanted to rely on the most, we may be reluctant to seek any kind of healing through another person. Love gone sour or scornful can wound our hearts and break our spirits. Too many of us have experienced or witnessed deliberate cruelty or violation from other people—the unconscionable neglect, enmeshment, or abuse that threatens to annihilate or disintegrate the psyche.

Our willingness to rely on others for comfort, guidance, and support and to learn from others how relational resilience really works can easily erode if we remember a sometimes loving, sometimes raging alcoholic father chasing us through the house with a kitchen knife, or returning home from a vacation with Dad to discover that Mom had moved out, with no explanation ever given.

Our higher brains can later extend compassion — and even forgiveness — to people whose behaviors have disappointed or wounded us if we come to understand that they, too, have probably suffered in relationships in ways that shaped their behavior. And we can recognize that we may also have disappointed and wounded others along the way. But repeated toxic experiences in relationships and the wariness that results can skew our perceptions of ourselves and others, derail our capacities for trust and self-acceptance, and leave us mired in anxiety and shame. Instead of processing new experiences with naturally curious engagement, we may defensively withdraw. These conditioned neural patterns can block our ability to learn about resilience from healthier relationships.

Nonetheless, if we want to become more resilient, we need to learn how to use new experiences in genuinely resonant relationships, including new ways of relating to the self, to rewire our patterns of relating. This is the *choosing* part of harnessing neuroplasticity. Developing resilience requires rebuilding the resonance circuit in our brains that puts the maturation of the prefrontal cortex back on track. It means undoing any history of relational troubles and traumas that may still create mistrust and defensiveness.

Resilience allows us to use relationships as positive resources, instead of relying only on our own survival responses. We want to move from neural cement or neural swamp into a more flexible mindset that lets us develop relational resilience and relational intelligence — the interpersonal skills that allow us to meet all the storms and surges of our lives, not just the relational dramas and traumas. To develop this intelligence, we need to learn to use interpersonal neuroplasticity as a powerful agent of recovering relational resilience.

The Power of the True Other

At a conference on attachment and relationships, the keynote speaker told us: "All this talk therapy is just an excuse to hang out long enough for the relationship to do the healing." One hour a week with a trained and empathic professional can be helpful, sometimes essential, but we have more than a hundred waking hours in the rest of the week to seek out beneficial new experiences on our own — with friends, partners, and pets, in memory and in imagination — to create new circuitry in our brains that helps us know and value who we truly are.

The speediest and most reliable way to strengthen the prefrontal cortex, and begin to recover the resilience of our true self, is through experiences with people who can be, as the clinical psychologist Diana Fosha puts it, true others to our true self.

True others are those who can see and reflect our true self back to us when we have forgotten, or perhaps have never known, who we truly are. They remember our best self when we are mired in our worst self and accept without judgment all of who we are. True others are not necessarily the people closest to us, though they may be: they are the people most attuned to us, those most accepting of our innate goodness, our essential worth as human beings. For many people, a true other can be a spiritual figure or deity; for others, it may be a counselor, teacher, or friend. When someone who is acting as a true other genuinely sees us at our best, we can see ourselves in that light, too. This mirroring helps us rediscover our resilient self.

The power of the true other can be seen in the example of the Irish playwright Oscar Wilde when he was imprisoned in England in 1895 for homosexuality. As Wilde was walking through the throngs of jeering hecklers on his way to prison, his publisher and friend, Robert Ross, quietly bowed and tipped his hat to him. Wilde later recounted in his autobiographical work *De Profundis* that his friend's gesture of respect was what enabled him to endure his two years of imprisonment with his courage and dignity intact. When Ross acknowledged Wilde's true self, Wilde's resilience came to the fore.

Having other people reflect our best self to us can happen in the simplest of ways. A few months after I moved my eighty-one-year-old dad out to live near me so that I could care for him as his health declined, he had a stroke severe enough to land him in the hospital for a few days and in a skilled nursing facility for a while after that. One morning, he became suicidal. That behavior was more than the nursing facility could take responsibility for. At 5:30 AM the staff called me to come and pick him up. In his confused mental state, and despite his frailty, he had managed to climb onto a second-story deck overlooking the courtyard and had threatened to jump.

When I arrived, my dad was waiting in the lobby. Getting him into my car to take him home was no problem, but I was completely bewildered about what to do next. Would he be safe at home? Did I need to move him to a board-and-care facility? Before I got in the car myself, I burst into tears. Right there on the curb in the parking lot,

I collapsed and sobbed. All my fear and confusion about his failing health welled up and spilled over. The nurse who had discharged my dad saw my collapse out the window, came out of the building, sat next to me on the curb, and gently took my hand. For the next fifteen minutes, she never said a word. She just held my hand and gently stroked my back as I cried out wave after wave of grief and anguish.

Eventually, as the tears subsided, I looked into the nurse's eyes and saw someone simply seeing me and my pain, caring for my pain and all the pain of all the family members who had ever gone through what I was going through, all the pain of the human condition. In that moment I knew that my struggle was completely seen, understood, and accepted. In that moment, she was the true other to my true self, and her unspoken empathy allowed me to regroup. Her presence conveyed to me I that could find my way through this dark time and helped me recover my confidence.

In this instance, I was fortunate that the true other showed up for me. But rather than just hope or wait for someone to turn up randomly on their own, you can deliberately seek out true others; you can deliberately choose the new relational experiences that will rewire your brain for more inner security and resilience.

Creating Inner Safety and Trust

The process of being seen, understood, and accepted by an attuned, empathic other engenders a sense of genuine self-acceptance, a feeling that we are profoundly okay. We feel safe enough, strong enough, sure enough to venture courageously into the world and develop the competencies we need to deal with life's challenges.

Among my favorite stories is one I heard from the meditation teacher Jack Kornfield. A seven-year-old boy and his family went to a restaurant for dinner. When the waitress asked the boy what he wanted for dinner, he replied without hesitation, "A hot dog and French fries!" His mother interrupted, telling the waitress, "He'll have meatloaf with mashed potatoes and gravy." After the waitress had taken the parents' orders, she turned to the boy and asked, "Do you want ketchup and mustard on your hot dog, son?" As the waitress was leaving, the boy turned to his parents and said, "She thinks I'm real!"

When others take us seriously, honoring our existence, we become real to ourselves. Through supportive recognition by others, we begin to reap the benefits of a secure attachment we may not have had early on; we can deepen any inner security we've been able to encode. The rest of this chapter discusses skills that help you to do this and presents a series of experiential exercises to help you remember your own strength, resourcefulness, and wholeness — the nature of who you are and were, deeper than any conditioning that might have obscured or derailed that essence. Because authentic relationship is critical for restoring this connection to your true self, all of the exercises involve interacting with others, whether face-to-face with a real person or in your imagination. Both are equally effective in conditioning new neural pathways. Following each exercise is an explanation of the neuroscience underlying it.

Skill 1: The Healing of Presence and Deep Listening

*The most basic and powerful way to connect to another
person is to listen. Just listen. Perhaps the most
important thing we ever give each other is our attention.....
A loving silence often has far more power to heal and
to connect than the most well-intentioned words.*

— RACHEL NAOMI REMEN, MD

When we want to listen deeply to another person, we prepare ourselves to give them our full attention. We temporarily set aside our own needs and agendas. We stop rehearsing what we're going to say in response to what we anticipate they are going to say. We become present, opening our mind and heart to the person underneath the words, underneath the bragging or the complaints. We become curious about what the person is saying and not saying, what might need more time or deeper trust to be voiced. As Henry David Thoreau said,

"The greatest compliment that was ever paid me was when someone asked me what I thought, and attended to my answer."

We can bring the same attentiveness and contemplative listening to ourselves. We can practice tuning into our own experience, moment by moment. We can notice tension, irritation, restlessness, impatience, and boredom, or calm, peace, delight, joy, and awe. As we listen more deeply even than the level of our breath, body sensations, feelings, and thoughts about ourselves, we can drop into a quiet space of no chatter, no agenda, no nagging doubts, no habits of perceiving or interpreting ourselves. We can enter a spacious stillness so calm and clear that we begin to sense the wholeness of our true being.

As we learn to listen skillfully, grounded in that wholeness, we are conditioning in our brains a new way of being with ourselves and with others, creating the safety and trust that is part of our psychological platform of resilience.

Exercise 1: Deep Listening

When we shift our attention toward listening, our whole world changes. Learning to listen is equal to learning to love.

— RUTH COX

This exercise is done with a partner. Decide who will be the speaker and who will be the listener.

1. The listener asks the speaker a question (samples below); the speaker answers as honestly and thoughtfully as she can. The listener listens silently, though attentively and appreciatively. The listener then simply says, "I appreciate your letting me know that," and asks the same question again. The speaker answers the question again from a different

angle or from a deeper level of understanding and inner truth. The listener listens as before and, when the speaker is finished, again says, "I appreciate your letting me know that," and again repeats the question. If the speaker doesn't respond right away, the listener simply maintains a receptive silence. This questioning and response can continue for as long as the speaker is still discovering new understandings or feelings in response to the question.

Here are some sample questions. Choose only one and keep asking it.

What brings you joy in your life?

What has brought you sorrow?

What worries you now?

When have you found courage in dark times?

What are you grateful for?

What are you proud of?

2. When the speaker is done (and thanks the listener for listening), the two of you switch roles. When you have both experienced listening and being listened to, you can debrief, sharing what you noticed about your experience in each role and what you discovered about yourself.

3. Take a moment to integrate this new learning into your ongoing sense of self in relationship to others, creating more safety and trust in relationships. Let yourself take in the good news that exercises like deep listening are strengthening your prefrontal cortex and allowing more new conditioning as you go along.

The Neuroscience of Why Deep Listening Creates Safety and Trust in Relationships

The anterior cingulate cortex — the structure we use to focus our conscious attention — also functions as a switching station between the brain's left hemisphere (primarily responsible for processing our thoughts) and the right (primarily responsible for processing our feelings). The focused attention of deep reflection in response to a repeated question and being attentively listened to (whether in our own minds or by someone else) helps integrate the processing of the brain's two hemispheres and helps us probe our thoughts and feelings at a deeper level. We often "hear" ourselves in a new way and then, via the prefrontal cortex, integrate these new understandings about ourselves or others.

This kind of deep listening can lead to the compassionate receptivity that is needed in moments of great loss, in realizations of truths we don't want to hear, in times of disorienting change and transition. Compassionate listening requires us to set aside everything that is not simply presence and openness. We listen to the whole being of another with our whole being, and we attend to the whole being of our own self.

Skill 2: Sharing with Others

*Kindness is more important than wisdom, and the
recognition of that is the beginning of wisdom.*

— THEODORE RUBIN

Sometimes we find it easier to listen to the sharing of another than to share something about ourselves. The exercise below offers a safe way to build on the skills of listening you just learned in order to build skills in speaking from your heart to another.

Exercise 2: Sharing Kindness

1. Invite a friend, an acquaintance, or a friendly coworker to do this exercise with you. Take two minutes each to share an experience of kindness that has happened to you today

already, or earlier in the week, or earlier this year, even back in the third grade: a moment when someone held open the door, picked up something you dropped, smiled as you walked down the hallway, sent a supportive email when you were going through a hard time — any behavior that registered in your consciousness as support from the universe, something that gave just a little lift or a little steadiness.

2. Take another two minutes each to explore what it's like for you to be sharing this story with your partner, receiving kind attention, resonance, and support.

3. Take a moment in silence to notice any effects in your body and mind from doing the exercise, such as a sense of buoyancy, comfort, or relaxation.

You can do this exercise with variations — recalling moments of courage, flexibility, or patience — with great benefit to your brain and to your capacities for resilience. Each time you explore a quality necessary for resilience, you are intentionally conditioning that quality more deeply in your neural circuitry.

The Neuroscience of Why Sharing with Others Creates Safety and Trust in Relationships

This exercise brings the vagus nerve into play. Its function in the brain's resonance circuit is to help regulate the lower brain's assessment of the level of safety, trust, connection, and belonging you experience in any situation. Every experience of a positive, nourishing connection with another person improves this capacity, increasing the sense of ease and well-being in relating to other people. Sharing these moments explicitly with others, as in step 1 and 2 of this exercise, strengthens the attunement and empathy functions of the entire resonance circuit in the brain, supporting your resilience in interacting with others safely, in dealings that seem not so safe, and in navigating the world in general.

As you remember experiencing a moment of kindness, your brain lights up all the networks of that memory: the visual image, the emotions, and the body sensations, as well as the thoughts and beliefs. You convey the entire experience to your partner through your facial expressions, body language, and tone of voice as well as your words. As your partner attunes to you, the mirror neurons in his brain pick up the nonverbal signals of your inner experience and begin to register in his brain as his own inner experience of your inner experience.

When your partner shares with you his experience of hearing your story and conveys empathy for your experience, he is creating what is called an intersubjective experience of the connection between the two of you, which both your explicit and implicit processing systems take in. Your mirror neurons, picking up the signals from your partner, let you know you are seen, accepted, and understood. Even a few seconds of this sharing and mirroring strengthen the resonance circuits in each of you, allowing you to engage more easily and skillfully with other people.

When you and your partner debrief about your experiences, you are encoding the content of the stories and examples into your explicit memory and enhancing your relational intelligence. Equally significant, you are encoding the knowledge of how to do something: strengthening in your implicit memory the procedural learning of how to create more safety and trust in relationships. By sharing moments of relating skillfully, you are strengthening the circuits that will allow you to rewire old patterns and support your relational intelligence. You become more competent in connecting to others — one of the five Cs of coping.

Deep listening and sharing kindness have used new conditioning to rewire your brain. Repetition of these exercises, or experiences like them, will reinforce the new learning in your brain's circuitry in the direction of deeper resilience.

Skill 3: Experiencing the Innate Goodness of Yourself and Others

Be kind, for everyone you meet is fighting a hard battle.

— PLATO

Just as listening to others, listening to ourselves, and being listened to help us recover a sense of trust and confidence about ourselves in relationships, experiencing goodness — in ourselves and others — deepens that trust and confidence while creating more openness, receptivity, and flexibility in the brain. We learn to access that sense of goodness through deconditioning — the process of brain change that allows us to relax old, conditioned patterns of how we relate to ourselves and others; letting go of opinions, judgments, and defenses; and returning to a clear sense of our core innate goodness, coming home to the innate nobility and wholeness that is an essential component of our resilience.

The two exercises below, drawn from the Buddhist wisdom tradition, will help you access a sense of this innate goodness, which will become part of your psychological platform of resilience.

Exercise 3: Cultivating Loving Kindness to Experience Innate Goodness

Loving kindness practice (*metta*) is an ancient practice of goodwill from the Buddhist tradition in which we express warmhearted wishes for the happiness and well-being of other individuals and for ourselves, even when that's difficult. Through this practice we can learn to keep our hearts open to people we may dislike and even to parts of ourselves we may dislike. The practice leads us into a larger consciousness, to a broader perspective, independent of our personal needs or expectations, helping us meet events and other people in our lives with more openness, flexibility, and resilience.

Loving kindness practice involves the repetition of phrases of well-wishing through several categories of people, from easier to more difficult. Typically it begins with expressing wishes for ourselves. Because of our conditioning, it is sometimes easier to feel the flow of loving kindness for someone else than it is for ourselves. If that is true for you, go ahead and begin the practice by directing your well-wishing toward a benefactor or friend, and then include yourself in the practice when you are ready.

The phrases are formulated silently to yourself. However, the meditation teacher Sylvia Boorstein suggests singing the phrases to yourself: a simple melody makes the practice easier to remember and more fun to do. Moreover, singing involves more integrated brain functions than speaking does. The result of the practice is more peace of mind and heart, greater contentment and well-being. Over time, we come to increasingly know and inhabit these states of mind as who we truly are.

1. Choose three or four phrases of well-wishing to repeat silently in your mind. The traditional phrases include the following: may I be happy; may I be peaceful; may I be strong in body and mind; may I have ease of mind and heart. Practitioners have modified the phrases through the ages to include: may I be safe from inner and outer harm; may I be free from suffering, from all causes of suffering, from causing any suffering; may I be kind to myself; may I trust my goodness; may I love and accept myself just as I am.

    You can invent your own phrases; many people do. I have developed phrases that have worked powerfully for me and for many clients and students: may I have compassion for myself as I endeavor to open my heart; may I know that I am held, safe and secure; may I know that I am able to trust; may I know that I am loved and cherished; may I know that I am able to love others with understanding, compassion, and forgiveness.

2. Repeat your chosen phrases of well-wishing for five minutes, three times a day, for three days, or whatever rhythm fits into your life. The important thing is the sincerity of your intention to use the practice to evoke and encode the states of mind and heart that are full of loving presence, spacious awareness, and openness to the true nature of ourselves and all beings. With enough practice, these states of mind become traits of being.

3. Begin another three-day cycle, now extending the well-wishing to other people. The Buddhist tradition identifies specific categories of people to receive this well-wishing, starting with people who are easy to open our hearts to and extending to people who are more difficult. Choose one specific person in each category to practice with, repeating the practice again for other individuals.

    Benefactors: people who have helped you in some way, who have seen the best in you and helped you bring out that best, such as parents, teachers, mentors, therapists, siblings, and friends.

    Dear friends: the people who, as one unknown author has said, "know the song of your heart and hum it back to you when you've forgotten the words."

    Neutral persons: people whom you may encounter regularly but don't know personally: people who deliver your mail, check out your groceries, walk their dogs in your neighborhood, or vacuum the carpets at your place of work. You don't know their joys and sorrows. You don't know if they are good or bad. You only know that they are human and subject to all the forces and challenges of human life, and that they have an essential worth as human beings, too. The power of the practice is to feel the loving kindness flowing from your heart to a neutral person, not because of who they are or what they may have done for you, or even in recognition that they are also vulnerable to suffering of the human condition, but simply to honor their true nature.

Difficult persons: people we are most likely to have negative, even contemptuous, opinions of and are most likely to contract our hearts against. They may include the coworker who is always snippy or the politician whose behavior we find reprehensible. This is where the rubber meets the road. Sending wishes for strength, happiness, and ease even to a difficult person can train our minds and hearts to stay open, calm, wise, and skillful in dealing with them or other people like them. We come to understand that our state of mind and heart does not depend on them, on their behaviors, or on their changing their behaviors. If you lose your focus while practicing with a difficult person, return to wishing well to an easier category of people, to reestablish the flow of goodwill from your heart. Build up a head of steam, and try again.

All beings: everyone, near and far, known and unknown. This last step in traditional loving kindness practice opens our hearts "as wide as the world."

4. At any stage of this practice, take a moment to notice any changes in your own well-being. You may feel an ease or openness that signals more receptivity to other people and to experience in general. This receptivity occurs at the neural level, too: deconditioning makes it easier for your brain to rewire.

The Neuroscience of Cultivating Loving Kindness to Experience Innate Goodness

Loving kindness practice concentrates the attention of our minds, not so much on the person to whom we are offering the well-wishing (the object of the practice) or on the phrases themselves (the vehicle of the practice), as on the flow of goodwill arising in our own hearts that is the reliable outcome of the practice. With practice, that goodwill can seem effortless. We experience that flow of goodwill as evidence of the loving, caring, and goodness of our true nature, deeper than all of our personal conditioning.

That flow of goodwill causes the brain to shift into the defocusing mode of processing, in which deconditioning takes place: a more spacious and open state of consciousness. In this state, we can let go of any stories about ourselves or other people and any personal expectations or needs. This defocusing mode of consciousness helps our brain stay more receptive to new experiences, making it easier for us to encode new insights and more wholesome patterns of relating into our neural circuitry. This new relationship to relationship supports the development of the five Cs of coping. With practice, we become calmer, clearer-sighted, more connected, more competent, and more courageous.

Skill 4: Honoring the Innate Goodness of Others

Loving kindness is considered in the Buddhist tradition to be one of four "sublime attitudes," states of mind and heart that develop naturally when you are in touch with your true nature and that lead to the deepest happiness. The other three are compassion, joy in the welfare of others, and equanimity. Together, these four attitudes help you keep your heart and mind open in the face of all kinds of adversity and suffering.

The next exercise leads you and a partner through an experience of all four of these sublime attitudes. Although the exercise is done in silence, you maintain eye contact throughout the exercise. The gazing, even without words, can evoke a profound sense of intimacy and trust as you open up to the nobility of your common humanity. This perspective is important for learning to relate to others resonantly and skillfully.

Exercise 4: Honoring the Innate Goodness of Others

1. Invite a friend to do this exercise with you. Sit across from each other so that you can maintain eye contact. Do the entire guided meditation together in a spacious silence.

2. Simply gaze into your partner's eyes, allowing yourself to see in her the nobility of her true nature, the innate goodness and radiance of her being. Silently wish her well, sending the expressions of loving kindness: may you know the deepest happiness; may you have ease of mind and heart. Let yourself know that at the same time, your partner is sending you expressions of loving kindness as well. Let yourself take in the kindness being offered.

3. Then allow your awareness to shift. Imagine what human sorrows your partner might have experienced in her journey, what losses, what griefs, what pain of the human condition. Silently begin to send her expressions of compassion: may your sorrows be held in loving awareness; may your sorrow ease; may you feel my care for your suffering. Let yourself know that, at the same time, your partner is sending you compassion for your own sorrow and suffering as well. Let yourself take in the care and compassion being offered.

4. Then allow your awareness to shift again. Imagine what human joys your partner may have experienced: what accomplishments and competencies she might have achieved; what blessings of abundance and love she might have experienced. Silently begin to send her expressions of sympathetic joy, happiness for her happiness: may you fully delight in your delight; may you feel your joy deeply. Allow yourself to know that, at the same time, your partner is sending you expressions of joy. Let yourself take in the sweetness of her joy in your joy.

5. Allow your awareness to shift again, to expressing wishes for calm abiding and equanimity: whatever happens on your journey, may you perceive and respond to it with a calm ease of mind and heart; may you have deep inner peace. Allow yourself to know that, at the same time, your partner is sending wishes for equanimity and calm abiding for you as well. Let yourself take in the calming energy of her well-wishing.

6. Allow your awareness to shift one more time, to simply being, noticing whatever is going on for you right now: awareness of your inner experience, and awareness of your awareness. Notice and reflect on any changes in your inner, subjective sense of self. You may notice a sense of spaciousness, less defensiveness, more openness.

The Neuroscience of Honoring the Innate Goodness of Others

The steady eye contact of this exercise activates the fusiform gyrus, a small structure in the right hemisphere of the brain that recognizes faces and reads their emotional expressions. Research has found a correlation between high activity in the fusiform gyrus and low activity in the amygdala when we perceive a sense of safety in another person. Specifically, the perception of safety and trust in the facial expressions of another can calm our own nervous system.

When you deliberately maintain eye contact with another person while experiencing and expressing positive emotional states like kindness, compassion, joy, and equanimity, you are evoking experiences of safety and trust that encourage your brain to relax and open into the neural circuitry of a defocusing state. The deconditioning of this state allows new experiences of relationship — of safety, respect, honoring, and trust — to be wired into your circuitry more easily.

Skill 5: Rewiring Negative Views of Yourself

If we are to rewire our sense of self to acknowledge our strengths and competencies, we need to be able to accept the goodness that others see in us. But we may find it much more difficult to receive the love and compassion in the previous exercise than to give it. We may "smallify" ourselves, as my friend Daniel Ellenberg would say, rather than let the love and goodwill of others nourish and resource us. We may receive compliments quite regularly: "You handled that attorney's questions really well." Or "Nice job getting the teachers and parents to talk to each other." But beliefs we hold about ourselves from previous experiences in relationships might cause us to block or deflect these comments and reply, "No, not really; I actually thought I was lousy" or "Anyone could have done that; it was nothing special." We need to be able to take in the positive views others have of us and encode them into our neural circuitry in order to rewire our old views of ourselves, especially when we might believe something quite different.

When you see someone looking at you with unconditional positive regard, mirror neurons evoke the sense of goodness within you that the other person is seeing. I present the next exercise in the form of a guided visualization so that you can do it easily on your own, anytime, anywhere. Practicing letting yourself take in the love of others is an important step in rewiring any negative views of yourself that may interfere with your resilience and sense of well-being.

Exercise 5: Rewiring Negative Views of Yourself through Seeing the Goodness That Others See in You

1. Sit or lie comfortably. Allow your eyes to gently close. Focus your attention on your breathing. Rest comfortably in the simple presence of awareness. When you're ready, let yourself become aware of how you are holding yourself

in this moment. Are you feeling kind toward yourself? Are you uneasy with yourself? Are you feeling critical of yourself? Just notice, just be aware and accepting of what is, without judgment — or if there is judgment, notice that.

2. Then, when you're ready, bring to mind someone in your life who you know loves you unconditionally, someone in whose presence you feel safe. This could be a teacher or dear friend; a partner, parent, or child; or a beloved dog or cat. It could be a spiritual figure — Jesus or the Dalai Lama, or your own wiser self. Or it could simply be a memory from any time in your life when someone accepted you as you are and loved you.

3. Imagine yourself sitting with this person face-to-face. Visualize the person looking at you with acceptance and tenderness, love, joy. Feel yourself taking in his or her love and acceptance of you.

4. Now imagine yourself being the other person, looking at yourself through their eyes. Feel that person's love and openness being directed toward you. See in yourself the goodness, the sacred humanness that the other person sees in you. Let yourself savor this awareness of your own goodness.

5. Now come back to being yourself. You are in your own body again, experiencing the other person looking at you again, with so much love and acceptance. Feel yourself taking in that love and acceptance. Take the love deeply into your own being. Feel it in your body. Notice how and where you feel that love and acceptance in your body — as a smile, as a warmth in your heart — and savor it.

6. Take a moment to reflect on your experience. You are learning to recondition past negative views of yourself. Set the intention to remember this feeling any time you choose to.

The Neuroscience of Rewiring Negative Views of Yourself

This exercise uses our mirror neurons to do some reverse engineering. When we intentionally evoke the sense of being seen by someone who loves us and is looking at us with loving kindness, with appreciation, with compassion, our mirror neurons begin to fire in response. We can feel those feelings in our own bodies, even if we are holding quite different, contradictory feelings about ourselves at the same time. Imagining the other person's kindness begins to rewire our previously conditioned views of ourselves. This reconditioning strengthens our prefrontal cortex in its function of attuning to and being empathic with ourselves and, of course, with others.

Because this form of reconditioning with mirror neurons is powerful, it's important to spend time with people who see our goodness, our capacities, our resilience and mirror them back to us; likewise, it's important to protect ourselves from people who hold negative views of us. Chapter 9 picks up this thread again.

Skill 6: Befriending Yourself

The psychological self is made up of many selves, an integration of different patterns of neural firing that encode various memories or mental representations of different aspects of the "self." Your self might be made up of the self who was brave enough to run back into the burning house to save the family dog, the self who was generous enough to bring casseroles three nights in a row to the neighbors with newborn triplets, and the self whose nose got pushed so far out of joint at not being invited to a second cousin's wedding that you didn't speak to that side of the family for two years. These many selves can manifest a wide range of resilience in their connections with others. Resilience depends as much on how skillfully we relate to all these inner aspects of ourselves as it does on how intelligently we relate to others.

Resilience can be impaired by old messages that tell us we can't possibly run our own restaurant or can't start over again when our restaurant burns to the ground, by old voices that tell us we'll never get a PhD and don't deserve to anyway, or by old parts of us that are stubborn, shy, mean, devaluing, and not fully on board with this resilience thing.

Resilience requires acknowledging, allowing, and accepting all of the rebellious or reluctant parts of the self simply *as* parts of the self. It requires honoring their reactions as their best strategies to protect us from harm — perhaps misguided or outdated now, but at one time deeply believed to be necessary, even adaptive and brilliant. Embracing these inner parts and integrating them into an authentic sense of self is one of the capacities of the mature prefrontal cortex, one that is essential to strengthening our inner base of resilience.

Befriending ourselves simply means being willing to look at all parts of ourselves — the good, the bad, the ugly — with honesty and clarity, with kindness and tenderness; to open our hearts and minds to the truth of this multiplicity of selves, without flinching, without self-hatred or condemnation, and with an eye to appreciating how we have come to become who we are.

Many techniques are available to help us become aware of all the patterns we call voices, parts, aspects, or facets of our selves; engage in a dialogue with them; and accept, honor, and integrate them into one coherent narrative of the authentic, whole self — even the ones that seem harmful or bad at first glance. The next exercise is a simple guided visualization developed by Virginia Satir, a family therapist who specialized in self-acceptance and self-esteem. The exercise uses the wiser self (see chapter 4) to conduct a sophisticated and productive inner dialogue with these parts. You might want to keep paper and pen handy to jot down notes as you go through the exercise.

Exercise 6: Befriending Yourself by Accepting the Many Parts of Yourself

1. Settle comfortably in your seat. Allow your eyes to gently close. Focus your attention on your breathing. Rest comfortably in the awareness of simply being.
2. When you're ready, imagine you are outside a theater.

Imagine the building, the doors, the posters outside. Walk up to one of the doors, open it, and walk into the lobby. Open another door and walk into the empty theater. Walk all the way down to the first or second row and take a seat in the center of the row. An empty stage lies in front of you. All is quiet.

3. Now imagine that the first figure to come out on the stage is your wiser self, standing in the center. This figure represents all the qualities you aspire to: wisdom, strength, courage, compassion, competence, acceptance.

4. Now imagine other characters coming onto the stage one by one. Each of these imaginary characters embodies a particular quality in yourself. These characters could be people you know, yourself at a different age, people you know from the movies or history or literature, animals, or cartoon characters.

   The first character embodies a quality in yourself that you really, really like. Take a moment to let that character take the stage. Notice and relate to that character kindly and remember it (perhaps make a note).

   A second character comes on stage embodying another positive quality in yourself. Again let that character materialize on the stage and remember it.

   A third character comes on stage embodying yet another positive quality about yourself. Let the character materialize, and remember it.

   Look carefully at these three characters, which embody three different, positive qualities in yourself, standing with your wiser self. Take a moment to notice, relate to, and remember them all.

   Now bring a fourth character to the stage that embodies a quality in yourself that you really don't like all that much. In fact, you wish it weren't part of you, but you know it is.

Let this character materialize and take a moment to notice and relate to it kindly, and remember it.

Bring on a fifth character that embodies another negative quality in you.

Bring on one last character embodying just one more negative quality in yourself.

Take a moment to materialize all these characters, notice and relate to them, and remember them; jot them down.

5. Now you have onstage your wiser self, three characters embodying positive qualities, and three characters embodying negative qualities. Ask each character in turn what special gift he or she brings to you by being part of you: ask the positive ones first, then the negative ones. As you listen to their responses, notice what lessons you learn from their being a part of you. Each one has some wisdom or learning to offer.

6. Next, ask your wiser self what gifts and lessons these parts have to offer you. Listen carefully for the answers.

7. Briefly thank each character for coming to be with you. Watch as they leave the stage one by one, the wiser self last. Then imagine yourself getting up out of your seat and walking back up the aisle, through the lobby and back outside the theater. Turn around to look at the theater where all this happened. Then slowly come to awareness again of sitting quietly, and when you're ready, open your eyes.

8. Take a moment to remember and embrace the lessons of each of these six characters, especially the negative ones: each is an integral part of you, essential to your wholeness.

The Neuroscience of Befriending Yourself

When we don't accept all the aspects of who we are, it requires effort on the part of our prefrontal cortex to keep the unwanted parts of ourselves out of awareness, outside the coherent narrative of our-selves. When we deliberately become receptive to those parts of ourselves we may have pushed away or forgotten and allow them back into the sense of our authentic self, all of the energy that was used to keep them out of awareness is available to use for more ful-filling purposes, helping us be more responsive and resilient. And any wisdom from their efforts to keep us safe from harm is now available to guide us rather than derail us. We can take wise counsel from the thirteenth-century Sufi poet Rumi:

The Guest House

This being human is a guest house.
Every morning a new arrival.
A joy, a depression, a meanness,
Some momentary awareness come
As an unexpected visitor.
Welcome and entertain them all!
Even if they're a crowd of sorrows,
who violently sweep your house
empty of its furniture,
still, treat each guest honorably.
He may be clearing you
out for some new delight.
The dark thought, the shame, the malice,
meet them at the door laughing,
and invite them in.
Be grateful for whoever comes,
because each has been sent
as a guide from beyond.

The prefrontal cortex allows us to create the coherent narrative of ourselves: this is who I am, this is how I got here, this is how I choose to develop next. All of the exercises in this chapter strengthen the prefrontal cortex to function even more efficiently in encoding new strategies for resilience. At the same time, the exercises help you deepen your capacity to trust yourself and others. That trust opens myriad options and opportunities for well-being.

Pulling It All Together

You have just completed an important phase of learning to use relationships to rewire your brain for resilience and move in the world with competence and confidence. This rewiring can happen even when experiences in past relationships have made us wary of trusting others.

- We can use the power of interactions with a true other to strengthen the prefrontal cortex and recover a sense of our true self and a secure inner base of resilience.
- You can repeat the exercises as often as you wish to enhance your capacities for deep listening, relational engagement, loving kindness, honoring the nobility in others, taking in the goodness that others see in you, and befriending yourself.
- All of these exercises strengthen the resonance circuit in your brain, which creates a sense of safety and trust in relationships, relationships that you can use in turn to increase your resilience.

CHAPTER EIGHT

Creating Inner Security
and Confidence

Being deeply loved by someone gives you strength,
while loving someone deeply gives you courage.

— LAO TZU

IN READING ABOUT less-than-secure attachment styles in chapter 2, you may have noticed that you missed out on some of the experiences that would have naturally encoded resilient coping styles into your neural circuitry. Nearly half of us do. You would have then missed out on some of the experiences that lead to development of what the attachment theorist John Bowlby called the *internal secure base*, the psychological capacities of resilience that are the outcome of secure attachment. Dan Siegel, creator of the discipline of interpersonal neurobiology, refers to these capacities as FACES: the ability to be *flexible*, *adaptive*, *coherent*, *energized*, and *stable*. These capacities, whether instilled from the beginning of our brain development or because of skillful rewiring through other relationships later in life, allow us to feel competent and confident as we navigate the bumps and bruises of the world. This base of inner security is a vital protection against trauma. It is also dynamic, more of a flow of processes (a verb) than a solid entity (noun). Neuroscience locates the neural substrate of that internal secure base, as you might expect, in the prefrontal cortex.

If you haven't yet had the help of enough true others to aid you in claiming the birthright of what I call your inner base of resilience, you can use new experiences in new relationships to recover it now. And the process builds on itself.

Research studies of the past decade have consistently demonstrated that this inner base of resilience is marked by specific relational capacities:

- a sense of safety and trust in relationships with one's self and others, which supports neuroplasticity in the brain and keeps it open to learning;
- a flexible focus of attention on oneself, others, and the world, which permits flexibility in responses to life events;
- a flexible interdependence with others that balances a healthy independence (autonomy) with a healthy reliance on others (affiliation);
- an appreciation that healthy relationships are integral to happiness and a sense of competence engaging in relationships, believing that relationships will most likely work out and that you can act in ways that will make them work out.

The findings of the research are echoed in the words of Tenzin Gyatso, the fourteenth Dalai Lama: "Consider the following. We humans are social beings. We come into the world as the result of others' actions. We survive here in dependence on others. Whether we like it or not, there is hardly a moment of our lives when we do not benefit from others' activities. For this reason it is hardly surprising that most of our happiness arises in the context of our relationships with others."

The exercises presented in the previous chapter — reclaiming your goodness, taking in the love and cherishing offered to you now, rewiring old messages that cause you to doubt yourself — form a good basis for developing resilience in relationships. Wiring into your brain new patterns of bonding, belonging, and relating give you even more options and choices in how you respond to ongoing catastrophes and kerflooeys in relationships and in general. This chapter explores ways to evoke the new experiences of yourself in relationship to others that allow you to build on this psychological platform of resilience. A sense of inner security allows you to develop the competencies you need to realize your potential and to navigate your world.

Skill 1: Nourishing the Inner Base of Resilience

Receiving the unconditional love of another is essential to developing the "earned" secure attachment that recovers our internal secure base. The unconditional love of another says, "I may not agree with all of your ideas or approve of all of your behaviors, but I love you, no matter what." It's what a securely attached baby receives, whether it's fussing and refusing to eat or cooing in satisfaction. It's what we can receive later in life when someone loves and supports us, whether we just won the big game or lost it by two points. As the prefrontal cortex processes the experience of unconditional love, it establishes and fortifies the sense of well-being and goodness that is the base of our resilience.

Receiving the love and understanding of another person for all aspects of ourselves, including our less positive qualities, may be a new or rare experience for many of us. That someone else might be accepting and even loving of our negative aspects may seem completely counterintuitive, too. But when we create experiences that let us feel unconditional love, we nourish an inner base of resilience. We begin to claim our birthright of resilience.

Exercise 1: Taking In the Love of Others to Nourish the Inner Base of Resilience

1. Ask a friend to help you in this exercise, someone who knows both your best and your worst qualities, or enlist

someone willing to work from a list you provide of these qualities you have identified on your own.

2. Sitting face-to-face, ask your partner to share the positive qualities that he sees in you, or those you have listed, saying for each, "I see your [generosity, open-mindedness, courage], and I really appreciate that about you." Maintain eye contact with the partner during this step.

3. Let in the feeling, "This is true about me. This is okay about me. I can love and appreciate this part of me. I can love and appreciate all of me." Close your eyes, if you wish to, while you are accepting this feeling. Notice what happens in your body and mind as you receive this care from another.

4. Your partner begins to identify your less positive qualities, saying, "I see that you can be [stubborn, jealous, bitter]. I accept this part of you as part of being a human being; I value this part of you, too, and honor it as an important part of you."

5. Again, your job is to let in the appreciation and acceptance, without disputing or diminishing what your partner is saying.

6. Continue receiving the sharing until you feel done. Take a moment to notice any changes in your inner sense of yourself, and experience any increased inner sense of well-being and goodness. Thank your partner for his collaboration. (You may switch roles and repeat the exercise if you both choose to.)

The Neuroscience of Why Taking In the Love of Others Nourishes Our Resilience

When we seek out new experiences in relationships that frame both our strengths and our vulnerabilities as part of being human, we create new circuits in the brain that encode these new views of ourselves (new conditioning). The prefrontal cortex can integrate these new views into the coherent narrative of the self, using them to rewire old views we held before. These views become new reference points to guide future actions. They become the core around which we can reorganize a sense of ourselves as secure, strong, and resilient. We can experience trust in ourselves rather than doubt, and pride rather than shame or devaluing. In addition, feeling safe in the love and acceptance of others enhances the neural flexibility we need in order to create other new circuits.

Skill 2: Taking In the Good to Nourish the Inner Base of Resilience

Evolutionarily and culturally, we are hard-wired and conditioned to look first for what's wrong, what's negative, and what's potentially dangerous in any situation. Because of the brain's negativity bias, we can become, and remain, quite negative about other people and our relationships with them. However, it is possible to rewire our brains for positivity instead. This is particularly important if our experiences of others in relationships have been wounding or disappointing. To strengthen the inner base of resilience, we need to look for and delight in positive experiences of ourselves in relationships with others.

Rick Hanson, the author of *Buddha's Brain*, uses the phrase "taking in the good" to refer to the process of pausing to let positive experiences sink deeply into the mind and body. By focusing attention on the moments of generosity, patience, and honesty that we experience in our relationships with others, letting those positive moments register within us, our brains develop habits that move us beyond surviving to thriving. In the next exercise, we practice deliberately evoking positive experiences in relationships, receiving them deeply, and then reinforcing them by remembering them later. All of these steps serve the process of installing new, significant relationship patterns in the brain, strengthening the inner base of resilience.

Exercise 2: Taking In the Good to Nourish the Inner Base of Resilience

1. Practice noticing moments of kindness and understanding as they happen in your day. For instance, someone lets you cut in front of him in line at the corner deli when you're desperate to get change before the meter maid tickets your car. Someone notices that you picked up the trash left by a park bench and smiles as you walk by. A colleague stops you in the hall to say "Good job" after a presentation or offers you a handful of cherries from her lunch. A new neighbor brings you homemade lasagna after you've spent six hours moving into a new apartment in the pouring rain, and then checks the next morning to make sure you're okay.

2. Let the experience register in your mind and body. Notice how this moment of connection makes you feel: perhaps acknowledged, included, or happy.

3. Take in the felt sense of this goodness in your body: a warmth, a relaxation, an opening. Notice what fills your heart: perhaps gratitude, joy, peace.

4. You can reinforce the taking in of the good by telling supportive friends about this moment later, or by imagining telling your circle of support. You can remind yourself again through journaling or in an end-of-the-day review of "three good things I'm grateful for today." This repetition reinforces the encoding of the event in your neural circuitry; you can draw on it again and again as nourishment for your inner base of resilience.

The Neuroscience of Why Taking In the Good Nourishes Our Resilience

If we are so busy that we don't take the time to take in the good, we miss out on vital nourishment for the base of resilience. We receive the good like water running through a sieve. Research indicates that savoring a moment of experience for at least thirty seconds strengthens the traces of neural firing in our memory. Taking in the good encodes networks that involve body sensations, emotional tone, and visual images as well as our conscious thoughts, and so we are encoding new circuitry implicitly as well as explicitly. As we remember and repeat this encoding many times a day over a sustained period, we create a memory bank of positivity that becomes a great support to our base of resilience.

These new experiences of taking in the good rewire our sense of self-acceptance, fill the holes in our heart, and strengthen our inner stability and flexibility. Through this new conditioning, we create new understandings about relationships that can contrast sharply with our previous templates or schemas. It becomes easier to override or set aside old, ineffective patterns. It becomes easier to feel that we belong, that we matter, and this feeling deepens our confidence in ourselves in relationship to the world.

Skill 3: Listening to the Intuitive Wisdom of the Wiser Self

My client Matthew came to his therapy session one evening torn between two possible courses of action at his job. Both were good opportunities, but they pulled him in two very different directions. One was a transfer to Tokyo to manage several new branches of the large retail clothing chain he worked for. The other was a promotion within the headquarters of his company; he wouldn't have to move, and the somewhat greater responsibilities came with slightly higher pay.

The first choice appealed to Matthew's curiosity and sense of adventure but brought up concerns of selfishness. Was it fair to ask his family to uproot themselves and live in a foreign country for two years? The kids would have to adjust to new schools and a new culture. The second choice appealed to Matthew's need for stability and security and a desire to be a good provider for his family, but it brought up concerns of going stale in a job he was already competent at and comfortable with.

I asked Matthew to settle into a comfortable position, take a few deep breaths, and relax into the state of mindful presence he had practiced with me many times before. I suggested he call upon his wiser self to listen to the concerns of each of the competing parts or voices within him: his desire for adventure, his desire for stability, his worries about selfishness, his worries about stagnation. After a few minutes, I asked him to drop below the level of all those voices, past all the layers of conditioning, roles, identities, and defenses, to the sense of his essential goodness that his wiser self embodied. In this process of deconditioning, Matthew could listen to the voice of his wiser self and let the grip of the conflicting parts of him relax.

By the end of our session, Matthew knew clearly that at this juncture in his life, his deepest yearning was for adventure. When he presented the result of his explorations to his family that weekend, they each could feel the genuineness of his enthusiasm stirring their own enthusiasm as well, and all readily voted for a two-year adventure together in Japan.

We can listen to the deep, intuitive wisdom of our wiser self for guidance about conflict within ourselves, as Matthew did, and for guidance in conflict with others as well. The following exercise shows how.

Exercise 3: Listening to the Intuitive Wisdom of the Wiser Self

1. Find a time and place to sit quietly without interruption. Settle into a comfortable position, take a few deep breaths, and relax into a state of mindful presence. Let any thoughts or concerns fade into the background. Then bring to your awareness a sense of your wiser self, the part of you that embodies your essential wisdom and goodness.

2. Bring to mind someone you are currently having difficulties with: a neighbor who turns up the television too late at

night; a coworker who misses important deadlines; a sister-in-law who dominates every discussion at the dinner table. Imagine that you can introduce this person to your wiser self and then stand to the side as you overhear the conversation between them.

3. Listen to how your wiser self handles the conversation with the difficult person: what it says, how it handles the energy of the difficult person. You are overhearing your own inner wisdom being patient and skillful with the difficult person.

4. When the conversation between your wiser self and the difficult person is complete, notice how the difficulty is resolved. Notice what you overheard, what you learned, what advice you are taking in from your wiser self.

5. Let the difficult person fade from the scene. Imagine that your wiser self turns to you, offers you a word or phrase of advice, and offers you one symbolic gift you can hold in your hand to remember this conversation by. You may choose to write down your reflections for future reference.

The Neuroscience of Listening
to the Intuitive Wisdom of the Wiser Self

Relaxing into the defocusing mode of processing in the brain allows you to "surprise the unconscious" and access the intuitive wisdom of your wiser self. The defocusing network, which operates especially on the right side of the brain, shifts our focus to the big picture, where we can comprehend things holistically and connect the dots in a new way. The right hemisphere of the brain also processes the rules of social relationships and our sense of self in relation to others. When we relax into the defocusing network, we can access these rules of relating in a more flexible way. In that process of deconditioning, our wiser self can intuitively create new options to solve problems in relating. You may not be able to access this intuitive wisdom very often at first or to trust it when you do. But the more you practice listening to your wiser self, the more you strengthen the internal secure base that it informs and guides.

Skill 4: Rewiring Difficult Experiences in Relationships

A teaching story in the Buddhist tradition can guide us in repairing and rewiring any troubling experiences in relationship in the present or traumatizing memories that still hijack us from the past. If you take a teaspoon of salt, dissolve it in a glass of water, and then take a sip of the water, the water tastes disgusting — it's too salty to drink. But if you take a teaspoon of salt, dissolve it in a large freshwater lake, then dip the glass into the lake and sip that water, the salt has dissolved in the larger lake; there's no taste of it at all.

We can dissolve teaspoons of relational upset or trauma in the vast lake of mindful empathy, positive emotions, and our own deep goodness through reconditioning. Old memories of difficult experiences seem to dissolve. They no longer have the power or charge they once had to derail our resilience.

Because reconditioning is a powerful tool for altering the brain's circuitry, and because we want to make sure we're rewiring old memories and not reinforcing them, I'm going to remind you of the ground rules before you begin the next exercise.

1. Anchor your awareness firmly in the present moment. You are safe here and now and will still be safe even when you retrieve a troubling memory of what happened back there, back then.

2. Focus your awareness on your positive resources: positive self-regard, self-acceptance. Trust your innate goodness, and evoke the wisdom of your wiser self.

3. Start small! Work with a teaspoon of trouble, not a ton. Recall one small, specific relational instance when resilience went awry:

- you were chosen last for the neighborhood softball team, and the sting of not being good enough lingers to this day;
- you were a little flip in your response to someone's money worries, responding with a quick slap on the back and a "Keep your chin up," and now they've ignored you for two weeks;
- your sister-in-law just can't seem to hear that you won't be coming to her house for Thanksgiving, and you resent her obliviousness to your own wish to celebrate with friends instead.

With practice, over time, reconditioning can indeed dissolve a ton of salt, but please let your brain feel successful at dissolving the pain of smaller memories first.

Exercise 4: Imagining a Wished-For Outcome to Rewire Difficult Experiences in Relationships

This exercise creates the resource of a better outcome to recondition a troubling or traumatizing memory.

1. Find a time and place to sit quietly without interruption. Focus your attention on your breath, beathing calmly and deeply into your heart center. Call to mind a particular moment of ease and well-being, a particular sense of your own goodness, or a moment when you felt safe, loved, connected, and cherished. Or think of a moment when you were with someone who loves and believes in you. Remember this moment in as much detail as you can, in as many levels of your body and brain as you can: a visual image, the feelings in your body that the memory evokes, any thoughts you have about yourself now as you remember the sweetness of that moment. Let yourself savor this moment in a mindful and compassionate "holding" of the memory.

2. When you feel bathed in the good feeling, and still anchored in the awareness of safety in the present moment, call to mind a moment when things went awry between you and another person. It might be slight or terrible, but if it's terrible, break down the experience into little chunks. (Again, start small.) As you reimagine that moment, remain in your observer role rather than reliving the experience. Evoke this memory to light up all the neural networks — visual images, body sensations, emotions, thoughts, or beliefs at the time. Recall memories of what you said and did; what someone else said or did; who else was there; how old you were and how old the other person was; what you were wearing and what that person was wearing. Maybe you wish you had said or done something different at the time. Maybe you wish someone else had done something different, even if that could never have happened in real life.

3. Then begin to visualize a wished-for outcome, even if this never could have happened in real life: what you would have said or done differently; what the other person could have done differently; what someone else not even in the original scenario could have said or done. If you simply wish that none of this had happened at all, you can imagine what would have happened instead. Let the new story unfold as you would have wished, in as much detail as you can. You are creating a scenario that completely disconfirms or contradicts what happened before.

4. Hold the two scenarios in your awareness at the same time, or switch back and forth between them, always refreshing and strengthening the newer, more positive scenario. After a few moments, let go of the old memory and just rest your attention on the new scenario. Let your mind play out this new scenario, and then notice how you feel. Notice any emotions or thoughts or beliefs about yourself that come

up now, and if they are more positive and resilient, let them soak in. Then bring your awareness back to the present moment.

The Neuroscience of Rewiring
Difficult Experiences in Relationships

Using this technique does not change what happened, but it does change our relationship to what happened. It doesn't rewrite history, but it does rewire the brain. This kind of careful reconditioning can rewire a shame-based sense of self, dissolve self-doubt and smallifying, and help the inner critic retire. Altering your brain circuitry through reconditioning creates a stronger neural platform of resilience in the internal secure base and allows a new relational intelligence to emerge. The relational intelligence we explore in the next chapter allows us to deal with even intrusive, withdrawn, or hostile people resiliently in any situation.

Pulling It All Together

In this chapter, you have learned how to choose new experiences that help you strengthen your inner base of resilience in order to fully realize your potential and skillfully navigate your world.

- Taking in the unconditional love and acceptance of others helps our neural circuitry encode both the calm and the courage that are part of our internal secure base. We feel confident exploring new relationships, new experiences, and new ways of taking care of business in the world.
- Taking in the good connects us to the resources of our inner goodness, inner strength, and inner competence that equip us to face difficult situations.

- Listening to our wiser self helps us see options and choices more clearly as we contemplate big decisions.
- Knowing how to rewire old, painful memories stops them from plaguing us and helps us feel competent and confident about continuing to rewire our brains for resilience.

CHAPTER NINE

Developing Relational Intelligence

The moment we cease to hold each other,
the sea engulfs us and the light goes out.

— JAMES BALDWIN

RELATIONAL INTELLIGENCE is an umbrella term I use for the people skills that allow us to navigate our world, especially our peopled world, competently, effectively, and resiliently. Similar to Daniel Goleman's notion of social intelligence, relational intelligence allows our brains to create bonds with others that sustain us through thick and thin. Research shows that these bonds provide us with a deeper sense of happiness and well-being than anything else in the human experience. They are among the resources that sustain our resilience.

The skills of relational intelligence include empathic listening and speaking, wishing for the happiness and well-being of ourselves and others, taking in the good, and befriending all parts of ourselves and others — all presented in previous chapters. They also include reaching out for help, setting healthy boundaries, negotiating changes in behavior, repairing ruptures, and being willing to forgive. In this chapter you will learn to develop these skills. Studies show that these relational intelligence skills are more predictive of our success as human beings — meaning resilience and well-being in the workplace as well as in relationships — than IQ.

All of these skills build on and reinforce the five Cs of coping. Reaching out for help keeps us connected to the resources we need to find a new job or a good doctor or the right tutor for our kid. Setting limits and boundaries actually helps us stay calm in relationships, knowing we won't be intruded upon or have to do something that goes against the grain or could be harmful to do. Negotiating change builds our competence in getting our needs met. Knowing how to repair a rupture in a relationship helps us find the courage to take risks, confident that we can repair and even strengthen the bond with another person if need be. Forgiveness requires the mindful empathy that allows us to see the larger picture clearly, holding our own behaviors and those of others, resilient or not, in a larger compassion that supports resilience.

Skill 1: Reaching Out for Help

A sense of disconnection or isolation from other people, not knowing that other people can be a source of support in times of need, can impair the functioning of our social brain and undermine our capacity for resilience. We want to be able to act independently and autonomously — that is one of the great benefits of building or restoring our internal secure base — but interdependence is integral to human social life, and we also need to feel that it's okay to turn to other people for support.

Researchers at the University of Michigan conducted a simple experiment to measure the effect of receiving help on a person's estimate of a difficulty. Participants standing at the bottom of a steep hill were asked to estimate its height; their estimates were recorded. Next the same participants were given heavy backpacks and asked to estimate the height of the hill again. The estimates were considerably higher. The backpacks were then removed, and the participants were paired up to climb the hill together. This time their reported estimates of the height of the hill were considerably lower than the original estimates. Help...helps.

The biologically hard-wired drive "to seek physical proximity to a caregiver in times of perceived threat or danger" (see chapter 1) spurs the attachment behaviors that catalyze the development of all of the human brain and the maturation of the prefrontal cortex in particular. Reaching out for help — for material resources, for spiritual and practical wisdom, for relational support and guidance — remains a cornerstone of resilience lifelong.

Our nervous systems have evolved to be affected by the presence of people around us. This means others can help us regain our equilibrium when they are more stable and centered than we are. Someone simply being present in the same room helps calm our nervous system, even if she is doing something completely different from us. We're preparing our tax returns; she is reading the paper. Her presence helps us stay calm and productive, stabilizing the nervous system so that we can remember our own inner resources and connect to the resources offered by others.

For many of us, asking for and accepting help is much harder than giving it. We may not know how to ask for help, we may believe that asking for help is a sign of weakness, or we may have come to believe, from experience, that there's no point. At the other extreme, if we have not developed enough self-sufficiency, we may be constantly asking for help and driving people crazy. Reaching out for help in relationally intelligent ways is a sign of resilience. You don't need to wait for something bordering on catastrophe — a teenage son arrested for drunk driving, a muscle spasm in your lower back that keeps you in bed for three days, a storm that blows a huge tree down onto the roof of your house — to practice asking for help.

Exercise 1: Reaching Out for Help

1. Set the intention to focus your awareness on your automatic tendencies to either reach out for help or to avoid asking.

Recall a time when something you were facing suddenly turned out to be more complicated or difficult than you expected: the lost wallet led to identity theft; the strange spot on your hand turned out to be melanoma. As you evoke your memory of facing something difficult, notice what your own reflexive response was: turning to others, turning away, or turning inward. Notice how you feel now as you remember coping in that way.

2. Then, whatever your automatic style, deliberately imagine asking others for help and support, and imagine them responding quickly and skillfully. Their practical help would be welcome, but just their attention and presence may be enough to help you feel connected and supported. Notice your response within as you experiment with reaching out. Have some compassion for yourself if this new conditioning of reaching out in this way causes any initial discomfort.

3. Practice this reaching out for help a number of times in your imagination, in various scenarios. Then gradually, consciously, begin asking for help from others in your daily life — trusted others at first — to experience the benefit to yourself. Reaching out for and accepting help get easier with practice and steadily rewire the brain into a new resilient habit.

The Neuroscience of Reaching Out

When we reach out for help, we use our brain's resonance circuit to activate what is called our relational engagement system, a complex neural circuit that uses the stability of another person's nervous system to help us stabilize our own. Once our own nervous system is back in balance, our prefrontal cortex is free to look for options and solutions and to use all the resources that are available. So reaching out for help isn't about finding people with all the answers, or having other people do everything for us. It's simply about using the stability of other people's brains to stabilize our own, so that we can be resilient in finding resources and making choices.

Skill 2: Setting Limits and Boundaries

Developmental psychologists have found that the human brain is capable of distinguishing between self and others by six months of age. The capacity of theory of mind (see chapter 1) takes that development further as we mature. More important for taking our place in the world as independent, resilient human beings, by four years of age our brains are capable of recognizing and accepting that other people may be having thoughts and feelings different from our own. Your thought, belief, impulse, feeling, or reaction to a topic, event, or reality may be completely different from mine at the same moment — and vice versa. And that's okay.

Theory of mind allows us to develop and maintain an inner subjective reality — a sense of self — that is separate from other people's opinions and expectations of us. It allows us to be ourselves and other people to be who they are, regardless of our needs or projections. We each have our own inner subjective reality, whether we're fully or only fuzzily in touch with it.

Theory of mind is essential to the brain's capacity to differentiate our experience from anyone else's experience. It is a form of mental clarity that leads to relational intelligence. If I get irritated at missing a flight and assume that you are, too, rather than noticing that, in fact, you're not irritated at all — you're already talking with an agent to get on the next flight — I may miss an opportunity to skillfully negotiate our next steps.

This capacity to differentiate our own thoughts, feelings, reactivity, and responses from another person's helps us step back from assumptions, rules, and expectations about how we and others *should* feel or behave. Stepping back from "should" is essential for responding flexibly — reminding us that different options are available and

that they are valid, a sine qua non of resilience. Setting limits —
trusting that we can set boundaries, regardless of another person's
reactions — also allows us to initiate communication and take risks
in relationships that otherwise we might not perceive as safe. We
learn to avoid either responding aggressively to protect ourselves or
acquiescing completely to another person's needs when they do not
reflect our own needs. This experience supports the brain's capacity
to stay open to learning and change.

Secure, resonant relationships enhance this capacity of theory
of mind; less secure or unempathic relationships typically don't. So
not everyone fully develops this capacity by age four. The exercise
below uses practice in setting limits and boundaries to strengthen
your theory of mind, which strengthens your relational intelligence
and resilience.

Exercise 2: Setting Limits and Boundaries

1. Ask a friend to help you in this exercise of finding the sweet
    spot in setting a limit or boundary, not tapping into aggres-
    sion or collapsing into being a doormat. The point of the
    brain training here is for you to be able to differentiate your
    needs and views from another person's and to assert them
    skillfully, not reactively. Settle into your own mindful empa-
    thy before you begin.

2. Identify one limit or boundary you've been reluctant to set:
    an earlier curfew for your daughter on school nights; a limit
    on interruptions from a coworker; saying no to a brother-
    in-law who expects to camp out in your living room rather
    than stay in a hotel when she and her family visit. Your
    friend plays the role of the other person.

3. Clarify in your own mind how setting this limit reflects
    and serves your own values, needs, and desires. Then try
    to understand the values, needs, and desires of the other
    person. Jot down notes if you wish. Notice any common

ground between the two of you; notice your differences. Notice your own experience; come to a sense of grounded-ness and presence in your body.

4. Initiate the conversation about limits with the other person. Begin by expressing your appreciation for their listening to you. State the topic; state your understanding of your own needs and of theirs. Check to see if your understanding of their point of view is accurate. Coach the friend in the role of the other person as needed, but keep the focus of the exercise on setting the limit, independent of the other person's reaction. Refresh your empathy by tuning into what you are experiencing in the moment and what the other person may be experiencing; refresh your mindfulness to be aware and accepting of what is happening.

5. State the terms of your limit, simply, clearly, and unequivo-cally. You've already stated the values, needs, and desires behind the limit, so you do not have to justify, explain, or defend your position. This is *your* limit. Reiterate the terms of your limit as many times as is needed for the person you are talking to — your role-playing partner — to understand and accept it.

6. In this exercise, your role-playing partner does accept the limit. Notice how you experience this success: notice any changes in your view of yourself in relationship and in your view of your skills in relational intelligence.

The Neuroscience of Setting Limits and Boundaries

Theory of mind is a complex mental capacity that involves the pull-ing together of functions of the focusing (self-referencing) network. The same brain structures we use to construct our own sense of self — the prefrontal cortex, the anterior cingulate, the insula, and the hippocampus — allow us to create a mental representation of another person's self, or at least some aspects of their experience. This process is known as mentalizing. The focusing network integrates information we pick up about the other person from brain stem–based resonance. The reading of emotional meaning by the right hemisphere and the cognitive understanding of the left hemisphere lead to an empathic articulation of the other person's experience.

Mentalizing involves more than thinking *about*; it means being able to generate a clear cognitive understanding of the other person's reality as different from our own. As you practice various techniques to strengthen the prefrontal cortex, you may notice the capacity for theory of mind growing as a result.

Skill 3: Negotiating Changes in Behaviors

When we experience conflict or disagreement in a relationship, often we can see clearly what the other person is doing wrong, but we find it much harder to see clearly how what *we* are saying or doing may be hurting us, the other person, or the dynamic of the relationship. The other person may be able to let you know (skillfully) what he sees you doing that is problematic: lacking clarity about your own needs or limits, withdrawing into a shell instead of staying engaged in dialogue, or acting in a belligerent way (strategies that may seem completely natural and justified to you).

The chances are that your part in any impasse stems from habits of reacting learned from previous relationships. You might tend to keep your own needs or desires close to the chest to avoid provoking an angry response; as a result, the other person has no clue where you stand or what you need. You might have a habit of avoiding a difficult conversation in order to preserve a relationship, even if the remaining connection feels increasingly tenuous. Or your automatic response to the discomfort of a dilemma might be telling the other person off in no uncertain terms, without giving him a chance to present his side of the dilemma. If you acknowledge the accuracy of these observations, and identify the old pattern that isn't working in the current situation, you can use the process of reconditioning to undo old behaviors or patterns of relating by completely rewiring the neural circuitry that underlies them.

In negotiating positive change in any relationship, mindfulness — seeing clearly what we are saying or doing, and tolerating what we are seeing — is an essential tool. Self-empathy and self-compassion — for why we are saying or doing what we are saying or doing — are also essential. Taking responsibility for our part in creating any snafu or impasse in a relationship deepens our relational intelligence and lays the groundwork for asking for change in another person's behavior as well.

Exercise 3: Negotiating Changes in Behaviors

1. Identify a problem in the dynamic between you and another person. Perhaps communication between you and a coworker has unraveled to the point that deadlines are being missed. The sting from a careless comment by a friend has strained the connection between the two of you for more than a week. It's been two months since you've moved out, but your former landlord still hasn't returned the security deposit, and your attempts to recover the money have only led to stalemate.

2. Summoning up your willingness to be ruthlessly honest and clear with yourself, let yourself see clearly what you might have said or done that might be contributing to the current impasse.

3. Make a conscious choice to act in a different way to rewire the old circuitry. For example, you might experiment with stating your needs clearly to your coworker. This not only reopens communication but will also cause your neural patterns to fire in a new, even contradictory direction, which gives your brain the opportunity to rewire the old circuitry. You might ask your estranged friend to participate in some

deep listening (see chapter 7), not only to reengage in a dialogue with a friend who is important to you but also to give your brain the opportunity to use the new experience (engaging) to trump the old pattern (withdrawing) and thus rewire or even completely dissolve the old circuitry. Or you might take a friend with you the next time you talk with your former landlord to calm your nervous system as you learned to do in exercise 1, giving your brain the opportunity to rewire a pattern of belligerence into a more effective pattern of communication.

4. Notice any changes in the dynamics of your relationships as you take responsibility for your part in them and deliberately choose to recondition the neural circuitry underlying habitual patterns of reactivity. Notice any changes in your own sense of relational competency and relational intelligence. All of these changes in your sense of self are a form of reconditioning.

The Neuroscience of Negotiating Changes in Behaviors

Reconditioning works best when we can light up every channel of the associated neural network: sensing the body sensations of withdrawal and of engaging, feeling the emotions of fear or anger and then of trust or calm, noticing the thoughts that accompany avoidance as opposed to deep listening, or becoming defiant as opposed to asking for help.

In this exercise, when you choose to think, feel, or act in a way opposite to the way you have been habitually thinking, feeling, or acting, you are altering the firing of neurons in your neural circuitry and shaping that circuitry into new patterns and pathways. Many times, when the new behavior trumps the old, it triggers major rewiring, too. Suddenly the new feels so normal that we wonder why we ever thought otherwise.

This skill takes practice, but it pays off in being able to negotiate more skillfully when the boss asks us to work overtime two weekends in a row or when talking with an elderly parent about giving up driving. Resilience opens up options.

Skill 4: Repairing a Rupture

Researchers have discovered that even in "good enough" close relationships, we spend about one-third of the time in actual relating (attuned connection), about one-third in rupture (misattuned or disrupted connection), and one-third in repair (recovering the attuned connection). Repair is the most important phase of this rhythm, especially in terms of rewiring our patterns of behavior.

Years ago, I was visiting relatives in northern Minnesota on their summer vacation and witnessed a brilliant example of repair. My seven-year-old cousin Marty was fishing off the dock one morning. His mom, my Aunt Gen, came out to check on him, noticed his mouth was covered in jelly and crumbs from his morning donut, and scolded him for being so messy as she wiped his face clean. Marty's body visibly slumped in a sulk. As Gen started to walk back to the house, Marty's dad, my Uncle Ted, who had watched the whole scene, walked over to Marty, put his hand gently on his shoulder, and reassured him, "That's okay, son. Fish bite better with a dirty face anyway." Marty gave his dad a smile and a high five and joyfully went back to fishing.

Gen, who had watched Ted's skillful repair to Marty's self-esteem, decided to try to make amends with Marty, taking responsibility for causing a rupture in Marty's self-esteem as well as between the two of them. She went into the house for more donuts. Back on the dock, she handed one to Ted to eat and ate one herself. Gen intentionally left crumbs on her face, then asked Marty, "How's the fishing?" Marty looked at her, understood her attempt at repair, laughed, and gave her a big hug.

Skill in repair strengthens the security of our connections with others and our sense of mastery in relating. When we trust our competency at repairing a rupture and reconnecting in a relationship, we are more willing to take the risks that build trust in relationships and make them worthwhile. Repairing connection requires mindful empathy on at least one side of the rupture — and ideally on both — as well as the skills of relational intelligence already discussed. Through presence and deep listening, you create the sense of safety that allows the brain to stay open to new information and new understanding. When you see the goodness in yourself and the other person, you gain a larger awareness of empathy and understanding that can help both of you see options and choices. When you take responsibility for your own part in the rupture, as you do also when you are setting boundaries and negotiating change, you can more easily initiate and follow up on the repair. Repairing a rupture is practice in creating an outcome both of you wish for.

Exercise 4: Repairing a Rupture

1. Identify a person you feel comfortable asking to practice this exercise with you, and identify a sense of rupture or disconnect between the two of you that you would like to repair. The rupture could have been caused by a misunderstanding or miscommunication. (Small is a good way to begin.) Your focus will be on repairing the relationship, not repairing the misunderstanding, and privileging reconnection over deciding who's right or wrong.

2. Sit down together, face to face, and take a moment for both of you to come into a state of mindful empathy, each becoming aware of what you are experiencing in your own body and emotions in this moment, remembering what you value in this relationship and why you are motivated to repair it, and feeling compassion for both yourself and your partner.

3. Take turns expressing your experiences of the events that caused the rupture and the emotions you have experienced since. Listen deeply and carefully to your partner's experi-

ence of the events that caused the rupture and the emotions he or she has experienced since. Notice what's happening in your own body as you begin to understand and empathize with your partner's experience.

4. Now take turns expressing your understanding and empathy for the other person's experience. This conveying of empathy isn't about fixing or even agreeing. It's about conveying understanding, and experiencing that understanding as it resonates with the other person.

5. Notice your own experience as you receive your partner's empathy for your experience. Notice if receiving this empathy leads to a reengaged resonance, a renewed sense of trust, a sense of reconnection and repair. Share your experiences.

6. Acknowledge yourself and your partner for your efforts in this exercise. If there has indeed been a repair, acknowledge that, too.

The Neuroscience of Repairing a Rupture

Mindful empathy and a strong capacity to differentiate your experience from the other person's (theory of mind) are crucial to the success of repairing a rupture and reconditioning your neural circuitry. When you can remain mindful of your own experience, you can easily use the resonance circuitry in your own brain to empathize with the other person's experience. Your empathy also engages the resonance circuit of your partner if that person is able to acknowledge and accept the empathy. It is that experience within your partner's resonance circuit, of feeling seen and understood, that allows the reconnection and repair to occur. The resonance of feeling seen and understood actually relaxes the neural circuitry, allowing it to be more flexible and thus open to new information and to repair.

When both people are sincerely trying to repair a rupture, the safety they create for each other through the reengaging of the resonance circuits and the resulting flexibility of the neural circuitry make the repair happen much more easily and quickly. Success becomes self-reinforcing. As we're learning that we *can* repair a rupture, we increasingly trust ourselves to become competent in doing so.

Skill 5: Forgiveness: The Ultimate Repair

Forgiveness is not an occasional act; it is a permanent attitude.

— MARTIN LUTHER KING JR.

Most of us will experience injury, injustice, disappointment, or betrayal at some point in our lives. Staying caught in those experiences can block our resilience and our relational intelligence from developing. Continuing to feel judgment, blame, resentment, bitterness, and hostility against those who have caused us harm can cause us pain and suffering ourselves. The same can be true if we haven't been able to forgive ourselves for harm we have caused others or ourselves. In order to rewire the behaviors of complaining, criticism, disgruntlement, and contentiousness we can so easily get stuck in, we can use deconditioning to open ourselves to the genuine understanding, compassion, grieving, and forgiveness that are needed to move into resilient coping and relational intelligence.

When we drop below the level of story, below the level of our personal emotional pain, into the deep inner knowing of our own goodness, we can remember the inherent goodness in all human beings, regardless of the conditioning that overlies and obscures it. In the mode of defocusing, where deconditioning takes place, we access inner states of kindness, compassion, and goodwill; we evoke the state of processing in the brain from which it is possible to forgive.

Forgiveness does not mean condoning, pardoning, forgetting, false reconciliation, appeasement, or sentimentality. It is a practice, daily and lifelong, of cultivating our own inner peace and wisdom that allows us to see that our pain is part of the pain of all human beings universally, to reset our moral compass, and to remain compassionate even in the face of injustice, betrayal, and harm.

Exercise 5: Forgiveness

This formal forgiveness practice is adapted from an exercise learned from the Buddhist meditation teacher Jack Kornfield.

1. Sit comfortably, allowing your eyes to close and your breath to be natural and easy. Let your body and mind relax. Breathe gently into the area of your heart, letting yourself feel all the barriers you have erected and the emotions you have carried because you have not forgiven yourself or others. Let yourself feel the pain of keeping your heart closed.

2. Breathing softly, move through each of the following possibilities for forgiveness. Begin reciting the suggested words, letting the healing images and feelings that come up grow deeper as you repeat the phrases of forgiveness.

3. Seek forgiveness from others with the following words: *There are many ways that I have hurt and harmed others, have betrayed or abandoned them, caused them suffering, knowingly or unknowingly, out of my pain, fear, anger, and confusion.*

    Let yourself remember and visualize the ways you have hurt others. See the pain you have caused out of your own fear and confusion. Feel your own sorrow and regret. Sense that finally you can release this burden and ask for forgiveness. Take as much time as you need to picture each memory that still burdens your heart. And then as each person you have hurt comes to mind, gently say: *I ask for your forgiveness, I ask for your forgiveness.*

4. Seek forgiveness for yourself with the following words: *Just as I have caused suffering to others, there are many ways that I have hurt and harmed myself. I have betrayed or abandoned*

myself many times in thought, word, or deed, knowingly or unknowingly.

Feel your own precious body and life. Let yourself see the ways you have hurt or harmed yourself. Picture them, remember them. Feel the sorrow you have carried from this and sense that you can release these burdens. Extend forgiveness for each act of harm, one by one. Repeat to yourself: *For the ways I have hurt myself through action or inaction, out of fear, pain, and confusion, I now extend a full and heartfelt forgiveness. I forgive myself, I forgive myself.*

5. Find forgiveness for those who have hurt or harmed you with the following words: *There are many ways I have been harmed by others, abused or abandoned, knowingly or unknowingly, in thought, word, or deed.*

You have been betrayed. Let yourself picture and remember the many ways this is true. Feel the sorrow you have carried from this past. Now sense that you can release this burden of pain by gradually extending forgiveness as your heart is ready. Recite to yourself: *I remember the many ways others have hurt, wounded, or harmed me, out of fear, pain, confusion, and anger. I have carried this pain in my heart long enough. To the extent that I am ready, I offer you forgiveness. To those who have caused me harm, I offer my forgiveness, I forgive you.*

Gently repeat these three directions for forgiveness until you feel a release in your heart. For some great pains you may not feel a release at first; instead, you may experience again the burden and the anguish or anger you have held. Touch this softly. Be forgiving of yourself for not being ready to let go and move on. Forgiveness cannot be forced; it cannot be artificial. Simply continue the practice and let the words and the images work gradually in their own way. In time you can make the forgiveness meditation a regular part of your life, letting go of the past and opening your heart to each new moment with a wise loving kindness.

The Neuroscience of Forgiveness

Forgiveness is a powerful practice that begins to ease the shift between the focusing mode of processing in our brain — the self-focused, narrowly focused, past- and future-oriented mode that could be described as the mode of "me" — to the defocusing mode of processing — the more present-oriented (even timeless), more expansive (even universally oriented) mode that could be described as the mode of "we." The defocusing mode allows us to see other people's struggles and suffering as well as our own from a larger and more compassionate perspective. When we are caught in habitual, self-limiting patterns of resentment and hostility, we can let ourselves drop into that merciful spaciousness from which new, more adaptive responses can emerge.

Pulling It All Together

The exercises in this chapter develop many skills of relational intelligence that help ensure that your actions in relationships, and your many ways of engaging with the world, are constructive and effective.

* Increasing mastery of the three processes of brain change develops your internal resources, allows you to trust yourself to know what to do with whatever is coming at you, and helps you recover more quickly from stress or grief. You can feel competent in relating to other people, setting boundaries when needed, and getting the guidance, comfort, and support you need to navigate the storms of life.

* You can stay open to all life experiences — whether bumps

on a pickle or full-blown catastrophe — and respond more adaptively and resiliently.

- Research indicates that every resilient behavior we do ripples out from us, the way ripples spread out from a stone thrown into a pond, touching first the person most directly affected, and then another person affected by the first person, and then another — at least four people deep. In effect, every time you choose to harness your brain's neuroplasticity to recover your own resilience, the benefit of that brain change is reaching others in wider and wider circles.

PART FOUR

KEEP CALM AND CARRY ON: RECOVERING RESILIENCE THROUGH RESOURCES OF THE BODY

CHAPTER TEN

Losing and Recovering Our Equilibrium

Serenity is not freedom from the storm but peace amid the storm.

— AUTHOR UNKNOWN

"KEEP CALM AND CARRY ON" was one of the mottoes of the British government during World War II. When we feel we are under siege ourselves, enduring our own personal version of the bombings during the Blitz, we need to call on the CEO of resilience and use body-based tools (somatic resources) to regulate the progression of worry, fear, and panic in our nervous system that could cause us to freak out or fall apart. The somatic intelligence that flows from a well-functioning prefrontal cortex allows us to stay calm, stay steady in our wise mind, and deal.

That place of calm steadiness that the prefrontal cortex reliably returns us to is a physiological state known in modern neuropsychology as the *window of tolerance*. This is our baseline state of physiological functioning when we're not frightened, stressed, overtired, or overstimulated. When we're in this window, we're grounded and centered, neither overreacting to other people or life events nor failing to act at all. Being able to meet the storms and struggles of our lives from that place of steadiness, and being able to return quickly to that window when we are pushed out of it, is the somatic prerequisite of resilience.

In this chapter, you will learn ways to strengthen the capacity of the prefrontal cortex to regulate the reactivity of the lower brain, with its rapid assessments of potential harm and survival responses of connect — or fight-flight-freeze, submit-collapse. You will also learn why it is normal for the prefrontal cortex to have difficulty in regulating that reactivity and how both the legacy of early conditioning and our biological legacy of the stress response can put the prefrontal cortex temporarily out of commission, sometimes for longer than is good for us.

Chapter 11 offers many experiential exercises that help you quickly recover the functioning of the prefrontal cortex and return to that baseline of calm equilibrium — the window of tolerance. You'll learn how to:

- use body-based resources like breath, touch, and movement to quickly return your nervous system from overreaction or shutting down to your baseline equilibrium, the calm that allows you to carry on;
- resonate with the calm in someone else's nervous system to calm your own;
- use relational resourcing to activate the release of the natural hormone oxytocin, the fastest-acting mechanism in the human brain to counter the effects of the stress hormone cortisol and return us to a state of calm and connection;
- use body-based tools to rewire old, conditioned responses to your survival reactions, so that they no longer derail your resilience.

Chapter 12 shows you how to build on the stable base of your window of tolerance to use your own body-based wisdom to further develop many skills of somatic intelligence:

- priming the brain to be less reactive to stress in the future by creating both a neurochemical buffer zone and explicitly encoded "memories for the future" that can protect you from the slings and arrows of your personal outrageous fortune;
- using implicit body memories as well as explicit cognitive memories of previous resilient coping to help you cope resiliently now;
- expanding the window of tolerance so that you're better able to handle stress;
- working with another important neurochemical circuit — the dopamine system — to help alleviate the anxiety, fear of failure, and doubt and risk involved in trying something new.

Once you can use the somatic intelligence of your prefrontal cortex to manage your body's automatic reactivity to danger or threat and reliably maintain an inner equilibrium, you can act in the world with skill and conscious response-ability. You can carry on.

The Window of Tolerance and Equanimity

*Praise and blame, gain and loss, pleasure and
sorrow come and go like the wind. To be happy,
rest like a great tree in the midst of them all.*

— Buddha's Little Instruction Book

Window of tolerance and *equanimity* are terms from two different paradigms of brain change. Both refer to the physiological and mental state necessary to recovering resilience, stabilized by the prefrontal cortex of the brain. The term *window of tolerance* was coined a decade ago by Dan Siegel, based on the past twenty years of research into the resolution of trauma and the development of new mindfulness-based, body-based therapies for trauma. In the much older Buddhist wisdom tradition, the mindful cultivation of the practice of equanimity is a reliable way to access the same zone of equilibrium. When we are in our window of tolerance or in equanimity, we do not react disproportionately to disruptive changes in our circumstances. And if we do react (survival responses can trigger us to act or collapse in less than a second), we are likely to remember to pause and become mindfully aware of our body's initial reactivity. With practice, we learn not to react to our reactions. When a cup is balanced on the edge of a table, it's in equilibrium. We have equanimity if we don't lose our own equilibrium when the cup falls and shatters. With equanimity, we can respond to the shatterings of life with careful reflection and wise choices.

I see the window of tolerance and equanimity as the physiological and spiritual constituents of the inner base of resilience (see chapter 8), which also allows us to stay in our window of tolerance and calmly meet the stressors and pressures of our daily lives.

You may already be able to sense, at times, a physiological state of peace and ease, of being calm and relaxed, yet engaged and alert. (One of the exercises below is designed to help you enter this state.) When the prefrontal cortex is functioning well, we can easily maintain this natural equilibrium. We're not too revved up; we're not too shut down.

One lunchtime, my client Serena saw a small group of boys playing soccer in a neighbor's yard as she rode by on her bike on her way to the gym. She instinctively slowed down and kept her eye on their game. But suddenly the soccer ball flew from behind a parked car into the street, and one of the little boys darted out after it. Serena swerved to avoid hitting the boy, hit the bouncing ball, and went headfirst over the handlebars onto the pavement. She landed on her right shoulder, fracturing it on impact.

Serena had had falls from her bike before; she knew to keep her body still and breathe slowly into the pain. She managed to think clearly enough to ask one of the older boys to get her cell phone out of her backpack and to explain to him how to call the emergency services. By the time a neighbor dashed out to help, the ambulance was already on its way. Serena asked the neighbor to store her bike for her and to call and ask her sister Anita to meet her at the hospital. Serena was able to stay lucid and coherent at the hospital as the doctors x-rayed her shoulder and fitted her with a sling. She had Anita cancel the two sales calls she had scheduled for that afternoon; she even thought to schedule her first physical therapy appointment before she left the emergency room. Serena's prefrontal cortex managed her body's stress resiliently, enabling her to ask for and get the help she needed as quickly as possible.

Skill 1: Maintaining Equanimity

For 2,500 years, Buddhist practices that teach equanimity have helped practitioners such as Serena calm the body and the mind, allowing them to return to the window of tolerance, enabling them to perceive events clearly and respond wisely. Here's a simple practice to help you cultivate a sense of equanimity.

Exercise 1: Cultivating Equanimity

1. Sit or lie in a comfortable position. Settle your awareness into a sense of presence, relaxing into this moment, here and now.
2. Notice anything you are experiencing in this moment — the pressure of the chair or floor against your body, a realization that you forgot to buy toothpaste yesterday, an anxiety about paying tuition for the college your daughter has set her heart on attending, concern about early signs of dementia in an aging parent
3. Notice your reaction to what you're noticing. Notice your reaction to forgetting the toothpaste, the anxiety about the tuition, your concern about the dementia. Then notice any further reaction to those reactions, any judgments or worrying or planning in response to the initial reactions.

4. Choose to let go of all of that reacting and noticing the reactions. Return your awareness to simply being in this moment, breathing here and now.

5. Continue to practice noticing your reactions and your reactions to your reactions and then letting them go, returning to the window of tolerance. You are using the process of deconditioning to retrain your brain; be persistent.

There are many times when it's appropriate and necessary to focus on a problem and try to resolve it. This exercise is teaching your brain to choose to return to the window of tolerance as a prelude to any skillful problem solving later. If it seems impossible to find the calm of the window of tolerance at all, seek a place in your body that *is* calm — your elbow or your big toe. Find some place out of the vortex of worry and focus your attention there. Return your attention there when you let go of your reactions and your reactions to your reactions.

When you first begin practicing equanimity, resting in the window of tolerance may seem like only a tiny break from all the worry churning in your mind. Keep practicing; keep retraining the brain. The window of tolerance is your natural baseline state of equilibrium. When you persevere in the practice, you can attain a steady physiological state of equilibrium from which you can begin to solve your problems. Over time, equanimity practice helps you expand your window of tolerance to handle bigger stressors with calm; you become more and more resilient.

The Neuroscience of Why Cultivating Equanimity Returns Us to Our Window of Tolerance

The Buddhist tradition teaches that suffering is inherent in the human condition: no one is immune to sickness, old age, and death and a host of other losses. However, as the teachings add, we don't have to add to our suffering by reacting in ways that are harmful or inappropriate.

As we have learned, every experience of reactivity creates a pattern of neural firing in the brain. Repeated neural firings reinforce the pattern of reactivity, adding to our suffering. If we get upset watching the evening news and then stay upset through dinner, staying in reactivity is adding to our suffering and possibly to the suffering of people around us. If we react to being upset by shutting down and withdrawing, or collapsing into helplessness, then we aren't engaged in resolving the stressors, either: we're reinforcing the patterns of not acting. Returning our awareness to our window of tolerance gives the brain a breather from reactivity. When the firing patterns in the brain are calm again, yet engaged and alert, we have created the state of mind from which we can solve our problems wisely and efficiently.

Recovering Our Balance through the Balance of Others

We learned in chapter 1 that fear — the body's response to a stressor — triggers the drive for attachment, our inborn reaching out for help and protection from another person. If, in our early years, our parents were able to soothe our fear with comforting touch, words, and behaviors, our developing nervous system learned to calm down and stay actively engaged, too. In effect, our parents' prefrontal cortex regulated our own. Through positive experiences, our developing prefrontal cortex learned how to perform this most basic function for resilience — regulating the stress response — on its own.

When that conditioning goes well, the developing prefrontal cortex can recognize the rev-up of stress or the shutting down in reaction to stress. It can direct the use of neurotransmitters to calm the lower brain's alarm center, the amygdala, and stay in the window of tolerance. (You will learn in chapters 11 and 12 to activate the release of these neurotransmitters.) And the prefrontal cortex can still use the regulation of another person to stay within the window of tolerance, too.

Skill 2: Resonating with the Calm of Others to Calm Ourselves Down

Because of the efficiency of the relational resonance circuit, which allows us to pick up the physical and emotional vibe of another person, just being near a person who is calm, in his or her window of tolerance, helps us return to our own window of tolerance. For example, Joe's silent presence and equanimity helped Nathan and Dan return to a calm state. The nurse who sat with me in the parking lot after my dad's stroke helped me recover my equilibrium. Someone being present in the room with us helps us relax and get our taxes done, and the calm presence of someone else by our side helps us believe we can get to the top of the hill. It's a wise harnessing of our neuroplasticity to have someone nearby who can help us stay calm if we've just witnessed or caused a car accident or there's a bomb scare in the building where we work. At any moment when we know we are revving up and need to return to our window of tolerance, we do well to find someone whose calm can calm us down, too.

Exercise 2: Resonating with the Calm of Others to Calm Ourselves Down

The next time you're in a situation that might cause your own nervous system to rev up and push you out of your window of tolerance, like flying during a thunderstorm, you can practice picking up the vibe of someone else's calm to keep yourself calm. In this exercise, it's the physical proximity of the calmer person that is helping your regulate your own nervous system, even if the person is not someone you're close to personally. Of course, you can rely on the calm of people who know you well to help yourself calm down, too. You can even use memories of people who care about you and support you to calm yourself.

1. Pick a partner for this exercise. If you're in a public place, this person may not even know you've chosen her. First

notice and name the stress response in your own body —
mild, moderate, or severe.

2. Tune into the calm you can pick up from the other person;
synchronize your breathing with hers, if you wish, and
receive her calming energy into the energy field of your
own body. Continue receiving her calming energy until you
do feel calm again.

3. Reflect on your experience. Notice whatever calming your
body was able to do.

Trust the calming; you can learn to do this more and more easily with practice, and each time you do it, you are rewiring your
brain for resilience. By using the calm of another person to help you
calm yourself, you are developing one of the five Cs of coping —
learning how to stay calm in a crisis.

The Neuroscience of Resonating with the Calm of Others to Calm Ourselves Down

Dyadic regulation is a term used to describe how the calm in one
person's nervous system can regulate and calm down the nervous
system of another. (*Dyad* in this context refers to two people interacting with each other.) Dyadic regulation is the process by which
the brain of a calm, well-regulated parent teaches the brain of a fussy
baby to calm down and soothe itself: it provides the conditioning
that enables the baby's prefrontal cortex to learn to regulate its autonomic nervous system (ANS). Dyadic regulation is operating any
time a friend soothes another friend over the loss of a romance or the
death of a pet. It operates when a calm person takes charge and leads
others to safety from a burning building without panic breaking out.

Dyadic regulation can also help us reengage with ourselves, with
others, or with a stressful situation when our survival responses take
us in the direction of numbing out or collapsing into helplessness.

The reassurance of someone who is comfortably in his or her window of tolerance can encourage us to regroup and try again, too.

Two structures in the brain contribute to effective dyadic regulation. One is the vagus nerve in the brain stem, where all resonance begins. The ventral branch of the vagus nerve perceives safety, trust, and calm in situations where there might be danger or life threat and can then slow down our heart rate and breathing or help us stay connected when our own response might be to collapse. A strong vagal tone in a calm person can evoke a similar response in the brain stem of another person. This vagal regulation is not cognitive or conscious. (Though, of course, thinking our way to a sense of safety and calm can work, too; it just happens more slowly.) Strengthening our own vagal tone by interacting with well-regulated people is one way that the brain learns to regulate itself and return to its window of tolerance.

The other structure is the fusiform gyrus, the small structure in the right hemisphere of the brain that the prefrontal cortex uses to recognize facial expressions. Studies have shown that when one person sees calm in the facial expression of another person, activity in the amygdala — the fear center — in the first person calms down. The functioning of both of these structures is developed through eye contact and mirror neurons, as in relationships of secure attachment and between a true other and a true self.

Losing Our Equilibrium Is Normal; Recovering Our Equilibrium Is Learnable

The involuntary revving up and shutting down that the prefrontal cortex is regulating are the normal, hard-wired survival responses of the lower brain that keep us alive, both as a species and as individuals. (See chapter 1.) The amygdala — the central alarm system of the lower brain — assesses in a very rapid, fairly primitive way signals of safety, danger, or life threat. If it detects no danger, we remain in equilibrium: we keep calm and carry on. If it detects possible danger, it relays that information through the insula to the prefrontal cortex for a more comprehensive (though slower) assessment. When the prefrontal cortex decides for itself on the most resilient, flexible response, including the possibility of connecting to others for help, it sends its own signals back down to the amygdala, regulating the unconscious revving up or shutting down of our nervous system and bringing us back into the window of tolerance. (The prefrontal cortex gets significant help in its assessment from the vagus nerve in the brain stem, which can activate the brain's resonance circuit to help us connect with others and act as a brake on the amygdala.)

While the prefrontal cortex is evaluating information coming from the amygdala, the amygdala is already activating the two branches of the autonomic nervous system — the sympathetic and the parasympathetic — to act like the gas pedal and brakes of a car. The sympathetic activates us to get us moving. The parasympathetic deactivates us to stop us from moving. (See table 4.)

Table 4. The Window of Tolerance

Sympathetic activation	When fear is regulated or absent: interest, curiosity, exploration, play, productivity, enthusiasm	When fear is not regulated: fight-flight-freeze response; too revved up; agitation, anxiety, panic
Window of tolerance	Physiological baseline of equanimity: calm and relaxed; engaged and alert	
Parasympathetic deactivation	When fear is regulated or absent: relaxation, reverie, daydreaming, napping, falling asleep after making love	When fear is not regulated: submit-collapse response; fainting, dissociation, numbness

The sympathetic nervous system (SNS) is the branch of the autonomic nervous system (ANS) that mobilizes our bodies to act. When the amygdala responds to a sense of danger with fear, the SNS can move us to connect with others, if our early experiences in attachment relationships conditioned the brain to do that. If the brain learned that reaching out to others led to comfort, soothing, and protection — which is the evolutionary function of secure attachment — then our automatic survival response will be to connect. The nervous system is calmed down by the presence of a calm other, and we return to our window of tolerance. From there we are free to go off and explore and play.

When there's no fear, the SNS can still activate us to *move* in the world, experiencing interest, curiosity, enthusiasm, and joy, while remaining in the window of tolerance. A well-regulated activation is what fuels creativity, productivity, exploration, play, and all manner of engaging and bonding with others. Our daughter can be nervous and excited about her upcoming piano recital but stay within her window of tolerance. She can feel relieved and relaxed when it's over, still within the window. We're alert and engaged, but not in trouble.

If connection to others has not become the automatic response to fear, the sympathetic nervous system moves us into the mode of fight-flight-freeze. We move to fight against the danger: in a car accident, this might lead to yelling at the driver who rear-ended us. We move to flee from the danger, perhaps driving away from the scene of an accident if we hit the other car. Or, even if our nervous system is revved up, our body might freeze, like a deer in the headlights, not moving or talking until the police arrive.

These automatic survival responses can be conditioned into habitual responses. We lash out at someone who disparages our carefully constructed way of being in the world before we think about consequences or consider his or her point of view. We panic when we realize our wallet is not in our pocket and start running around out of an urgent sense that we need to do something, but if we act without thinking, we might make things worse. If we are locked in automatic patterns of survival responses because of years of conditioning or past traumas, we may always walk away from an argument and refuse to engage, or we may always pour gasoline on the fire of any argument, yelling and refusing to listen. These are not resilient responses.

The other main branch of the autonomic nervous system, the parasympathetic nervous system (PNS), has a largely deactivating function: it slows us down or even shuts us down to prevent us from moving. When there's no fear, the parasympathetic branch relaxes us into not moving, as in the deep calm we can experience in some forms of meditation, taking a nap on the beach, and falling asleep after making love. Our bodies are calm and relaxed, still within the window of tolerance, but not necessarily engaged and alert. (Mindfulness practice, as a form of meditation, keeps us very much within the window of tolerance, calm and relaxed as well as engaged and alert.)

When we experience fear — and if connection to others has not become the automatic response — the parasympathetic branch may act to immobilize us through modes of submit or collapse. We submit to the danger, not asserting ourselves with the driver who hit us, or we collapse, numbing out, becoming paralyzed and dissociated, not "there" to deal. These automatic deactivating survival responses can be conditioned, too: we may have learned to give in in an argument without standing up for ourselves, so that we find ourselves without a backbone when we need one.

When the lower brain senses life threat, a primitive branch of the dorsal vagal nerve sends signals from the brain stem to the heart, lungs, and gut to shut down almost completely. People can faint from the sudden drop in blood pressure caused by this reaction, the body's early survival response of playing dead so the lion won't eat you.

Why It's Sometimes Difficult to Return to the Window of Tolerance

All these survival responses are normal and, in their own way, resilient: they keep us alive so that we can thrive another day. But glitches in these survival responses can make it hard to come back into our window of tolerance.

Glitch 1: Fast-Track Survival Responses
Preempt the Slow-Track Reflection

The brain structures responsible for triggering our survival responses — the brain stem, the autonomic nervous system, the amygdala, and other structures of the limbic system — operate in milliseconds, always outside our awareness. For millions of years, our brains have been hard-wired to react instantly to perceived threat or danger. We can jump out of the way of a speeding car or catch a falling child without having to think about it. We turn away from someone who gives us the creeps in one-tenth of the time that our higher, "thinking" brain needs to even register anything about that person. Much as we evolved to play dead so the lion wouldn't eat us, we can quickly disappear in a fog of dissociation so no one can find us.

The prefrontal cortex operates on a slow track. It takes three to five seconds to register that an event has occurred. The advantage of the slower processing is that the prefrontal cortex has the capacity to complete a far more comprehensive assessment and generate far more options, far more choices, far more flexibility in how to respond. Because the lower brain operates so much faster than the higher brain, it can cause us to respond to an event before the higher brain even knows anything is happening. In the time it takes the prefrontal cortex to decide whether what's lying in our path is a snake or a stick, the amygdala has already caused us to jump aside. (The slow track can sometimes be very slow: we've all experienced something taking days to dawn on us, or needing a week or two to connect the dots between one insight and another.)

Slow-track processing is not a problem if the prefrontal cortex catches the lower brain's reactivity quickly enough. Sometimes, however, our survival responses can hijack us into an inappropriate response before our prefrontal cortex manages to do the necessary reflection. When we feel threatened, we can reactively shake a fist in somebody's face, storm out the door, or freeze like a deer in the headlights. Or we might cave in or fall apart. Training our brains to pause before reacting, to give the prefrontal cortex the few seconds it needs to process the situation — as we learn to do in equanimity practice — is essential to responding resiliently.

Developing equanimity requires an understanding of our past conditioning. The amygdala operates entirely outside of our conscious awareness and can use only past conditioning to assess a situation and signal the ANS what to do. Given the brain's negativity bias, the amygdala is more likely to generate a stress response, perceiving danger or threat even where there may not be any.

The prefrontal cortex has its own conditioned patterns, too. Early experiences of fears not being regulated may slant its interpretations and responses toward the negative. This is precisely why the experiences that conditioned our earliest patterns of response can be so powerful. For the rest of our lives, both the amygdala and the prefrontal cortex continue to draw on these conditioned patterns to evaluate new situations. So our body's stress responses are rooted not in any particular event but rather in the meaning the brain attributes to that event and our conditioned response to that perceived meaning.

If our earliest experiences did not condition us to regulate our survival responses effectively, the prefrontal cortex may have not fully developed its capacities for self-regulation. We may need hours to calm our bodies down after an outburst of anger, causing more harm in the meantime. Or we may have learned survival strategies for coping with potential harm that were brilliant in the schoolyard but don't work so well in the office. We may automatically remove ourselves from any situation that seems threatening, missing out on opportunities to engage with new people at work or school, or to move our lives forward in a resilient way.

Glitch 2: Stress Responses Can Knock
the Prefrontal Cortex out of Commission

The hormone cortisol is the neurotransmitter of the stress response. Its release in the body gets us moving to save our lives. The signal to release cortisol comes from the amygdala. In perceiving a possible threat, the amygdala essentially asks, "Have we seen anything like this before?" It compares the current experience to its bank of implicit memories and within nanoseconds returns an answer: "This is okay or even good," or "This is bad or even dangerous." This hypervigilant processing of experience never stops, even in our sleep. (In our window of tolerance, it leads to pleasant dreams; outside that window of tolerance, it results in nightmares.)

The amygdala assesses not only perceived physical or external stressors but also psychological ones, like a new romantic interest failing to call back, not having enough money in the bank to pay this month's mortgage, or a gash on the leg that isn't healing. If it assesses the stressor to be dangerous or threatening, it immediately activates the release of the stress hormone cortisol, which immediately signals the body: "Don't just sit there; do something!" Or, if somewhere along the way we learned that taking action was itself a dangerous thing to do, that conditioning may stop us dead in our tracks so that we do nothing.

The effects caused by unregulated surges of cortisol can temporarily knock out the functioning of the prefrontal cortex. When I'm already late for work and I can't find my car keys, if I stress about that, for sure I won't be able to see them even when they're right in front of me. If we're not in our window of tolerance — for example, if we're tired or already stressed by other crises — a surge of cortisol coursing through our system can cause it to run amok. The amygdala can release cortisol, but it has no mechanism to turn it off; that is a function of the prefrontal cortex.

When the functioning of our prefrontal cortex is derailed by a stress response, even temporarily, we can remain stuck in a chronic state of alarm, agitation, hostility, rage, panic, or terror — or stuck in numbness, lethargy, or depression for a longer period of time than is good for us. In these states, reality testing becomes impaired, our judgment becomes compromised, and discernment and planning may be preempted by impulsive reactivity or by paralysis. Our explicit memories of resilient coping aren't available to quell the fear response. We have lost our balance; we have lost our resilience.

There are substantial costs to not being able to regulate the cortisol flowing through our system. Cortisol suppresses the immune system: the message to act now to escape a threat puts other systems in the body on hold. Studies show that chronic stress can increase the risk of contracting heart disease, lung disease, kidney disease, and cancer. "Stress kills" is no empty slogan.

Cortisol also destroys new brain cells and new synaptic connections among cells. This cell death especially affects the hippocampus, where new experiences are encoded into explicit memory, enabling the brain to learn. To encode new memory, the hippocampus has to generate new neurons and new neuronal connections. It is the most neuroplastic of all structures in the brain and thus one of the most vulnerable to the toxic effects of cortisol. By damaging the capacity for conscious learning from experience, a poorly regulated flow of cortisol impairs our ability to develop more adaptive, resilient responses; we default to the hard-wired survival response, causing a kind of vicious circle.

Pulling It All Together

- Everyone's resilience at times goes awry. There's no shame or blame in this. Our survival responses are biologically hard-wired, and less-than-optimal conditioning is the human condition.
- For the same reasons, losing our equilibrium at times is inevitable. This chapter shows the importance of learning to return to the physiological state of equilibrium — calm

and relaxed, yet engaged and alert — known as the window of tolerance, the somatic prerequisite of resilience.

- The prefrontal cortex regulates our body-brain's survival responses to stress — fight-flight-freeze or submit-collapse — so that we can return to the window of tolerance, which allows us to deal with stressors resiliently.

- With an understanding of the survival response, we can use skills of equanimity practice and dyadic regulation to help us stay both calm and engaged. We can recognize the adaptive activation of our autonomic nervous system (through the sympathetic branch), which leads to curiosity, exploration, play, and creativity, and the fear-based activation, which can lead to the fight-flight-freeze response.

- We can also recognize the adaptive deactivation of our ANS (through the parasympathetic branch), which leads to relaxation, daydreaming, and sleep, and the fear-based deactivation, which can lead to collapse, numbing out, and withdrawal.

- Implicit-only, fast-track survival responses can operate so quickly that they preempt the slower functioning of the prefrontal cortex to regulate our reactivity, thus temporarily derailing our resilience. The unregulated flow of cortisol can further impair our capacities to recover our resilience.

In the next chapter you will learn tools and exercises to overcome these glitches in our nervous system's responses. The exercises use somatic (body-based) resources to retain or regain our equilibrium and then to recondition those responses. This is resilience in action.

CHAPTER ELEVEN

Recovering Our Balance through the Body

To touch is to give life.

— MICHELANGELO

THE EXERCISES IN THIS CHAPTER are designed to help you learn to use body-based (somatic) tools to bring the prefrontal cortex back online and bring you quickly back into your window of tolerance. Once you have recovered your balance, you can use more somatic tools to help you rewire old body-based memories that might derail your resilience now.

When Cortisol Runs Amok, Oxytocin Calms It Down: Activating Oxytocin Release

The hormone oxytocin is the neurotransmitter of the "calm and connect" response and is the brain's direct and immediate antidote to the stress hormone cortisol. The fastest way to regulate the body's stress response and return to a sense of calm is to activate the release of oxytocin in the brain.

When oxytocin is released by the hypothalamus (in the limbic system) into the brain and bloodstream, cortisol levels plummet and blood pressure drops. Oxytocin is the neurochemical basis for the felt sense of safety and trust, of connection and belonging. When we know how to activate the release of oxytocin, we can quickly return to our window of tolerance and feel reassured that "everything is okay; everything is going to be okay."

Stephen Johnson, in his book *Mind Wide Open*, offers a dramatic story about the power of oxytocin to keep someone calm and in their window of tolerance. Stephen's wife had given birth to their son just two days before the 9/11 terrorist attack on the World Trade Center. From their apartment in downtown Manhattan that morning, Stephen could see debris and ash floating past the living-room window. While he was pacing the floor, half-crazed with anxiety, his wife was calmly nursing their son in the rocking chair. Childbirth and breastfeeding activate oxytocin release, generating a feeling of devotion between the mother and the newborn and a sense of blissful contentment. Stephen's wife was protected from the anxiety Stephen was experiencing by the oxytocin coursing through her system.

Oxytocin is a powerful helper in the process of maintaining equanimity and can be thought of as the neurochemical foundation of resilience. Researchers have demonstrated that a single exposure to oxytocin can create a lifelong change in the brain. The exercises below offer ways to intentionally activate the release of this neurochemical balm.

Skill 1: Activating the Release of Oxytocin through Touch

In a documentary film about Mother Teresa, I saw a two-minute segment of one of her nuns in a hospital in Beirut holding an eight-month-old baby who had been injured by mortar fire. He was screaming and thrashing about, his eyes darting here and there in pain and terror.

The nun was massaging his chest, cooing and calling to him until his eyes locked on hers. She continued gazing at him, massaging his heart, soothing him with her voice. In less than one minute his body relaxed; he calmed down and steadied his gaze on hers. He was still injured, but he was calm.

The fast way to release oxytocin and mitigate stress, even extreme stress, is through safe touch and warmth in a soothing relationship. Any warm, loving touch — hugs, snuggles, holding hands, partner dancing, cuddles with a pet, massage, or body work — can trigger the release of oxytocin and bring the body back into a state of calm. Even our own touch, as a reminder of the touch of others, can have this result.

Exercise 1a: Activating the Release of Oxytocin through a Head Rub

One fun way to trigger oxytocin release is a gentle, two-minute head rub. You can massage your own head, of course, and you can easily practice this exercise with a partner, friend, or coworker, sensual without being sexual. Use your fingers to gently massage the scalp, forehead, nose, jaws, and ears. The touch, warmth, and movement release the oxytocin in your brain, lowering your blood pressure and calming your racing thoughts. With a few moments' respite from stress and pressure, you are primed to cope more resiliently with the next stressor.

Exercise 1b: Activating the Release of Oxytocin through Massaging the Vagus Nerve

The vagus nerve, loaded with oxytocin receptors, resides in the brain stem. You can easily locate that region by placing your fingers at the back of your skull where the top of your neck nestles into the skull. A gentle massage to that part of the neck (you can easily do this yourself) can be a potent trigger for the release of oxytocin, increasing feelings of goodness and well-being throughout the day.

Exercise 1c: Activating the Release of Oxytocin through Hugs

Stan Tatkin at UCLA has found that when people feel safe with each other, a twenty-second, full-body hug is enough to release oxytocin in both men and women. Most of us don't feel comfortable with a full-body hug with anyone except a partner, immediate family, or closest friends. We do the A-frame hug of arms around the shoulders at best. The closeness of a full-body hug maximizes the effectiveness, so exchange a full-body hug with somebody you're comfortable with as often as you can. Twenty seconds is about three long, deep breaths, easy for you and your hug-ee to time on your own. Try changing head positions with each breath.

All of these exercises prime your brain to release oxytocin before a flood of excess cortisol knocks your prefrontal cortex out of commission. Safe touching with loved ones is the best possible antidote to stress and a great buffer against trauma.

Skill 2: Activating the Release of Oxytocin through Loving Connection

We may not always have someone around to give us a hug when we need it most. Fortunately, we are learning from neuroscience that we can also activate the release of oxytocin, calm down our stress response, and return to our window of tolerance by connecting or remembering connections with others. Feeling safe and loved in turn activates the release of oxytocin in the brain. We can intentionally change our neurochemistry to change our physiological state.

The earliest survival response to fear is to connect — in John Bowlby's words, to "seek physical proximity to a caregiver in times of perceived threat or danger." We can regulate our fear response by immediately turning to others for help in regulating our distress. When Samantha's mom calmed her down after Barney's over-exuberant doggy greeting, the regulating effect of oxytocin was at work. Even calling, emailing, or texting someone who is a touchstone of safety, asking for a response, can release the oxytocin if we are securely attached enough to that person.

We can give our brains baths of oxytocin whenever we are with someone we truly love and who truly loves us. Neuroscientists have demonstrated many times that even remembering or imagining someone we love, by whom we feel loved, is enough to release small but regular doses of oxytocin. This effect can come from feeling "held" by a spiritual figure or religious deity as well. When the oxytocin is flowing throughout our system, when we again feel safe in our body and in our world, we can once again think clearly and respond wisely.

As Dan Goleman says in *Social Intelligence*, "Repeated exposures to the people with whom we feel the closest social bonds can condition the release of oxytocin, so that merely being in their presence, or even just thinking about them, may trigger in us a pleasant dose of the good feelings that this molecule bestows. Close, positive, long-term relationships may offer us a relatively steady source of oxytocin release; every hug, friendly touch, and affectionate moment may prime this neurochemical balm a bit. Small wonder office cubicles are papered with photos of loved ones."

Exercise 2: Activating the Release of Oxytocin through Hand on the Heart

We come into the steady calm of our window of tolerance by experiencing moments of feeling safe, loved, and cherished and letting those moments register in our body and encode new circuitry in our brain. This exercise offers a way to evoke those feelings.

1. Begin by placing your hand on your heart, feeling the warmth of your own touch. Breathe gently and deeply into your heart center, taking in a sense of calm, peace, goodness, safety, trust, acceptance, and ease. You may elaborate these feelings as you wish. Breathe in a sense of contentment,

well-being, kindness for yourself, gratitude for others, self-care, and self-love.

2. Once that's steady, call to mind a moment of being with someone who loves you unconditionally, someone you feel completely safe with. This may, of course, be a partner, child, or parent; but if the dynamics of those relationships are complicated and the emotions mixed, you may choose any true other to your true self: a dear friend, a trusted teacher, a close colleague or neighbor, a therapist, your grandmother, a spiritual figure like Jesus or the Dalai Lama, or your wiser self. Pets are also great for this exercise.

3. As you remember feeling safe and loved with this person or pet, see if you can sense in your body the positive feelings and sensations associated with that memory. Really savor a feeling of warmth, safety, trust, and love in your body.

4. When that feeling is steady, let go of the image and simply bathe in the feeling itself for thirty seconds. Savor the rich nurturing of this feeling; let it really soak in.

You can do the first part of this exercise — quickly placing your hand on your heart — thirty times a day if you need to: when you hear bad news on the phone, when you're about to open an envelope from the IRS, when you're stuck in gridlock, when you realize you just left your laptop on the bus, when you see the disappointment in your son's face after telling him you can't take him to the baseball game tonight after all.

You can incorporate the second part of the exercise — feeling loved and cherished — at least a dozen times a day: before you get out of bed, over your first cup of coffee, before a serious conversation with a parent or a boss, regrouping after a potential contract or romance falls through.

A variation of this exercise comes from the Buddhist meditation teachers and authors James Baraz and Tara Brach: place your hand on your own cheek and say gently, "Oh, sweetheart!" The touch and kind intention of yourself toward yourself will also release oxytocin.

I teach couples to practice this exercise any time things feel calm and loving between them. (One couple did it every time they passed each other in the hallway.) By practicing it when things are going well, you can wire in a new coping strategy that can then be brought into play any time your old coping strategies flare into a fight (survival response) or bring you to the precipice of one.

The Neuroscience of Activating
Oxytocin through Hand on the Heart

Breathing deeply, gently, and fully activates the calming branch of our autonomic nervous system, the parasympathetic branch. The parasympathetic modulates the body-brain's fight-flight-freeze response when we feel threatened or agitated, helping to keep us in our window of tolerance. Breathing, or *pranayama*, has been a core practice in yoga and meditation to relax the body and steady the mind for over 3,500 years.

Breathing positive emotions into the heart center steadies the heart rate, restoring the equilibrium of the body so that we can remain present and engaged. Neural pathways from the heart to the brain signal the brain directly to release the oxytocin, which evokes a sense of safe connection with others; the oxytocin immediately reduces our stress.

In evoking a memory or image of feeling loved and cherished, we activate the prefrontal cortex, which triggers the hippocampus to search for explicit memories of moments when we have been held, soothed, protected, encouraged, believed in, times when we have reached out for help and received comfort and support. In chapter 5, I tell the story of the calming effect of using an imaginary circle of friends to alleviate my anxiety during eye surgery. Thinking of my friends caused the release of oxytocin in my brain; the calm caused by the release of oxytocin lasted through the entire surgery. That event in turn has become a memory I can use to soothe my anxiety in any new situation.

Through safety and trust in connection, we come back into our window of tolerance. From there, with our higher, thinking brain calm and alert, we can mobilize quickly, act skillfully, and take care of business.

Other Body-Based Ways to Return to the Window of Tolerance

Besides activating the release of oxytocin, there are other, slower-acting tools that help you to return to your window of tolerance: body-based tools that "remind" the prefrontal cortex how to come home to this state of calm and reinforce our steadiness there. Although these are somatic exercises, your higher brain has a role to play, too: a sense of mindful awareness and compassionate acceptance will make the exercises easier and more effective.

Skill 3: Somatic Resourcing through Breathing

The autonomic nervous system regulates our heart rate, our rhythm of breathing, and our digestive processes without any conscious processing whatsoever — thank goodness. But we can consciously use our breathing to activate the parasympathetic branch of the ANS. We do this in meditation and yoga when we breathe deeply to calm the body and the mind. We can consciously affect our heart function: researchers have found that when we breathe a sense of positive emotions — goodness, safety — into the heart, the heart rate not only slows down but comes into a stable and coherent rhythm that reliably supports resilience.

When we intentionally slow down and deepen our breathing, we are activating the parasympathetic branch of the nervous system in a positive way. We are conditioning the brain to calm down and return to our window of tolerance. Breathing slowly and deeply can deescalate a full-blown panic attack in a matter of minutes. Doing it throughout the day helps us establish calm rather than stress as our new baseline.

Exercise 3a: Deep Breathing to Relax the Body

1. Lie comfortably on your bed or on the floor, closing your eyes if you wish. Take a moment to come into a sense of presence, being here, in this moment, in this body. Notice the sensations of your head, your back, your pelvis, your legs, and your heels touching the bed or floor, feeling the groundedness of the earth itself supporting you. Place one hand on your heart, the other hand on your belly. You can also place a small pillow under your back behind your heart center, corresponding to the hand on your heart in front. Awareness of the space in your torso between the pillow and your heart can evoke the sensations of ease and well-being.

2. Notice the sensations and movement of your breath filling your belly as you inhale, rising through your lungs and chest to your throat and nose, then releasing through your throat, chest, and belly as you exhale. (Your heart actually rests on your diaphragm, so these long deep breaths give a gentle massage to the base of your heart as well.)

3. Notice the pauses between inhaling and exhaling. Allow your breath to expand, filling every part of your body, moving into your shoulders, arms, and hands, your sacrum, your legs, your feet. (When you focus the awareness of your breathing on a particular area of your body, you can consciously release tension in parts of your body that have been tightened by implicit memories of stress or trauma.) Become aware of your entire body breathing.

Over time, this exercise conditions a new, more relaxed pattern of breathing you can use in any posture — sitting, standing, and walking as well as lying down. As you bring a compassionate awareness to your breathing, notice whether you experience a spontaneous welling up of gratitude for simply being alive as well.

Exercise 3b: Breathing to Create Resonant Connection

Here's another simple exercise that uses breathing and touch to create a resonant connection between you and another person that can relax your reactivity and help you return to your window of tolerance. After two to three minutes you and your partner can switch roles.

1. Have your partner lie down comfortably on the floor with eyes closed. Sit comfortably on the floor nearby. Come into a sense of presence, of being with this person, here and now. Place one hand on his hand or forearm, the other hand on the crown of his head. Your partner breathes slowly, deeply. Begin to synchronize your breathing with his breathing. Simply breathe together for two to three minutes, noticing the life force of the breath entering and leaving his body and yours. You are strengthening the capacities of your resonance circuit and dropping into a shared equilibrium, an equanimity for two.

2. A variation of this exercise is to contemplate the reality that the molecules of air entering and leaving your lungs are the same molecules of air entering and leaving your partner's lungs, and indeed, the same molecules of air entering and leaving the lungs of anyone in the same room, in the same car or bus or plane, in the same office or store or theater or world. To open up to this kind of intimacy with beings all over the planet can radically expand our minds and open our hearts, creating a larger perspective and relaxing our bodies into the window of tolerance.

Skill 4: Using Somatic Resources to Rewire Old Somatic Memories

The body stores somatic memories of previous stress and trauma: the tension in our arms if we have had to protect ourselves from intrusion; a clenching in our fists or jaw from when we wanted to strike out or speak out in self-protection but learned it wasn't safe to do so; the collapse in our gut when we have been shamed or humiliated. We can use the exercises below to release these implicit memories, without even needing to bring them to conscious awareness to do this reconditioning. These somatic exercises help us return to and stay in our window of tolerance and rewire old patterns held in the body that might push us out of that window of tolerance. From our regained equanimity, we can choose how we want to consciously address any past stress and trauma as well as current stressful situations.

Exercise 4a: Rewiring Old Somatic Memories through a Body Scan

This exercise is a simple and reliable way to increase both awareness and compassionate acceptance of whatever you might be experiencing in your body at any given moment.

1. Lie comfortably on your bed or on the floor. Feel the back of your head, your shoulders, your back, your hips, the backs of your legs, and your heels touch the ground. Let your body relax and sink into the ground supporting it.

2. Begin by bringing your awareness to your feet. Say hello to the big toe of your right foot, listening for any aches or pains in the toe, compassionately wishing it a sense of comfort and ease. Say hello to all the toes on your right foot, the arch, the ankle and heel, carefully noticing the sensations in each part of the foot. Do the same thing slowly for every part of your body up through your torso, hands and arms, and every part of your face and head; to each ear, each eye, your nose, all the tender parts of your mouth; to the hair outside of your scalp and to the phenomenal brain inside your scalp that is allowing you to be mindful and compassionate in this moment. As you scan your body, bring a compassionate caring and acceptance to any part of it that needs comfort and ease. You

can slow way down, mindfully notice, and send compassionate caring to each knuckle if you have arthritis, or to scars from an old football injury. The body scan is a practice to mindfully, lovingly inhabit all parts of you, to become safely aware of every experience of your entire body.

3. Practice being especially mindful and compassionate toward sensations in the belly, in the heart center, in the throat and jaw, and in the genitals, areas where we can hold unconscious somatic memories of tension, shame, anger, or fear. Use your mindfulness and compassionate acceptance now to hold any distressing sensations or memories. Say hello; listen for aches and pains, physical or psychological, and send care and the intention for comfort and ease to any troubled memories held in the body.

4. End this practice by becoming aware of the energy field of your body as a whole — your whole body breathing, in equanimity, alive, relaxed, and resilient. Creating a larger awareness and acceptance of your body creates a safe setting for working with any somatic memory that arises and then deconditioning or dissolving it.

The Neuroscience of Rewiring Old Somatic Memories through a Body Scan

The anterior cingulate cortex is the brain structure we use to focus attention on anything — in this case, on physical and emotional pain. You may have noticed places in your body that felt tight, rigid, or painful. When we focus our awareness on physical sensations, we are also helping areas that hold emotional pain to relax and release tension. We don't even have to know the story behind the pain or give it a name: the mindful empathy of the body scan is rewiring the circuitry that holds the pain.

A variation of the body scan is the relaxation-response exercise, popularized by Dr. Herbert Benson, a cardiologist at Harvard Medical School and pioneer in mind-body medicine. It takes advantage of the fact that our bodies cannot be anxious and relaxed at the same time. The alternating tension and release of tension in the muscles of our bodies helps bring the entire autonomic nervous system back into the window of tolerance. Allow seven to ten minutes for this exercise. It can be done sitting (great for a long bus or train commute) or lying down. Many people eventually become so relaxed doing this exercise that they fall asleep before completing it. In time, you will strengthen your capacity to stay in the window of tolerance, both deeply relaxed and fully alert.

Exercise 4b: Rewiring Old Somatic Memories through the Relaxation Response

1. Breathing gently and fully, begin by curling the toes of the right foot, holding that muscle tension for the count of seven. Slowly release the tension as you count to fifteen, breathing gently. Then curl the entire arch of the right foot as though pointing the foot, holding that muscle tension for the count of seven. Gradually release the tension as you count to fifteen. Then flex the foot, toes back toward the leg, holding that muscle tension for the count of seven. Slowly release as you count to fifteen.

2. Continue tensing and relaxing various muscles of the body, progressing through your entire body as you tense and count to seven, then gently release as you count to fifteen. The counting focuses attention, allowing the worries and concerns of the day to fall away. Breathing into each area of the body as you let go of the tension helps that area relax.

3. Tense the lower right leg, and let that go; tense the upper thigh of the right leg, and let that go. Tense the hip and buttocks muscles of the right leg; let them go. Repeat for the left leg. Move through the torso, tensing and relaxing parts of the chest and belly in turn. Tense the fingers of the

right hand into a fist, then relax them; tense the forearm, the upper arm, the shoulder, then relax; repeat for the left hand and arm. Tense the muscles of the back, the neck, the face, and release. You can also reverse the exercise, starting at the head and working down to the feet.

4. End the session by blowing air through your fluttering lips — blowing a nice raspberry. This is yet another way to activate the PNS (who knew?). Savor the sensations of relaxation as you breathe gently. Rest one full minute — or longer — in this relaxed state.

Exercise 4c: Moving the Body to Rewire Difficult Emotions

This is a simple experiential exercise I learned from the psychologist Natalie Rogers to mindfully and compassionately use varying body positions to rewire (recondition) difficult emotional and mental states.

1. Identify an afflictive state that you would like to explore, process, and shift. It could be an emotion like fear, anger, or sadness; it could be a mental state like confusion or agitation. Come into awareness of the body sensations, images, feelings, and thoughts of this state.

2. Allow your body to lead you and come into a body posture that embodies this state. Stay in this posture for thirty seconds. Don't do a lot of thinking or figuring out here: just let your body express what you are feeling, or the state of thinking you are working on. For example, you might allow your body to assume the posture of collapse: perhaps bending over, curling shoulders inward, hiding your face in your

hands. Feel your way into your body's experience of this posture.

3. Now, without thinking, without going to your head at all or putting anything into words, allow your body to lead you into a posture that is the opposite of this state. Remain comfortably in this second posture for thirty seconds. For example, your body might select a posture opposite to collapse that involves standing tall, spine straight, arms outstretched in exuberance. Feel your way into your body's experience in this posture.

4. Without thinking, return to the first posture, and hold it again for fifteen seconds. Then resume the second posture again and hold it for fifteen seconds.

5. Allow your body to find its way into a posture that is midway between the first two. The middle posture may incorporate elements of the other postures, or it may feel entirely new.

6. Take a moment to notice the sensations and feelings in this middle posture. What are you experiencing? Notice any differences between the postures, between the states they embodied. Reflect on your experience. What shifted? What state are you in now?

The first time my client David did this exercise, he began by exploring an embodied sense of depression. "I expected the opposite of my feeling of depression would be joy, or something that felt happier. But it wasn't. It was reverence. I never would have thought of that; I never expected that. But it felt right somehow." David's experience of reverence helped him be more flexible and resilient in coping with his down moods. From this bodily experience of moving through depression to reverence, he also knew that he could choose to rewire his mental state.

*The Neuroscience of Moving the Body
to Rewire Afflictive Emotions*

The body has its own wisdom and knows how it needs to move to "correct" something. You use this somatic wisdom intuitively when you take a break from working too long at your desk or from weeding too long in your garden and get up and stretch or go for a brisk walk around the block. We can access this intuitive body wisdom by letting the body move first, without thinking, and then reflecting on what the movement might mean. This exercise is a prime example of how we can use our body's wisdom to rewire our brains from the bottom up.

Skill 5: Rewiring Negative Body Memories

Part of what determines whether we are able to choose adaptive strategies in a moment of threat, like activating the release of oxytocin, or fall into default patterns of reactivity, with cortisol coursing through the body, is the implicitly encoded patterns of response we have learned. Our resilience can be thrown off when old, trauma-based somatic memories push us out of our window of tolerance, sometimes without our even knowing what has happened or why we're suddenly so reactive.

My client Andrea created her own somatic resource to recondition her survival response to problems involving technology. She had already done a lot of work on early childhood traumas and had come to a fairly strong place of equanimity. And yet she could still have a sudden startle response when a document she was working on at the computer suddenly disappeared into cyberspace, or her plane reservation disappeared from the check-in screen at the airport. The revving up of Andrea's nervous system and the subsequent cursing at the computer — not pretty, not equanimous, not useful — was creating a technophobia that was derailing her resilience in coping with modern life.

We began by searching Andrea's explicit memory for an early, frightening experience involving machines or appliances. One memory came readily to Andrea's mind: her family had moved to a new home when she was three and a half. The living room was empty except for a radio. Andrea thought she must have accidentally turned the volume on the radio up rather than down, for her dad suddenly came charging into the living room and pulled the plug from the wall. Her mom was in the bedroom on the other side of the living-room wall, not feeling well, and her dad may have feared that the loud music would disturb her. His dramatic reaction had clearly upset Andrea.

We began searching for positive memories related to that event that Andrea could use to recondition any lingering trauma from it. She remembered how she used to stand on her dad's toes so that the two of them could dance. We speculated that perhaps Andrea had turned up the radio that morning so she and her dad could dance together around the empty living room. The somatic memory of Andrea dancing on her dad's toes, and the accompanying sense of love, safety, and trust, could evoke the flow of oxytocin that could calm the automatic startle response in her brain to difficulties with technology.

Andrea began practicing lifting up her toes as though she were dancing on her dad's toes, saying out loud, "Toes up!" and then pairing that physical gesture with the surge of oxytocin from remembering the joy of those moments with her dad. The next time Andrea's body went into a startle response at the computer, she lifted her toes off the floor, telling herself, "Toes up!" and the reaction instantly stopped, leaving her calm and able to cope. Andrea had found a somatic way to break the pattern.

Exercise 5: Rewiring Negative Body Memories

You can experiment with a very simple form of reconditioning for rewiring those body-based negative memories, based on the technique of somatic experiencing developed by Dr. Peter Levine.

1. Identify a place in your body where you might be holding a somatic memory of a trauma or something that simply feels negative or unpleasant: a churning in the stomach, a tense jaw, a tightening in your back or shoulders. Notice the physical sensations.

2. Now locate a place in your body that is not feeling any distress or trauma at all — maybe your elbow or your big toe. Notice the physical sensations of being in the window of tolerance: feeling calm, relaxed, at ease. If you are currently experiencing the body-based sensations of any trauma, this window might be quite small. Focus attention on that calm, untraumatized place in the body, steadily feeling the sensations there of ease and relaxation.

3. Now switch your attention back and forth between the physical sensations of the place in the body that is not traumatized at all and the physical sensations of the place in the body that is holding the network of the trauma memory. When you switch between awareness of the two different body parts, you are practicing a technique called *pendulation* (like the pendulum of a clock swinging back and forth). It's a way for you to recondition a trauma memory through body sensations alone.

The Neuroscience of Rewiring Negative Body Memories

As you focus your attention on the physical sensations in your body, you are lighting up the networks encoding the memory of the experience, a process essential to rewiring it. As in the reconditioning described in chapters 2 and 3, when the sensations of the untraumatized place in the body are stronger than the sensations of the trauma memory, the trauma memory can be rewired. With practice, you can draw on a somatic resource to completely dissolve a trauma memory held in implicit memory in the body.

Pulling It All Together

You have just learned nearly a dozen body-based skills that will help you stay in, or quickly return to, the state of equilibrium in your body-brain so that you can respond to the startles and upsets in your life with greater equanimity and resilience.

- You have learned how to activate the release of oxytocin — through touch and loving connection — to use the brain's direct and immediate antidote to the stress hormone cortisol to help you return quickly to your window of tolerance.
- You have learned to use somatic resources like breathing, body scanning, progressive muscle relaxation, and movement to remind the prefrontal cortex how to regulate the body into calm.
- You have learned ways of strengthening the prefrontal cortex to use positive somatic resources to rewire negative experiences held in body memory.

Being able to remain calm in the face of difficulties is one of the five Cs of coping, and it makes it far easier for your brain to learn new strategies of deploying the other four Cs. Somatic resourcing also creates a platform for learning additional skills of somatic intelligence, priming your brain to preempt your reactivity before it even arises, to learn more self-confidence from previous experiences of competence, and to be willing to risk making mistakes and trying something new. As you practice these techniques, they keep rewiring your brain for more resilience.

CHAPTER TWELVE

Developing Somatic Intelligence

You can't stop the waves, but you can learn to surf.

— JON KABAT-ZINN

A MASTER MONK is meditating in a temple with other monks. Suddenly a fierce bandit storms into the temple, threatening to kill everybody. The other monks flee, but the master monk remains, calmly meditating. Enraged, the bandit shouts, "Don't you understand? I could run you through with my sword and not bat an eye!" The monk calmly replies, "Don't you understand? I could be run through by your sword and not bat an eye."

This teaching story from the Buddhist tradition has always struck me as the epitome of how priming the brain prepares a practitioner to maintain calm in a crisis. This is one form of the somatic intelligence — wisdom of the body — we are building in order to recover our resilience. However metaphorical and however great a stretch of the practice of equanimity it represents, the story illustrates how priming can regulate our reactivity, even in the most extreme situations. The monk's brain was primed by years of mindfulness and compassion practice to remain calm in the face of life threat; modern neuroscience might say that his prefrontal cortex could regulate any reactive response from his amygdala. While we might not strive for that level of equanimity, and hopefully we will never face such a dire situation, we can learn to use our own mindful empathy and compassionate reflection to strengthen our equanimity by learning to prime our brains, too.

Skill 1: Priming the Brain to Remain Calm in a Crisis

Priming simply means preparing the brain to feel a certain emotion or a physiological state that could be adaptive in an anticipated situation: to feel proud or confident before walking into a meeting with the boss, to boost your assertiveness when defending yourself in court, to remain grounded and open-minded when hearing your doctor discuss results of the latest lab tests.

There are many strategies for managing emotions and physiological states after they arise. Priming is different: it's preemptive, creating an emotional or physiological state that prevents fear or anger or shame from arising. Here we set the intention to remain calm and then use priming as a tool to do so. We can effectively prime the brain to meet stressful situations by achieving a state of calm and equilibrium beforehand. We can use the oxytocin response in particular to prime the brain to be less reactive to future stress because the release of oxytocin, activated whenever we remember someone we care for or who makes us feel cared for, acts as a buffer against stress even before it occurs.

An excellent example of this kind of priming was reported in a study by James Coan at the Laboratory for Cognitive and Affective Science at the University of Wisconsin. In the study, three groups of women subjects knew they were going to be administered a slight but unpleasant electric shock on their ankles. Their brain functions were monitored using an fMRI scanner. The control group of women subjects, who were left alone in the scanner, registered anxiety before and pain during the test. Women holding the hand of a stranger (the lab technician) registered less anxiety and less pain. But the group of women holding the hands of their husbands registered the least anxiety and pain, and in some cases, no anxiety or pain at all. The pleasurable security of holding the hand of someone who loved them released oxytocin, reduced their stress, and overrode both anxiety and pain. These women instead reported experiencing peacefulness throughout the procedure. Holding hands with someone they felt safe with primed or conditioned their brains to remain in the calm and relaxed, yet engaged and alert, state of the window of tolerance. It turned off the threat switch in the brain and overrode anxiety and pain, even in a situation that was stressful to others.

Phil Shaver discovered similar benefits to priming before stress in a study at the University of California, Davis. Subjects were shown photographs of disturbing material. Those who were instructed to think of a situation in which they felt safe and loved before seeing the photographs showed far less stress reaction than subjects in the control group who were not primed in this way. Consistently, the oxytocin released in remembering someone the subjects loved or felt safe with acted as a buffer against a stressful trigger a few minutes later.

My client Claudia shared with me a dramatic example of the power of priming. Late one night she had to drive home through a pelting rainstorm. She had touched base by phone with her partner before setting out, so oxytocin was already flowing in her brain and body. As she was driving in the fast lane of the freeway, the left front tire of her car suddenly caught the shoulder of the road. The car skidded onto the shoulder. Claudia overcorrected, and the car swerved across four lanes of freeway traffic to stop in the mud off the shoulder on the other side.

It was all over in fifteen seconds. No one was hit, no one was hurt, and no damage was done. Claudia simply got back on the freeway and drove home. She felt grateful for the miracle of her life and grateful to be going home to a loved one. But she felt no trauma or stress, not even for a minute. Her brain was primed and her nervous system was buffered by the oxytocin. Sue Carter of the Chicago Psychiatric Institute, one of this country's primary researchers on oxytocin, reports, "People under the influence of oxytocin don't have the same stress response that others do; bad news rolls off them more easily."

One way to prime your brain to face a challenging situation that you know is coming — such as a medical or legal procedure or confronting a difficult person or group — is to cultivate a virtual circle of support to call on in your imagination. Priming the brain in this way makes it easier for you to stay in your window of tolerance when an accident or catastrophe takes you by surprise.

Exercise 1a: Prime the Brain by Beginning the Day in Loving Connection

Beginning the day with a sense of loving care and connection is a fantastic way to build our brain's buffers against stress. It's as important for our emotional health as a nutritious breakfast is for our physical health. It's great if you can wake up in the morning cuddling a sweetie, or immediately hug your children or a pet, or wrap your arms around yourself with a squeeze of self-acceptance and encouragement. The touch provides a sense of comfort and connection before you meet the challenges of the day; you're primed to live the day from your window of tolerance.

Exercise 1b: Prime the Brain by Beginning the Day in Ease and Well-Being

If that sweet send-off is not available in the morning, it can still be an excellent practice to not get out of bed until you can evoke within yourself a sense of loving connection from the past, or even a fantasy about the future, that evokes a sense of ease, safety, and well-being. As with Sean, whose story appears in chapter 5, that may take a few breaths, or a few minutes; sometimes it can take thirty minutes or more. But it's worth priming the brain to meet the challenges of the day from a place of calm, relaxed engagement. Set the intention to start the day in your window of tolerance, no matter what happens later.

As we practice staying in our window of tolerance to meet the challenges we anticipate throughout the day, we are priming our brain to stay calm when called upon to face challenges we don't anticipate, as well.

Exercise 1c: Prime the Brain by Returning to Your Window of Tolerance

1. A simple introductory practice is to check in with yourself periodically to discern whether, in fact, you are in your window of tolerance. If you are, your body feels calm, relaxed, yet engaged and alert — not agitated, not shut down. You feel present, settled, and balanced. When you're not in your window of tolerance, you notice the unease; you feel "off." With practice, you can learn to recognize the difference instantly.

2. When you notice you're not in a state of equanimity, stop doing what you're doing as soon as you can — there's not much point and some risk if you're moving forward without being grounded in your base of resilience.

3. Breathe and place your hand on your heart to calm your body. Draw on your practices of mindfulness and self-acceptance. Hold whatever is happening in the moment with as much awareness and compassionate understanding and empathy as you can muster. Call on your relational resources. Evoke the memories of feeling safe and loved until you saturate yourself with oxytocin. You'll probably return to your window of tolerance quite suddenly, because once the oxytocin reaches an effective level, its effect is immediate.

Doing this usually isn't hard; it's remembering to do it that's hard. Perseverance teaches us that these practices do work, and when we know that they work, we're more likely to remember to do them the next time we need them.

When I first began checking in with myself in this way, I had to stop every five minutes and intentionally return myself to a state of equanimity. But each time I did the practice, the interval of feeling calm lasted longer. As you become more successful at returning to your window of tolerance, take in the good feeling of the inner calm and peace before rushing off to do the next thing. Give your brain the thirty seconds it needs to rewire this experience of calm into its circuitry so that staying within your window of tolerance becomes a new habit, a source of new resilience.

Skill 2: Developing Current Confidence from Previous Competence

I once hiked with my friend Donn up a steep trail on Mt. Tamalpais, near my home, following many switchbacks for more than half an hour to reach a grand viewpoint. Belatedly I realized that if we were to take the same switchbacks down the mountain, I would get back to the parking lot too late to pick up my goddaughter at her gymnastics practice. Donn asked if I could bushwhack straight down the mountain. After years of backpacking in the high Sierra, my automatic response was "Sure I can!" Down the steep hillside I went, surefooted; Donn quickly followed. We arrived at the parking lot in less than fifteen minutes.

Saying "Sure I can!" is an important somatic resource of resilience. Researchers have found that the greatest predictor of success — in anything — is a previous track record of success — in anything. In other words, we don't have to have faced the same challenge before to feel confident that we can deal with what we're facing now. We have resilience when we know that we have dealt successfully with *anything* before. The feeling of confidence about bushwhacking down a mountain becomes an inner resource encoded in the neural circuitry of our brain that we can call on whenever we need to bushwhack through any difficult terrain: getting an aging parent to write a will or tracking the thousands of details involved in moving overseas.

Confidence is a somatic memory of competence. Interestingly, research shows that even if we have an inflated sense of that earlier competence, it still serves as a resource of confidence now. We get through an "uh oh!" by remembering "uh oh!s" we've gotten through before and by evoking the visceral feeling of "Sure I can!" that came from that success. We may experience that feeling of "I can!" as a feeling of groundedness, a trust, a security. Standing tall, sensing our weight through our spine and hips and anchoring our feet on the earth can ground in the body this resource of trust and reassurance in our competence and mastery.

Research also shows that for purposes of somatic resourcing, it's not so much the size of a previous success that matters as the genuine sense of competence or mastery that comes from it. Succeeding at something we accomplished all on our own (painting the living room, repairing a broken lawnmower, helping an athlete feel better about herself after her mistake cost the team the game) creates a sense of ownership of the success. Once encoded in the neural circuitry, that feeling can be even more effective at creating confidence (and thus resilience) than playing a small part in a larger organizational effort with no sense of ownership of the final outcome. If we're hammering nails in a Habitat for Humanity building project, it's the "Sure I can!" from the three walls and a door frame that we built ourselves — the sense of competence in our own work rather than the sense of accomplishment at the completion of the entire house — that becomes the somatic resource of confidence that we can draw on later when we need to rebuild a business or a marriage.

Exercise 2: Wiring In Current Confidence from Previous Competence

1. Identify areas of your life where you would like to have more of the feeling of "Sure I can!" They might include returning to school after thirty years in the workforce, buying into a franchise, or facing an empty nest when your youngest child has moved away.

2. Identify three moments in your life when you actually had that sense of "I can!" in your body — a visceral sense of confidence arising from a moment of competence. Reflect not so

much on what you did, because that will change with circumstances, but on how you felt when you realized that you
had done it. Remember, we're talking moments here, not
major events: opening a stuck jar lid for your mom, intuit-
ing which way to turn to find the train station in a strange
city, knowing just what to say when your child experienced
a disappointment. Modest but genuine successes can mean
just as much for rewiring the brain as those that are more
dramatic.

3. Focus on the sense of mastery those successes brought you.
   How does that remembered sense of mastery feel in your
   body now? Take in the feeling of "I did; I can" as a body-
   based resource.

4. Try to bring that visceral sense of "I did; I can" into the
   present and apply it in the areas where you would like to
   feel this confidence more often. Even the slightest success at
   doing this reconditions your brain toward resilience.

The Neuroscience of Wiring In Confidence

Our brains begin encoding experiences of mastery into schemas or
templates of "I can!" almost from the moment we're born. A baby
can typically grasp a toy at two months of age, reach for people at
four months, hold its own bottle at six months, and give a hug and
walk with support at twelve months. Each of these successes conditions the pattern of "I can!" into the developing brain, providing a
neurological underpinning for the inner sense of trust and security
that builds the base of resilience.

As we intentionally create an archive of explicit memories of
successful coping, we are strengthening that base and thus our capacity for resilient coping now. Any time the prefrontal cortex accesses
a memory that carries with it the somatic sense of "Sure I can!" it can
send an inhibitory transmitter — GABA — to the amygdala. This

inhibits the firing of the amygdala, signaling, in effect, that the prefrontal cortex is taking care of business and that the amygdala does not need to activate a survival response.

Remembering a moment of previous coping when we're facing a daunting task or situation can help us return to our window of tolerance, where we can cope more resiliently.

Skill 3: Reframing Incompetence as Competence

One of my favorite *Calvin and Hobbes* cartoons is an inspiring moment when Calvin trips and falls down the stairs and lands in a heap at the bottom, dazed and confused. Then he stands up, throws his arms up in the air as though welcoming applause, and says, "Ta da!"

My meditation teacher Sylvia Boorstein tells this story of one of her own "Ta da!" moments. She had arranged to meet a friend for an evening performance at Lincoln Center in Manhattan. She didn't want to take the subway from her hotel, but she thought the traffic was too heavy for a cab to get her there on time. She started to walk the twelve blocks. Realizing she was going to be late, she began to run. Sylvia started to feel embarrassed when she pictured herself as an old lady running down the street. Then she realized: "I'm 70 years old, and I can run down the street! In high heels! Great joy!"

You bounce back from adversity any time you discover or claim your competence within seeming incompetence, any time you reframe a potentially embarrassing moment as a moment of triumph. Your own reframing or perspective draws on a healthy sense of pride. You claim a sense of competence. "Sure I can!" "I am someone who can."

Exercise 3: Reframing Incompetence as Competence

1. Evoke a sense of confidence in your body, perhaps by remembering a "Sure I can!" moment. Take a moment to feel the strength in your body from this memory.

2. Then call to mind a moment of incompetence that might have caused some discomfort, embarrassment, or inconvenience: leaving the tickets for the concert on your desk at home or mixing up the birthday gifts you gave your two best friends. Notice any deflation of your body energy or collapse in your body posture as you remember this moment.

3. Pairing the memory of incompetence and the accompanying sensations of deflation or collapse with the memory of competence and the sensations of energy and strength may be enough to recondition and rewire the feeling of incompetence and bring you back into your window of tolerance. If so, great. If not, evoke a sense of "Ta da!" to help reframe that moment of incompetence as simply held in the context of your many competencies overall, not enough to undermine your resilience. You can acknowledge this moment as part of being human and still stay in your window of tolerance.

The Neuroscience of Reframing Incompetence as Competence

A sense of incompetence, real or imagined, can trigger our autonomic nervous system into the survival responses of submit-collapse. (For a discussion of the role shame plays in this collapse, see chapter 14.) In response to a sense of threat to our psychological survival, the parasympathetic branch of the ANS is overactivated, and this response deactivates the normal functioning of the sympathetic branch. The body begins to immobilize, shutting down for self-protection. The energy of the psyche begins to deflate. Pushed out of our window of tolerance, we lose momentum and our capacity to act.

When we reframe our behavior and our view of ourselves as competent, or even use a gesture of "Ta da!" to recover a sense of healthy pride despite a slipup, we reactivate our nervous system, recover our energy, and move back into our window of tolerance.

Skill 4: Training Our Brains to Risk Something New

Yes, risk-taking is inherently failure-prone.
Otherwise, it would be called sure thing–taking.

— TIM MCMAHON

Whenever we're about to venture into something new — moving across the country, getting married again, taking on a new job, finally fixing the leaky showerhead — we can feel a hesitancy, a pull-back within — a somatic feeling of "Uh oh! Strange territory! Don't know if I should be doing this!" — even though, consciously, we might very well want to forge ahead. Our resilience goes on hold.

Using the skills already presented in this chapter, we can get ourselves over the fear of failure or of making a mistake. We can use the beneficial effects of oxytocin from the support of other people to help us cross the somatic threshold between the comfort of the familiar and the discomfort of the new and uncertain. But there is also another powerful neurotransmitter whose effects we can harness to cross that threshold in the brain: dopamine.

Dopamine is the neurotransmitter of pleasure and reward. With the release of dopamine in the brain stem we feel good, we feel alive and energized, and we want more. Dopamine is actually partly responsible for the way we get into ruts, doing what makes us feel comfortable, getting better at what we've always been good at. The neurochemical reward we get from repeating successful patterns of behavior can hold us back from trying new strategies, from discovering new ways of being and coping.

The release of dopamine can lead to addictive behaviors, too: wanting more of what made us feel good before, even if it's not good for us. Maybe shopping makes us feel happier, so we run up charges on our credit card until our debt is out of control, or we try to relieve our stress with too much social drinking. Mindfulness is the key here — awareness that always involves discernment of the wholesome from the unwholesome and the effect of our choices on our resilience.

Dopamine operates on the basis of expectation. When the brain experiences what it expects to experience — when we turn on the kitchen faucet and water comes out — dopamine levels stay steady. If something unexpected happens — we turn on the faucet and no water comes out — the expectation is disrupted. The disruption switches off the dopamine and generates a slight unease in the body. A mistake has been detected. The brain directs us to stop moving forward until we know things are okay.

The insula, the structure of interoception that reads what's going on in the body, communicates this unease to the anterior cingulate cortex, the structure that focuses our attention and tracks errors internally as well as externally. Spindle cells in the anterior cingulate cortex — the fastest-transmitting neurons in our brain — pick up the unease of this disruption of dopamine release and instantly saturate the rest of the cortex with that feeling of unease. (Some neuroscientists refer to this function of dopamine as the "Oh shit!" circuit.)

Read Montague, professor of neuroscience at Baylor University, tells us, "You're probably 99.9 percent unaware of dopamine release, but you're probably 99.9 percent driven by the information and emotions it conveys to other parts of the brain."

We can interpret this feeling of unease as anxiety, which can automatically lead to refusing or deferring new challenges. It feels like a risk to try something new. We might talk ourselves out of trying a new entrée at a new restaurant in a new city, visiting a foreign country, or venturing into the foreignness of a new career or a new relationship. If we want to move forward, we need to come back into our window of tolerance. We need to know how to work skillfully with our dopamine system so that we are not stopped in our tracks by warning signals from our lower brain.

Bill Bowen, the developer of psychophysical psychotherapy, has studied resilience and the creative process for thirty years. He suggests that when confronted with anything new, our responses range from the survival reactions of fight-flight-freeze, which halt any positive activation, all the way to adaptive activation and the free-flowing expression of creativity. Somewhere on that continuum there is a somatic threshold that we feel viscerally, where our body and brain chemistry stops us from going forward even though consciously — mentally, emotionally, and spiritually — we are ready to dive in. It can take the form of writer's block; cold feet on the morning of the wedding; or the last-minute justification of "I don't know anybody at the party, and I'm too tired anyway." This somatic marker is the disruption of the dopamine circuit, which is telling us, "Uh-oh, this is not what was expected." That's true: it's not. It's new. But that doesn't necessarily mean we should stop abruptly.

"Do one thing every day that scares you" was Eleanor Roosevelt's sage advice. Wise practice from a stellar role model of resilience, who coped with the hardships of the Great Depression, the tragedies of World War II, and the infidelity of a husband who happened to be president of the United States.

When we deliberately face our fear of doing something new or risky, or confront deep doubts about ourselves as human beings, we come to the somatic threshold that might block us from moving forward. As the meditation teacher Jack Kornfield says, we can read that anxiety not as a warning to retreat to the familiar and comfortable but as a signal that means "About to grow!"

By facing the fear and intentionally crossing the threshold into action, we are deliberately choosing to evoke new experiences that recondition the anxiety in our nervous system. By pairing an old pattern of fear or block with a new, more positive pattern of courage and action, we contradict the old and rewire it. This is reconditioning at its finest.

Exercise 4: Do One Scary Thing a Day to Train Your Brain to Risk Something New

1. Identify one scary thing to do today to practice crossing that somatic threshold of anxiety and experience something new. For example, apologize to your teenager for not keeping a promise; create a realistic budget of income and expenses and then talk with your spouse about it; go up into the attic

with a flashlight to see what's scurrying around up there at night; make a doctor's appointment to find out what's really going on with that persistent cough; ask your boss to make good on a promise of time off for the extra time you put in last month.

2. Practice facing the fear today, and then practice doing one new, different scary thing a day every day for the next thirty days. Crossing the threshold into action at least once a day rewires into the brain a new default feeling of "Sure I can!" or "Wow! I did it!"

3. As you repeat this practice of doing one scary thing a day for several weeks, notice any shifts in the messages your body is sending you as you prepare for the scary thing and after you've done it. Notice any emergence of the sensation of "Sure I can!" Facing fear is ultimately easier than constantly navigating around situations that provoke it. We reset the default to honesty, courage, and resilience.

Skill 5: Wiring for Resilience by Making Mistakes

Knowledge rests not upon truth alone, but upon error also.

— CARL G. JUNG

Resilience is based on learning new, more adaptive ways of coping. Researchers have found that one of the best tools for recovering resilience now is to learn from mistakes in the past. The wisdom of Mullah Nasruddin's saying "Good judgment is based on experience; experience is based on bad judgment" can be a comfort when we're faced with AFGO (another fricking growth opportunity) or fear of one.

Our brain rewires from the experience of making a mistake. When our choices turn out to be problematic for ourselves or others, we can learn from them by asking, "What did I not see? What could I have done differently? What can I do differently now?" As the neuroscience writer Jonah Lehrer says, "We turn a regrettable moment into a teachable moment." We can learn to find the gift in the mistake in the form of a belief that "I am learning; I am coping."

It helps to debrief after a mistake by talking it over with other people. Different perspectives help us discover the gift in the mistake and reduce our agony or self-condemnation over it. When we're having to deal with consequences that we would never wish on ourselves or anyone else, we can find some equanimity in knowing we are strengthening our capacities to cope. We may not wish to have to become so bravely, tenaciously adaptive in our lives, but we can rejoice that we are.

Exercise 5: Wiring for Resilience by Finding the Gift in the Mistake

Failure is not fatal, but failure to change might be.

— JOHN WOODEN

1. Ask a small (safe!) group of friends to come together to "look for the gift in the mistake."
2. Each person shares common mistakes first, the sort of mistakes that anyone might make: getting distracted and running a red light; accidentally deleting all the emails confirming travel reservations; forgetting to enroll in a health insurance plan by the deadline and now having to appeal. Find some comfort (not judgment) in the universal imperfections of being human.
3. Expand your sharing to include mistakes that had bigger external consequences — putting off going to the doctor until "just a cough" landed you in the hospital with pneumonia for a week — or internal consequences — the guilt you feel because that hospitalization caused you to miss your daughter's graduation from college.

4. Let the compassionate reflection of others in the group, as well as your own, allow each person to "own" their mistake, discern what lesson could be learned from it, and find the gift in it, according to the following narrative:

this is what happened;
this is what I did to survive;
this has been the cost;
this is what I have learned;
this is how I can respond to life now.

Even if the gift is simply a deeper intention to pay closer attention as we career through our days, or to be kinder to ourselves in our imperfect humanity, we have found the gift.

The Neuroscience of Finding the Gift in the Mistake

One of the major functions of the prefrontal cortex is to integrate the many messages and stories we tell about ourselves and our behaviors — who we are, how we got to be here, what we're proud of, what we regret — into one coherent narrative. We have to come to terms with the whole shebang in order to rest easy in our window of tolerance. Reframing our mistakes as learning not only helps us learn — preparing us to cope more skillfully and resiliently the next time — but also helps us relax into the self-acceptance that contributes to our equanimity, enabling us to keep calm and carry on.

Pulling It All Together

Through the exercises in Part 4, you have learned many practical tools of somatic resourcing to regulate your survival responses and return to the window of tolerance — the physiological state of calm and ease — and to strengthen your prefrontal cortex to use somatic resources to rewire old patterns that can derail resilience. These tools include:

- ways to prime the brain to remain calm in a crisis through activating the "calm and connect" properties of oxytocin;
- ways to use previous competence (at anything) to wire in the sense of "Sure I can!" to face new challenges, to reframe a potentially embarrassing moment as a moment of triumph, to reframe potential incompetence as actual competence, and to transform a feeling of deflation or collapse from shame into a healthy pride that keeps you mobilized and able to deal;
- ways to train your brain to risk something new by doing one scary thing a day; you practice repeatedly crossing the somatic threshold that could block your taking resilient action;
- ways to find the gift in the mistake, learning the lessons of experience in order to make better judgments and choices.

As prime minister of England during World War II, Winston Churchill epitomized for many the capacities to keep calm and carry on. He taught us: "Success is not final; failure is not fatal. Success is moving from one failure to another without loss of enthusiasm. It is the courage to continue that counts."

Through these exercises, you are creating a bona fide somatic intelligence that allows you to carry on with confidence and trust in your competence.

PART FIVE

RECOVERING RESILIENCE THROUGH EMOTIONAL WELL-BEING

CHAPTER THIRTEEN

How Neuroscience Is Revolutionizing Our Thinking about Feelings

I don't think there's such a thing as a bad emotion.
The only bad emotion is a stuck emotion.

— RACHEL NAOMI REMEN, MD

ONE EVENING MY CLIENT Curt came to session fuming because his nine-year-old daughter, Cathy, had been punished at school for a soap fight in the girls' bathroom that she had neither instigated nor participated in but merely witnessed. Cathy had been hauled into the principal's office that morning along with three other girls. Her protestations of innocence were ignored, and she was made to pick up trash on the playground at afternoon recess as her punishment. Curt wanted to throttle the principal, haul him in front of the school board, and sue the district for what he perceived as the school administration's shaming and bullying of his daughter.

Every one of us has had our emotional well-being derailed by worry, irritation, or envy from time to time. We may have a pattern of comparing ourselves with colleagues or neighbors to determine our status in the pecking order. We may find ourselves hypervigilant any time we have to travel to a new part of town. Many of us also have our resilience derailed for long stretches by the toxic biggies: anxiety, anger, depression, shame, guilt. We may carry a fear of failure or potential embarrassment into new projects. We might be hypersensitive and reactive to even casual remarks about our parenting. Or we may feel stuck in a low-grade sense of the blahs. In these states, our capacities to see clearly, to find the courage to claim our competence, and to connect to the people and resources we need to create new options are thrown off. Our resilience is derailed.

In the preceding chapters, you learned ways to develop your somatic intelligence to resiliently manage your stress responses and return to the calm that can lead to coping well. In this chapter you will learn how to develop your brain's capacities to skillfully manage strong emotions like Curt's and prevent them from swamping your resilience. Chapters 14 and 15 offer techniques for using those emotions as gateways to resilient action and strengthening the emotional intelligence that allows you to relate to yourself and others flexibly, adaptively, and resiliently.

The desire to get rid of these problematic surges of uncomfortable feelings and move on is natural in the human psyche. For millennia both Eastern and Western philosophies and psychologies have taught that we can conquer our "primitive passions" or "destructive emotions" through the governance of the "higher," rational brain. Today, however, neuroscientists who study feelings and thinking (affects and cognitions) are reversing that propensity to privilege the higher, rational brain over the lower, emotional brain to guide our most important decisions. They are discovering that we are not evolved to be exclusively rational creatures. Our emotional brain is as important to decision making as our capacity for reasoning is. The emotional brain can make decisions faster than the rational brain, based on information that the higher brain can't directly comprehend.

According to Daniel Goleman, author of the landmark book *Emotional Intelligence*, "Emotions streamline our decisions at the outset by eliminating some options and highlighting others. Emotions guide us in facing predicaments and tasks too important to leave to intellect alone: danger, painful loss, persisting toward a goal despite frustrations, bonding with a mate, and building a family. When it comes to shaping our most important decisions and our actions, the emotional brain is as involved in reasoning as is the thinking brain."

Emotions as Gateways to Resilient Action

This chapter follows the lead of the most recent scientific discoveries, taking the view that our emotions are unparalleled mechanisms of human connection: they fuel the affections that bond us deeply to other people and reveal the vulnerabilities that are part of our common humanity. Emotions fuel the vitality that makes us feel fully alive and "juicy" and are themselves powerful catalysts of brain change. Our emotions, from the most basic — mad, sad, bad, glad — to the most complex — resentment, jealousy, pride — are motivational systems in and of themselves. Affects — the neurobiological roots of what we call feelings or emotions — are simply waves of body sensations that signal us, from the bottom up, "Pay attention! Something important is happening here!"

These sensations are filtered through the primitive emotional processing center of the amygdala. This, with its inherent negativity bias, can lay a bad rap on the meaning of these sensations as they pass through the insula to the more complex discernment of the prefrontal cortex, which can consciously perceive, process, and respond to them resiliently, perhaps with a different, more favorable interpretation.

Our task is to learn when to listen to these emotions as guides to adaptive behaviors — as when our unease helps us establish a boundary against someone's repetitive, intrusive phone calls — and when to manage them, so that we return to our window of tolerance and respond wisely. If someone else is selected to present the concerns of our local environmental action group to the board of supervisors, we might cope with our disappointment by staying engaged in the cause anyway, rather than withdrawing in a huff. We also need to learn when to realize that these emotions are based on an implicit memory of a previous situation that is no longer true, so that we don't have to react now the way we did then: just because the family we grew up in never talked to us directly about Uncle Fred's cancer and silenced our questions after he died, that doesn't mean we shouldn't tell our spouse what the doctor has told us today. Our response flexibility around our emotions allows us to harness their energy toward resilient action.

A story I heard from Heather Martin, a Canadian teacher of mindfulness, illustrates the harnessing the energy of emotions toward resilient action. A few winters ago, a huge snowstorm downed large trees and closed major roads in Toronto. One woman driving west to see her newborn granddaughter in a hospital on the other side of town found the road blocked by a large fallen oak tree. Another woman, driving in the opposite direction to see her dying father in another hospital, was stopped on the other side of the same tree. The two women got out of their cars and began sharing their common plight with each other.

After a few minutes of discussion, the two women decided they could trust each other enough to trade car keys. (If one of them had had a prior bad experience of trusting a stranger with something as important as their primary means of transportation, this story might have gone in a different direction.) Each one drove the other's car to the hospital to see her loved ones; they exchanged cars again once the storm had passed and the roads were cleared. In this case, the capacities of the two women to read and trust their own emotional signals led to a resilient solution to their dilemma.

All emotions are, in essence, impulses to act: *e-motion*. When processed and expressed well, all emotions lead to resilient action. For instance, anger can lead us to protect ourselves and our loved ones from attack, injustice, and oppression. Sadness can lead us to reach out and connect with resources that make life bearable and meaningful. Fear can cause us to stop, assess, regroup, and choose wisely. Healthy shame can help us learn the values and norms that keep us fully accepted by the society we live in and benefiting from its wisdom and resources.

Once we learn that we can reliably process and manage the

information each emotion is giving us, we no longer have to disregard our emotions or defend ourselves against them. We don't need to hide our innermost selves out of fear of shame or embarrassment; we don't need to automatically blame others for our own imagined inadequacies; we don't need to "go along to get along" when doing so diminishes our healthy pride in our own gifts and talents. That's the beauty of emotional intelligence. We become open to all of our experience, all of our feelings, our full humanness.

The prefrontal cortex is the manager of emotions. As you strengthen it to regulate your feelings, you can also allow it to incorporate the wisdom of emotions into your brain's decision-making apparatus. The prefrontal cortex can increasingly discern when it's appropriate to respond to a specific emotion with decisive action and when it's better to acknowledge it, move through it, and choose to experience other emotions that might be more effective guides to resilient actions.

Managing Emotions to Produce Resilient Actions

As you know, the prefrontal cortex integrates communication between the structures that process our feelings and the structures that process our thoughts. It connects the "feeling" right hemisphere with the "logical" left; it also links the subconscious, intuitive limbic system of the lower brain with the conscious, reflective cortex of the higher brain. This integration allows us to choose our actions wisely from both the bottom up and the top down.

When Curt's daughter Cathy arrived home from school in tears, Curt patiently listened as Cathy sobbed out her story. As he did so, the resonance circuit in Curt's brain was picking up all the cues. Mirror neurons in his brain were firing to evoke in his own body what Cathy was feeling in hers: bewilderment, hurt, and shame. Curt's insula was conveying signals of those body sensations to the right hemisphere of his higher brain, which interpreted their emotional meaning.

When Cathy told him about having to pick up trash from the

playground during recess, Curt noticed a shift in his own body. His amygdala was activating the survival response of fight. He wasn't feeling Cathy's anger: he was feeling his own. And even in that moment it felt like something more than simply a good dad wanting to protect his precious daughter from undeserved punishment.

As Curt sat in my office that evening, I could see he was still in fight mode. From across the room I could almost feel his blood boiling. I asked him if he was willing to try a couple of things to calm down. Even thought he was still in a state of "fume," he nodded agreement.

We started with Curt placing his hand on his heart and slowly breathing into his heart center a sense of the love and tenderness he was feeling for Cathy underneath the anger. As I noticed his face soften and his body relax, I asked him to simply notice and name whatever he was feeling in that moment: the enduring anger, his concern for Cathy, his desire to protect her, whatever else he could become aware of. Focusing on the experience of the present brought his prefrontal cortex and the closely related anterior cingulate cortex back into action.

I asked Curt how far back he could trace feeling this particular flavor of anger. Now Curt's prefrontal cortex was drawing on explicit memories stored by the hippocampus, asking, "Have I seen this before? Was it good or bad?" It was matching those signals — calls to action — with memories of how he had responded before and how well his responses had worked. Curt's eyes widened in surprise. He had forgotten that he had once been bullied in kindergarten by a couple of older kids. He had pushed back against those older boys until a teacher rushed out onto the playground to stop the fighting. Curt's right hemisphere could readily associate his experience of being bullied with his perceptions of Cathy's being bullied. His anger wasn't only a natural impulse to protect his daughter: it was what had fueled his actions to protect himself.

As I began to convey my empathy for Curt's experience in a way that resonated with him, Curt could begin to feel some empathy for himself. The meaning making of the left hemisphere began to kick in. Curt's anger today made perfect sense. He was gearing up to protect Cathy from what he perceived as bullying by the principal, fueled by his own implicit memories of having to do the same for himself. Now, as we explored the event more deeply, Curt's prefrontal cortex went to work integrating the meaning of his emotional experiences, past and present, with the rational search for the appropriate response. We finished the session by exploring how Curt could channel his anger into some wise action: how to use the energy of his anger to go to bat with the principal on Cathy's behalf.

Curt decided to stop by Cathy's school the next morning on his way to work and ask for Cathy to be released from class to meet with him and the principal. He told me later he managed to keep his cool in the principal's office, hearing the principal's side of things but also speaking up for Cathy, modeling for her how to speak up for herself. Curt was firm, clear, and persistent, finally persuading the principal to apologize for not listening to Cathy carefully enough the previous day and acknowledging that the punishment might have been excessive and embarrassing. Curt would have liked a public apology in front of an entire school assembly but was satisfied with what he had accomplished and modeled for Cathy about channeling his anger resiliently to get some good results.

Developing the Prefrontal Cortex as the Manager of Emotions

The prefrontal cortex learns to manage or self-regulate all the information coming from our emotions that leads us to actions, resilient or otherwise — you already guessed — by the experience of having those emotions managed by the prefrontal cortices of the people we interacted with when our brains were first developing (through conditioning). As we mature, other people continue to help us regulate our emotions until we really get the hang of it.

Let's say a baby in a high chair drops a favorite toy and then gets cranky because the toy is out of reach. The baby's crankiness is an early form of emotion signaling the need for resilient action.

If the parent picks up the toy and gives it back to the baby, maybe with a smile of understanding, the retrieval of the toy by an attentive and empathically responsive parent soothes the baby, bringing her back into her window of tolerance. The parent's prefrontal cortex is regulating the baby's prefrontal cortex and teaching it how to regulate its own emotions. Over time, experiences like this help the baby develop a strong neural platform for regulating her own emotions. And if stress disrupts her self-regulation, she will have learned from a securely attached relationship that it's safe to turn to others for help in regulating herself until she recovers and regulates herself again.

This early empathic regulation also teaches the baby's prefrontal cortex the value and the process of paying attention to the signals that prompt the need for action. Over time, the baby learns to take her own wise actions to bring her emotions back to baseline equilibrium. From the empathic regulation of the parent (or other closely engaged brains), her prefrontal cortex learns about the role of emotions and stays open to being guided by them.

When there's a lack of empathic responsiveness from the parent, however, that lack can affect the baby's developing prefrontal cortex in two ways. First, if the baby's crankiness and its call for action are ignored by an overly busy or emotionally clueless parent — or, worse, the growing child is criticized or shamed for wanting these important signals for action addressed — her prefrontal cortex does not learn either the value or the process of perceiving, interpreting, and responding to these signals. Instead, rather than keeping the neural connections between the feeling right hemisphere and the rational left hemisphere strong, flexible, and "plastic" so that they can communicate easily, the developing brain shrinks those circuits to prevent us from drowning in feelings it doesn't know how to regulate.

Neural connections between the higher and lower brain are similarly affected. As the underlying neural circuitry becomes less flexible, less teachable, and less "plastic," and more like neural cement, the signals of emotion no longer pass through the circuitry to communicate the need for action. In fact, because the developing prefrontal cortex has not been guided well in learning how to manage those signals, it develops a repertoire of defenses to make sure it doesn't receive them. Defenses — psychological barriers against feelings — can become as rigid and unteachable as the neural circuitry that underlies them.

When our brains refuse to listen to the information coming from our emotions (or the neural connections to do so remain underdeveloped), our ability to use our emotions wisely to guide our actions — our response flexibility — is greatly diminished. We don't receive the signals telling us to leave a bad marriage or a dead-end job; we don't receive the emotional signals that would tell us to reach out for help or repair a rupture with a good friend.

Second, if the baby's parents tend to be overly emotional and not well regulated themselves in response to the baby's emotions, if they are too preoccupied to respond well to her crankiness and her call for action is lost in the flood of their own emotions, or if the parents are too involved in the need to act for themselves and are unable to act on her behalf, the baby's prefrontal cortex simply fails to develop its own capacity to hold and manage the emotional signals coming from its limbic system. The neural channels in the brain stay open, but the circuits developing between the prefrontal cortex and the limbic system don't stabilize enough; her self-regulation is weak and ineffective. The actions informed (or misinformed) by the chaos in the nervous system (sometimes described as "neural swamp") may themselves seem chaotic and unpredictable rather than wise or resilient. She might impulsively begin or end a relationship, certain that real happiness lies just around the corner either way. She might adore someone one moment, then turn away in a rage when that person disappoints her the next.

When the prefrontal cortex cannot fully regulate emotions, we can develop all kinds of less-than-resilient strategies to cope with emotions we mistakenly experience as problems. When asked by a spouse not to raise her voice in front of the children, for example, someone might respond belligerently, "I am *not* angry!" — a response completely disconnected from her own signals that she is indeed angry. Someone lost in the heartbreak of a romance gone south can fail to engage in any reflection on the meaning of the breakup or fail to mobilize the wise action that would let him engage in a new, more meaningful relationship. We're all vulnerable at one time or another to having our resilience hijacked by powerful emotions. The tools you will learn in the rest of this chapter help you strengthen your prefrontal cortex so that it can function competently to manage your emotions and act resiliently.

Your prefrontal cortex has a big job to do reading and regulating the emotions perceived by the right hemisphere of your brain (body sensation, affect) and integrating the meaning of those signals with the rational left hemisphere (language and thoughts). In this section, you will learn to use techniques drawing on the three processes of brain change — new conditioning, deconditioning, and reconditioning — to develop proficiency in using both hemispheres to determine the most skillful response. You begin, once again, with learning new ways to safely regulate emotions to catalyze new conditioning of neural pathways in the brain.

Skill 1: Noticing and Regulating Your Emotions

Anyone can become angry — that is easy.
But to be angry with the right person, to the right
degree, at the right time, for the right purpose,
and in the right way — that is not easy.

— ARISTOTLE

Mindful empathy uses the circuit of reading emotions, described earlier, to attune to our body's experience of any emotion so that we can "read" our own emotional signals more accurately. For instance, as Curt discovered, the more familiar you are with the many nuances of anger — irritation, annoyance, indignation, wrath, outrage — the more comfortable you'll feel learning how to express or act on that particular flavor of anger. The exercise below offers practice in noticing and regulating the flavor of another emotion — sadness or disappointment.

Exercise 1: Noticing and Regulating Your Emotions

1. Sit quietly, letting your awareness settle comfortably into your presence in the moment. Breathe a sense of ease and well-being into your heart center.
2. When you're ready, recall a small, simple memory of feeling sad or disappointed. Say your best friend is traveling on sales calls all the time now, and while you're happy for his success, you miss hanging out with him.
3. Notice what you feel when you evoke this memory, where in your body you're feeling it, and how it feels: maybe tight, heavy, or sluggish. If you wish, you can describe it in terms of color, size, shape, texture (hard, soft, squishy?), and temperature.
4. Next, while remaining aware of this feeling, let yourself feel your own care for yourself, your own self-empathy. It's not easy being a human being, and sometimes this is what being a human being feels like.
5. Return your awareness to your being in the present, sitting quietly and receptively. Notice any changes in your feeling of sadness or disappointment as you recall the memory now. Notice that you can hold this feeling in the larger awareness of your mindfulness and in the loving acceptance of your self-empathy.

You can practice holding moments of all kinds of feelings, such as frustration, boredom, or uneasiness. The point here is to attune to the feeling in your body. Attuning to the feeling in different sensory dimensions helps generate the sense that you are managing the emotion — able to contain it, name it, and describe it — rather than perceiving it as something so big, bad, and amorphous that it is driving you or that you need to push it away. Calling on self-empathy reminds you that there's nothing wrong or bad about feeling as you do: in fact, the feeling indicates your own healthy yearning or longing for something you would like to have happen differently. Persevering in this practice strengthens your prefrontal cortex to help you manage your emotions without being derailed (neural swamp) or having to defend against them (neural cement). You are also conditioning a new, deeply felt sense of self, a confidence based on competence: I can do this; I can experience my feelings; I can manage them well, and I can use them wisely as gateways to action.

The Neuroscience of Noticing and Regulating Your Emotions

Studies show that repeated noticing and naming of our emotions increases cell volume in the corpus callosum, the integrative fibers linking the two hemispheres of the cortex, making it easier to integrate the intuitive meaning of the emotion with the cognitive understanding of it. Self-empathy makes this process safe, even with difficult or "negative" emotions.

Skill 2: Expressing Your Own Emotions and Reading the Meaning of Others' Emotions

Both expressing your emotions to others and reading others' emotional signals are essential for accurate and efficient communication among friends or foes. Curt was able to read Cathy's emotions, manage his own in response, and then use that understanding to guide his actions and structure his conversation with the school principal.

Exercise 2: Expressing Your Own Emotions and Reading the Meaning of Others' Emotions

This exercise requires a partner in order to activate the resonance circuit we use to read and express emotions well. You will practice feeling five of the most basic emotions and then conveying your experience of those emotions to your partner: anger (from irritation to rage), fear (from worry to terror), sadness (from "Oh, pooh" to overwhelming grief), joy (from delight to euphoria), disgust (from annoyance to contempt). The exercise is done without words to strengthen the ability of the right hemisphere of the prefrontal cortex — the emotional brain — to comprehend and interpret these signals without help from the language-processing part of the brain. Practicing with core emotions builds our capacities for attunement, which can then be refined later to read more nuanced emotions such as disappointment, jealousy, guilt, and curiosity.

1. Decide the order in which you will evoke each of five emotions — anger, fear, sadness, joy, and disgust — without telling your partner. Recalling previous experiences of each emotion is a quick and easy way for you to experience the emotion again internally.

2. Tune into your own experience of the first emotion you've chosen to work with, and then let your body wordlessly express the chosen emotion for ten seconds. Maintain eye contact with your partner. You can use gestures, facial expressions, and sounds — just not words. You may find yourself exaggerating your expressions at first; that's okay. Your partner notes which emotion he is reading from your expression but doesn't disclose it yet. Notice what happens inside you — self-attunement — as you communicate your own feelings to someone else. Notice whether the sense of the emotion increases, decreases, or changes into something else.

3. Without discussion yet, turn your attention inward again. Release the emotion you've been expressing with a few gentle, deep breaths into your heart center, evoke the next emotion on your list, and then display that second emotion to your partner for ten seconds. Again, your partner notes the emotion, but the two of you don't discuss anything.

4. Still without discussion, refocus your attention inward, evoke the next emotion on the list and display the feeling to your partner. Repeat the process for each emotion.

5. When you have displayed all five emotions, your partner shares his best guess at the emotion you were displaying each time.

6. Switch roles, so that your partner also displays five emotions in sequence. As you observe them, notice what signals you pay attention to — facial expressions, body language, the tone or rhythm of sounds — to distinguish one emotion from another. And notice what happens inside you as you perceive your partner's feelings.

7. When your partner has finished, reveal how you identified each emotion. Discuss any discrepancies.

This is a practice in developing empathy. Your expression of emotion is meant to convey meaning to the other person, and the attempt to read the other person's expression of emotion calls on the capacity of attunement. If all the guesses were accurate, congratulations to both of you! If there were discrepancies, take the chance to discuss what you perceived in each other's expressions of emotion that led you to a different interpretation. You are each strengthening the prefrontal cortex's capacities for expressing and attuning to emotions, the foundation of building more competence in communicating what you need, in developing the skills you need to get those needs met, and in empathizing with others as they express their needs.

The Neuroscience of Expressing Your Own Emotions and Reading the Meaning of Others' Emotions

We all rely on the fusiform gyrus in the right hemisphere of the brain to read the facial expressions of another person. The direct eye contact of empathic, responsive parenting stimulates the development of this structure in the baby's brain; we can strengthen the functioning of this structure through eye contact with other people lifelong. Research has shown that when our right hemisphere reads safety and trust in the facial expressions of another person, the amygdala calms down, and the stress response is reduced. Being able to read emotion in the facial expressions and body language of another is key to knowing how to respond to the behaviors driven by those emotions.

Despite the importance of communicating emotion, studies have shown that people don't always know what their facial expressions are communicating, because we can't read our own expressions unless we're practicing in a mirror. Exchanging feedback with another person can provide valuable information we might not have otherwise about whether the emotional messages we send are consistent with what we intend.

If we grew up in a household where empathic, emotional communication was not practiced or valued, then we might not have learned how to read someone else's expressions, either. Reading even positive emotions can seem challenging. (For people who have not developed this capacity through life experience, there are computer programs available that train the brain in how to read specific emotions, one by one.)

Skill 3: Managing and Shifting Emotions

A wave of emotion lasts only eight seconds on average, flowing through the body quickly. However, we can sustain the emotion, for good or ill. We can fan the flames of anger, for instance, by dredging up thoughts and stories that keep it foremost in our mind and even intensify it, blocking its evolution into a guide for resilient action. (We can also choose to sustain and reinforce positive feelings like joy and contentment. The skills and benefits of doing that are presented in the next chapter.)

Curt could have fueled his anger at the school principal by

remembering other times he had gotten angry at the same principal, or a different principal, or with anybody in authority. But because he was learning to be resilient, once his brain signaled him that he could take effective action, he could let go of his anger and focus on his skillful response. That is resilience: paying attention to the information coming from our emotions, regulating the emotions, then choosing how to respond.

Processing an emotion entails perceiving it, acknowledging it, being with it, taking whatever information is useful from it, and then letting the wave move through the body (as it naturally will if we don't grip it or feed it). One way to develop skill in this area is to expand our field of awareness to a consciousness that is larger than any belief or story about the emotion: not just to the big picture of the moment, although this is helpful, but to the context of all of life. We can access this bigger context through the process of deconditioning. When we drop into that state, we can still listen for the wisdom of the emotion — what it is signaling us to attend to and what action would be adaptive to take — but we don't have to wallow in the emotion itself; we don't have to drown in the neural swamp.

One of my clients was going through an emotional upheaval that was far more overwhelming than Curt's. Within a two-month period, Monica lost her income when the owner of the hardware store where she had worked for seven years sold the store to a national franchise, which replaced all the staff; her husband left her for another woman; and her beloved dog died. Wave after wave of fear, anger, and grief led to sleepless nights and a kind of paralysis about what to do next. Monica was able to manage those waves using several of the exercises presented here, including the one below, adapted from the Tibetan Buddhist practice of *tonglen* — a practice of compassion to relieve one's own suffering and that of others.

Exercise 3: Managing and Shifting Emotions by Practicing Compassion

1. Identify one particular challenge in your life, then identify one specific emotion arising from this challenge that

you would like to be able to live with, but not be over-whelmed by.

2. Find a place to sit or lie comfortably where you won't be disturbed for ten minutes. Come into a sense of presence in your body; find a place in your body where you can sense peacefulness and ease. (This may be your heart center; it may also be your elbow or your big toe.) Let your aware-ness drop below any stories, any worries, any concerns, into a sense of inner peace and rest. (Some practitioners describe this part of the practice as dropping below the storms on the surface of the ocean to the gentle flow of deep water thirty feet under the surface.)

3. From this place of peacefulness, call to mind your wiser self, the imaginary resource who knows you and loves you, who has compassion for your situation, who can empathize with all the emotions you are experiencing. Experience your-self *as* your wiser self, holding and managing with mindful empathy any heavy emotions you will be working with.

4. Establish a rhythm of breathing: as you inhale, breathe one small portion of the fear, anger, grief you are feeling into the larger sense of empathy and compassion that can hold it. As you exhale, breathe out that small portion of the nega-tive emotion, sending empathy and compassion to your-self as you release the emotion. (A slow breath takes about eight seconds, about as long as it takes a wave of emotion to course through your body — a nice evolutionary coinci-dence that we use to our advantage in this exercise.)

5. Continue this rhythm of breathing for five to ten minutes, simply letting in your emotion, letting it be, and letting it go.

6. As you bring this compassion practice to a close, notice any changes you may feel in your body, any deeper peacefulness from tapping into the mindful empathy and compassion that is larger than any of the emotions moving through it.

The Neuroscience of Managing
and Shifting Emotions through Compassion

In this deconditioning exercise, we're focusing on the power of shifting the processing of an emotion to the spacious, timeless consciousness of the defocusing network in the brain, where the emotion seems less solid and the story fueling the emotion begins to lose its definition. We begin to experience space between the waves of emotion. This awareness, enhanced by the empathy of our wiser self, allows the charge of the emotion to dissipate. The activation of the defocusing network in the right hemisphere also allows us to access our intuitive wisdom in order to choose what to do next.

The next chapter discusses the neuroscience of the "left shift": how the practice of prosocial emotions like compassion can increase neural activity in the left hemisphere of the brain. That engagement of the more rational left hemisphere allows us to regulate the negative emotions that can dominate the processing of the right hemisphere and to choose actions more wisely.

Skill 4: Resolving the Shutdown of Emotions

Depression, which is currently a major derailer of resilience for 20 percent of Americans, is technically not one discrete emotion. It is a physiological state that is a defense against feeling any emotions that might be too painful or distressing to bear. People experiencing depression tend to isolate themselves, because even the feelings of other people can seem overwhelming or intolerable, as can the feelings that their presence might evoke. The shutting down of all emotions leads to collapse. Depression effectively blocks any actions that our emotions would typically lead to. We become immobilized.

Modern science is discovering many ways besides medication to get people moving again when they are stuck in chronic depression: therapy, exercise, reaching out to help others in the community, and learning something new, like speaking a foreign language or playing a musical instrument.

We can also use the power of emotions to get us moving again. If we can allow ourselves to feel them, even negative emotions like anger can initiate action. In modern psychology, depression is considered anger turned inward — the caving in of the fight response to the point of inertia or collapse. Anger is one of the emotions people most commonly use to fuel themselves out of a depression and get themselves moving again. Declaring "I'm so mad I could spit nails" gives us more energy than retreating under the covers for weeks at a time.

But other emotions work to reverse depression, too, especially those emotions that reconnect us to others, to our feelings for others, and to their feelings for us. We can recondition the pathway in the brain that leads us toward collapse and the shutting down of feelings by pairing a feeling that leads to connection or action with the beginning of that slide. Similarly, we can pair a directly contradictory emotion with the desolation of the depression, if we're already in it, to help us back into connections with others and engagement in the world.

It might seem counterintuitive to use delight to recondition despair, but that's exactly what Monica did to cope with the loss of her beloved border collie. After Dewey died, I urged her to dig deep and find every memory of her delight in their connection: his exuberance when chasing a Frisbee in the park and leaping into the air to catch it; his friendliness when greeting other dogs and owners on the hiking trails near her home; the joy in her heart on hearing his bark as she came home after a long day at work. As Monica chose to recondition the despair that could have overwhelmed her, she again and again remembered the bubbling up of happiness and paired the feeling of those memories with the grief of her loss. Over time, the feelings of happiness and appreciation for all the good times took up more of her emotional and mental bandwidth, allowing the grief to fade and opening her heart to feelings of love. Soon she was ready to act: she brought a border collie–shepherd mutt home from the Humane Society to bring new joy and delight into her life.

Reconditioning her despair over losing Dewey was an important step for Monica in coming to terms with her other losses. Though it took longer, she was able to use a similar reconditioning process, focusing on love of family and friends, to release the incapacitating pain of her husband's leaving. Her growing skills in managing her losses eventually opened her up to reconnecting with friends and colleagues in her community and helped her find a job at a new solar-energy company.

Exercise 4: Resolving the Shutdown of Emotions

This exercise strengthens your capacities to feel and deal with your emotions. It requires preparation. The emotions you are going to work with may be painful, and you're experiencing them because of many different causes and conditions. Take a moment to get in touch with your own care for yourself. Acknowledge your own innate goodness. At first glance, this might seem impossible: when we're in the murk of grief, despair, or depression, we may feel unable to think of anything remotely resembling goodness, ease, well-being, or self-worth, and we might resent anyone asking us to try, as though they don't see our pain as real.

1. Anchor your awareness firmly in mindful empathy and compassion for your experience in this moment. Repeat to yourself: "May this suffering ease. May this suffering cease."
2. Evoke the presence of your wiser self to help you remember moments of goodness: joy in playing with a grandchild, satisfaction in changing the oil in the car or planting bulbs. Allow a sense of goodness to arise in your heart center, even in the midst of the difficult emotions. It's the body's sense of this goodness — along with joy, delight, satisfaction, and contentment — that will repair and rewire the grief, despair, or any other afflictive emotion, bit by bit.
3. Evoke one particular moment or aspect of the difficult

emotion you want to work with. If even one moment seems overwhelming, identify manageable chunks of the overall reality, and work with just one piece of the experience at a time. Focus your awareness on this one experience to light up all the networks of this one moment of the difficult emotion: sensations, images, the feeling of the feeling itself, thoughts about the emotion or about yourself for having it.

4. Evoke one particular memory of a moment that directly contradicts or disconfirms the moment of the difficult emotion you are working with: a moment of loving connection with a good friend, the joy of a winter sunset, the ease of relaxing in a hot bath. Imagine it as fully as you can to light up the associated networks of this opposing emotion, too.

5. Now hold the feelings of the two opposing emotions in your awareness at the same time (or switch back and forth), always using mindful empathy to strengthen the more positive, more resilient emotion. Gradually let the sense of the more difficult emotion fade or dissolve and rest your awareness in the experience of the more positive emotion and positive connection.

6. Repeat this exercise, pairing the same original moment of grief or despair with several different emotional experiences that directly contradict it until the charge of the afflictive memory fades or dissolves. Repeat this exercise with other moments of grief, despair, or depression connected to this particular event or situation until the emotional charge of the entire situation is manageable. You are no longer derailed: you can take effective action.

The Neuroscience of Resolving the Shutdown of Emotions

When our brains are learning how to regulate and manage emotion and strengthening the circuits that do so, they develop that ability through connections with other brains. Part of that learning is that *any* emotion can be managed and borne when we're not alone with it. What is shareable is bearable. The connection with other, well-regulated brains regulates our brain and strengthens the circuits we need in the prefrontal cortex to self-regulate.

When we pair a memory of feeling connected to resilient, regulated others, or evoke a memory of our own resilient and regulated wiser self or true self, we are drawing on the strength of those connections as resources. Our brain registers that we're not isolated or alone. Combined with mindful empathy that holds and cares for us in the process, we learn we can bear any emotion if we practice a little bit at a time. When that competency is strengthened, we don't have to disconnect from any emotion. We don't need to defend ourselves against emotions. We can integrate even intense and formerly painful emotions into our experiences of ourselves and into the neural circuitry of how we make decisions.

Pulling It All Together

In this chapter, you have learned skills to:

- help you experience, express, and manage your own emotions and read the meaning of your own emotions and those of others — new conditioning — that will help guide wise action;
- hold, or decondition, emotions in a larger awareness that will dissipate the charge of them so that wise action can intuitively emerge;
- choose to recondition afflictive emotions that block wise action, freeing up energy that lets you move in the world resiliently.

All of these skills help you move toward the five Cs of coping: staying calm the next time your boss criticizes your work or your mother-in-law criticizes your parenting; connecting to resources of people and practices the next time a sudden loss leaves you feeling bereft and alone; seeing clearly your neighbor's emotional needs for help and care the next time he has a hissy fit over garbage cans left in the driveway. These skills can guide you to an empathic and reflective response.

Over time, as you become more adept at managing emotions, including deeply difficult ones, you recover a sense of emotional competence, realizing, "I can do this; I *am* doing this; I am learning to deal with emotions skillfully." Claiming that sense of emotional competence creates a stable platform that helps you recover resilience and well-being and creates a solid foundation for emerging emotional intelligence.

CHAPTER FOURTEEN

How Positive Emotions Build Resilience

*A person without a sense of humor is like a wagon without
springs — jolted by every pebble in the road.*

— Henry Ward Beecher

The positive psychology movement has gained momentum in
recent years because of the research data showing the effect of positive emotions like joy and delight in enhancing our mental, emotional, and physical health and thus our capacities to cope. Scientists
have demonstrated that cultivating positive emotions can actually
undo the constricting effects of negative emotions on our behaviors, moving us beyond the narrow band of our default survival
responses to more resilient options. Deliberately cultivating positive
emotions can broaden and build our repertoire of possibilities. Joy
can spark the urge to play, to push the limits and be creative. Interest
can spark the urge to explore, take in new information and experiences, and expand the sense of self in the process. Laughter breathes
some space into grief. Contentment creates the urge to savor current
life circumstances and integrate that savoring into new views.

Positive emotions that broaden habitual modes of thinking or
acting also build personal resources that last beyond the moment of
the emotion itself, such as stronger social bonds and social support

and deeper insights that help place events in a broader context and alter worldviews. They even promote brain development and rewiring. Positive emotions are not simply an outcome of skillful coping; they are an instrument for building resilience.

Even more compelling data are available on the cultivation of prosocial emotions, that is, emotions evoked specifically in the context of relating to other people. Because the brain is a social organ, we are already hard-wired to use the emotions evoked in interactions with other people (or even remembering the emotions of interacting with other people) as gateways to prosocial behaviors and thus to wise, competent action. When we feel grateful, we are more likely to be altruistic to others. When we trust others, we are more likely to be generous. When we feel compassion, we are more likely to act on behalf of others. And, since new experiences and new conditioning create new circuitry in the brain, by choosing to focus attention on prosocial emotions, we evoke the brain's neuroplasticity to begin rewiring the brain in a more positive direction.

Skill 1: Cultivating Positive Emotions to Wire In New Patterns

In over one hundred studies to date, researchers have found that people who have a daily gratitude practice consistently experience more positive emotions; they are more likely to accomplish personal goals (thus demonstrating resilience); they feel more alert, energetic, enthused, alive; they sleep better; they have lower blood pressure; and they live an average of seven to nine years longer. Gratitude practice helps block toxic emotions like envy, resentment, regret, and hostility; it diverts attention away from stress and worry; it brings closure to unresolved traumatic memories; it strengthens social ties, letting people feel more connected to others, less lonely and isolated; and it improves a sense of self-worth.

A year ago, my sister-in-law phoned to tell me that my sixty-year-old brother had been rushed to the hospital with shortness of breath and pain in his chest. He was diagnosed with a blood clot in his right lung and several clots in both legs. When Mary handed the phone to Barry, I dove right into telling him how much I loved him, how glad I was that he was still alive. And then, in the midst of all the uncertainty and dreadful possibilities, I began to feel my own gratitude for our connection: although we were two thousand miles apart, he was still present in my life. With his life depending on an intravenous drip of blood thinner, it occurred to me to suggest he try a gratitude practice. (I'm a nerd immersed in the science of gratitude, I know, but I'm a quick-thinking nerd.)

Barry is a standoffish kind of guy, not inclined toward self-awareness practices of any kind. To my surprise, he started in, right there on the phone, grateful that Mary was there by his side, that the doctors clearly cared and seemed to know what they were doing, that his beloved poodles were safe at home, that the nurse brought him a drink of water as soon as he asked for it. It was a five-minute litany of everything he was grateful for, even as he hovered at death's door.

Barry didn't die, though the doctors insisted that he could have. The clots cleared two days later. My brother later told me he noticed a "disturbance in the force field" from so many of my friends sending prayers and blessings for his recovery. When he returned home, he became far more compliant with his doctor's suggestions regarding sleep, diet, and exercise. Whether or not Barry's gratitude practice actually saved his life, it certainly contributed to the conditioning of more resilient behaviors in his brain.

Exercise 1: Cultivating Gratitude to Wire In New Patterns

At times our own light goes out and is
rekindled by the spark from another person.
Each of us has cause to think with deep gratitude
of those who have lighted the flame within us.

— ALBERT SCHWEITZER

1. Take five or ten minutes to think of people who have helped you keep your life going: someone who helped you find

your reading glasses when you were hurried and distracted; a friend who sent a supportive email when your nephew crumpled a fender on your car; the grocery clerk who promptly swept up the jelly jars your exuberant three-year-old knocked off the shelf; a coworker who took over your duties when a nasty flu simply would not let you get out of bed.

2. Focus on any feelings of gratitude these memories evoke. Notice where you feel the sensations of gratitude as you let them resonate in your body.

3. Expand the circle of your awareness to gratitude for the people in the larger community who also help keep your life going: for example, those staffing your local hospital right now, ready to care for you if you slip in the bathroom and have to be rushed to the emergency room. You might include people staffing airports, pharmacies, fire stations, and gas stations and those testing water quality at your municipal reservoir. (For years my brother, Barry, was on call in his hometown to drive the snowplow at 3 AM so folks could get to work at 7 AM. I know how deeply he appreciated being appreciated for that humble service.) Practice gratitude for the people growing your food and recycling your garbage, for the entire web of life.

4. Reflect on your experience of practicing gratitude and the feelings your practice evokes. Notice any changes in your own emotions or thoughts about yourself as you focus on experiencing gratitude.

You can set the intention to do a three-minute gratitude practice every day for thirty days, focusing your attention on the people, circumstances, and resources that sustain your well-being every day.

Over time, this practice will lead you to experience other positive emotions more often, as well, and it will expand your choices of actions to be more positive, more resilient.

The Neuroscience of the "Left Shift" to Wire In New Patterns

Neuroimaging has revealed that cultivating experiences of positive and prosocial emotions such as gratitude, and focusing attention on those experiences, causes an increase in neural activity in the left hemisphere of the brain, exceeding the activity in the right hemisphere. This "left shift" indicates a shift in the brain from a stance of "avoid" to a stance of "approach" in responding to experience.

Because the right hemisphere of the brain develops significantly earlier than the left and thus has more neural connections to the survival-oriented lower brain, when it comes to processing emotions and responding with action, the right hemisphere and its negativity bias (engendering anxiety, depression, and shame) can block resilient action.

Because the left hemisphere is less connected to the lower brain than is the right, it is less affected by the lower brain's orientation toward survival. And because it can draw on memories from later in life when our coping has (hopefully) become more resilient, the left hemisphere can more objectively evaluate safety or danger in a new experience, and so it tends to respond more optimistically than the right.

Positive emotions strengthen the capacity to approach rather than avoid challenges and catastrophes we and others face. They increase curiosity and engagement with circumstances and support more open-minded, optimistic, creative coping. They undo lingering negative physiological responses, helping us return to our window of tolerance. The approach stance or sense of openness to experience not only makes us feel better but also creates a flexibility in the processing of our brains that makes it far more likely that we will find a solution to our problems. Focusing on positive emotions tends to fuel resilience by overcoming any learned helplessness, moving from languishing to flourishing, building enduring personal resources that rewire the brain in an upward spiral of greater well-being.

Focusing on positive and prosocial emotions is not meant to bypass or suppress dark, difficult afflictive emotions, not at all. We persevere in our practices of mindful empathy, learning to hold and process those afflictive emotions. We deliberately cultivate positive, prosocial emotions as a way to turbocharge the conditioning of new circuits and new habits, new states of mind and heart, so that they become enduring traits of resilience leading to resilient action.

Jack Gilbert counsels us in his poem "A Brief for the Defense": "We must have the stubbornness to accept our gladness in the ruthless furnace of this world."

When we intentionally and continually evoke experiences of gratitude, or other prosocial emotions like acceptance, patience, and equanimity, we strengthen the parts of our brains that allow us to respond to life events with an open heart rather than a contracted one, with resilience and care rather than fear, with approach and acceptance rather than withdrawal and shutting down. We get the benefit of feeling less worry, agitation, and depression and more joy, delight, satisfaction, and contentment.

Skill 2: Hanging Out with Emotionally Healthy Brains

Dan Siegel, the author of *The Mindful Brain*, once said at a conference focused on resilience and well-being, "Why are we all here at this conference today when we could be home learning everything we want to learn from a book? Because our brains learn better in the resonance, in the dialogue, with each other." Dan was pointing to an important key for positive brain change. Neuropsychologists know that resonant interactions with others prime plasticity in the brain. In contrast, isolation and lack of challenge and stimulation are the enemies of neuroplastic processes and brain health.

Because our brains are so profoundly influenced, for better or worse, by the quality of interactions we have with other brains, it's truly smart to spend time with other people who are intent on being and becoming resilient. Just as we can choose to engage in practices that create new neural circuitry to support new habits of emotionally positive and prosocial behaviors, we can choose to spend time with others who have shown by their behaviors that they have trained their brains toward those habits. Because our brains are so exquisitely hard-wired to pick up the emotional state of other human brains, we can use another person's deep joy or contentment to shift our emotional state in their presence. This dyadic deconditioning arises from the resonance of shared positive emotions. Again, focusing on the positive emotions does not mean that we bypass or dismiss the dark and difficult. Researchers have found that people who have cultivated genuine happiness and joy experience that happiness because of a deep appreciation and contentment with life; they feel joy no matter what.

Paul Ekman, a noted researcher and author of fifteen books on emotions, describes his struggle with intractable anger and rages: he had three or four "regrettable" episodes a week, by his own count, until he met the Dalai Lama in the year 2000. Paul was part of a Mind-Life Institute conference of Western scientists and Buddhist practitioners meeting in Dharamsala, India, to explore different perspectives on destructive emotions.

On the third day of the conference, observers were invited to ask questions of the Dalai Lama. Paul's twenty-year-old daughter, Eve, asked, "Why do we get the angriest at the people we love the most?" The Dalai Lama answered Eve's question (about expectations and the destructive compassion of an overprotective parent) while he simply held the hand of Paul sitting on the other side of him. He didn't speak to Paul directly as he talked with Eve; he simply offered the gentle touch of someone listening with compassion to another person's suffering. Paul said he experienced his whole body filling with a radiant warmth, absorbing the caring of the man whom many people believe to be the embodiment of compassion in this world.

Paul later reported that after this experience, he did not have another "regrettable" episode of anger for the next seven months — not even an impulse. As time has gone on, he sometimes feels the impulse of anger, but he feels no need to act on it. It's gone. Done. His personal reactivity has changed forever. Absorbing the Dalai Lama's deep peacefulness rewired the patterns of neural firing in Paul's amygdala, immediately and permanently.

We may not all have the opportunity to cultivate our prosocial emotions by holding the hand of someone as sophisticated in benevolence as the Dalai Lama. But we can deliberately seek out people whose capacities for prosocial behaviors are more developed than ours. We might find groups of people gathered for this purpose in churches and synagogues, yoga and meditation classes, and personal-growth and wellness workshops. Simply being in connection with people who are emotionally healthy can shift our emotional state and reprogram our circuitry.

Almost fifteen years ago, I consulted a homeopathic doctor about stress. He recommended that when I came home after a long day of seeing patients, I brew a full pot of hot tea and read poetry. I happened to be having six friends over for dinner that very weekend, so I emailed them suggesting they bring poetry to read together.

That was the humble beginning of our Gourmet Poets' Society, which has flourished for a decade and a half, with upwards of fourteen people meeting quarterly for a potluck dinner — with chocolate fondue as the staple dessert — and hours of reading poems aloud. The themes run the gamut of the human condition — love, death, delusion, celebration, injustice, triumph. However poignant the topic, there is always a buoyancy that comes from sharing tears as well as laughter. And everyone goes home with their circuits rewired toward love and gratitude.

There are many ways for us to rewire each other's brains, but sharing poetry is uniquely effective. Poetry's use of words to convey emotions through images and metaphors integrates the communication channels of the left and right hemispheres of the brain, helping us be receptive to the power of our emotions while simultaneously strengthening our capacity to regulate them. Reading (and writing) poetry is a reliable way of deconditioning old patterns of thinking and feeling, thus opening up new neural receptivity and allowing us to change more easily.

The poet and anthologist Roger Housden reminds us: "Great poetry calls into question not less than everything. It dares us to break free from the safe strategies of the cautious mind. It amazes, startles, pierces, and transforms us. Great poetry happens when the mind is looking the other way; the heart opens, we forget ourselves, and the world pours in."

Exercise 2: Finding Emotionally Healthy Brains to Connect With

These days, more and more connection with other people happens through social media. In rewiring your brain for resilience, it's truly more effective to find ways to spend time in the physical presence of other people. But if that's not possible in a busy life, or if the people you feel close to live a great distance away, connecting by phone or email can still rewire your brain in a positive direction. The following exercise helps you make the most of those connections with others.

1. Identify someone with whom you would like to share your experiences of positive emotions, to broaden and build your resilience repertoire. Ask this person to be your gratitude buddy or joy buddy, someone you will share resilience building with.

2. Arrange a regular process for checking in. Once a week for coffee? Once a month for a walk in nature? Every evening by email? Experiment and discover what works best for both of you.

3. When you check in, share moments of the positive emotion you're working with — laughter in the midst of trouble

or uncertainty; contentment in the midst of upheaval and change; friendliness in a hectic day. Recall how you felt when you experienced the laughter, contentment, or friendliness; notice how you feel now as you recall it.

4. Listen to your buddy checking in: notice how you feel hearing her experiences. It's most helpful when this sharing stays open and receptive, and focused on the positive emotion; this is not a time for giving advice or solving problems.

5. Notice how you feel after checking in. Take in the good of the experience to reinforce the rewiring in your neural circuitry.

6. Thank each other for the positive experience. You can notice the positive emotions continuing as you schedule the next time to check in.

Because cultivating specific positive emotions tends to lead to experiencing a broader range of emotions in general, and experiencing all emotions more frequently, you may notice that other positive, prosocial emotions develop — feelings of affection, respect, even love for your partner — as a result of this practice.

The Neuroscience of Connecting
with Emotionally Healthy Brains

People who have intentionally cultivated the left shift in their brain (though they might not choose to call it that) tend to have a more optimistic approach to problems and challenges in life. They are most likely well connected to the inner resources that allow them to cope well with the vicissitudes of daily living. Finding ways to spend time with people who seem to demonstrate the left shift gives you an opportunity to absorb some of their capacities to rewire your brain.

By checking in with your buddy in this exercise, you are using your entire resonance circuit to encourage your brain to shift to the left as well, to become more open to experiencing positive, prosocial emotions on a regular basis and, over time, gaining the benefits for yourself of better-regulated, more optimistic coping.

Skill 3: Using Positive Emotions to Heal Toxic Shame

Love makes your soul crawl out of its hiding place.

— ZORA NEALE HURSTON

We cultivate positive emotions to increase our capacities to take wise and resilient action in the world. In my work as a psychotherapist, I often see that resilient action is completely dragged down by the undertow of toxic shame. The next exercise shows how to harness the power of positive emotions, positive connections, and the innate neuroplasticity of your brain to recondition the neural pathway of shame: not to defensively get rid of it, but to proactively rewire it.

A client once asked me if I knew anything about "swamp." I replied, somewhat flippantly, "I have a PhD in swamp." I don't have a PhD in swamp or anything else, but I do have a long professional career of helping folks out of the emotional swamp that is the most powerful destroyer of our resilience: the sense of inadequacy and failure, of feeling not good enough or unlovable that is the territory of toxic shame.

Shame is not always toxic. Healthy shame can lead us toward actions that are resilient, as can its cousin, guilt. Both shame and guilt can arise when we feel we are or have done something that might exile us from our kin or tribe. Early in our evolution, exile or shunning was a death sentence: no one could survive alone on the Serengeti. We learn the norms of acceptable behavior through the conditioning of others' responses to our behaviors, our emotions, and ourselves. We learn to fit in. We internalize the values and moral precepts of our society and culture, and our reward is the feeling of safety that comes from belonging to that society. If we sense we are violating those precepts, the shame and guilt we experience tend to get us back on track. Learning to be resilient through healthy shame and guilt is supported early on in experiences of secure attachment. We learn to feel seen, understood, and loved for who we are, even if we do something bad as we are learning the cultural code. Developing a healthy pride in and acceptance of our essential, lovable self helps develop the neural circuitry that leads to trust, openness, more learning and growth, and more resilience.

Toxic shame takes root whenever we feel judged, criticized, rejected, or put down not only for what we do but for who we are. If we feel we have to be a certain way in order for somebody else to feel good about who they are, our developing sense of self can feel ignored, uncared for, or neglected completely.

There are actually neural cells around the heart that can feel the rupture of disconnection. The feeling of being unlovable or "bad," of having a "hole in our heart," has some physiological basis. When this happens, all the innate goodness we are programmed to develop goes into exile. As a colleague of mine says, all the eagerness and innocent exuberance with which we naturally move in the world gets "slammed mid-pirouette."

If this toxic shaming or guilting begins early enough, continues long enough, and remains toxic enough, we begin to smallify ourselves: the experiences build a self-reinforcing negative loop in our neural circuitry. We begin to perceive all of our experience through a filter of shame or guilt. When you think you've done well on a test and the grade comes back as a C-minus, the instant message from the inner critic is, "I told you you were stupid!" When you slip on a rug and fall down three steps before you catch yourself, another message comes: "What a klutz!" When you get distracted by a phone call and burn the steaks on the grill, it's "Can't you do anything right?" With enough negative experiences, we go into what the clinical psychologist and meditation teacher Tara Brach calls a "trance of unworthiness," experiencing a constant sense of failure rather than the pride in competence and mastery that leads to resilience.

Researchers have identified four processes that take place in the brain in the downward spiral of shame:

1. External criticism, rejection, or humiliation or the put-downs of the internalized inner critic shock or startle the sympathetic nervous system into a survival response, preparing us to defend ourselves or to flee a toxic situation.

2. The shock rapidly activates the parasympathetic nervous system's submit-collapse response, which cancels the response the sympathetic branch set in motion. Instead of mobilizing for action — fight-flight — we demobilize, collapsing or caving in for protection.

3. This collapse can evoke implicit memories conditioned by previous experiences. We land in the abyss of deficiency, the swamp of feeling "bad," unworthy, inadequate, or a fraud.

4. With enough repetition, the brain's response to these messages is to dissociate: to go numb, check out, or disappear. If no one can find us, no one can hurt us. We can even hide a shameful or guilt-ridden experience from our own awareness — split it off into its own disconnected memory pocket. We can "forget" that something we experienced ever happened and act as though nothing is wrong at all. This defensive hiding out, even from ourselves, contributes to our psychic survival, but the cost is high for ourselves and for those we relate to. The neural disintegration caused by toxic shame makes it extremely difficult to mobilize ourselves for any action at all. We undermine ourselves and close ourselves off from the love and support that would bring us back into connection and action.

My client Richard had set out driving to his best friend's engagement party in a pretty good mood. His job was satisfying: he was climbing the ladder as a regional division manager of a biotech company. His body was strong and healthy: he was one of the fastest swimmers in his master swim class. The tomatoes were ripening robustly in his garden. And he was making good time traveling, despite the crowded mountain highway. He was happy for his friend Toby, who was getting married to the woman he adored.

Suddenly, Richard felt a pang inside, as if someone had opened the door to a dark room. He could expect some teasing by a mutual friend at the party about his two failed marriages. Why couldn't *he* get it together? Richard began to slip into a cascade of misgivings and self-doubt. Should he have tried harder? Was there something wrong with him that caused two women to leave him? Would everyone at the party know he was a failure? The hope he harbored of meeting someone new at the party, having another chance, began to fade.

Even though Richard tried to switch the channel and think of something else, or even remember the good things about himself that he was recounting earlier, he began to sink into a black hole. His inner critic was relentless. Who was he kidding? He'd never be good enough to meet someone at the party today. In his fog, Richard didn't notice that the car in front of him had stopped abruptly. He "woke up" too late to put the brakes on and rear-ended the car in front. No one was hurt, but he totaled his small car and seriously dented theirs.

Even though a friend quickly came and rescued him, and everyone at the party was understanding and concerned about the accident, Richard found it impossible at first to take in their love and acceptance. He was sunk in a swamp of shame.

Shame has been called the "great disconnector." The best way to crawl out of the swamp of shame is to come into connection with another person who loves and accepts us exactly as we are, even if we sometimes have to conjure up that person in our imagination, and then to build on that love to come into our own love and acceptance of ourselves exactly as we are. As my colleague Ken Benau says, "To be seen or not to be seen; that is the question, and the answer."

Richard managed to find a few moments alone with Toby at the party and told him what had really caused the car accident. Toby had been Richard's friend since college, through all the dating, getting married, getting divorced, trying again, and "failing" again. Toby knew Richard's deep-down goodness, his sincere intentions to be kind and loving, and his willingness to learn what was getting in the way of those intentions. Toby also knew Richard's tendency to collapse into a "poor me" attitude rather than an empowered feeling of "I can do this."

As they talked, Toby reminded Richard of all the trust, affection, and respect they had shared with each other over the years. Richard could begin to listen as Toby framed Richard's longing to be in a healthy relationship as itself a healthy sign. "Look, man, after all you've gone through, you're still willing to take a risk again. I'm betting my money on you for sure; it will happen."

At the end of the conversation, Toby suggested that Richard join a men's group that he knew about, which was focused on connecting in healthy relationships. Because Richard could take in the sincerity of Toby's acceptance and affection for him, he could see the possibilities for healing and awakening in the suggestion. He was able to come out of his shame swamp and rejoin the party. Within a few weeks he had joined the men's group and began, in effect, hanging out with emotionally healthy brains. He also enrolled in several workshops on being authentic in intimate relationships, learning to focus on being his true self and seeing the true selves of other people.

You may think I'm making this next part up, but I'm not. After six months in the men's group and those workshops, learning many skills of healthy relating and accepting himself as a good enough potential partner, Richard hit it off with Lucy, the sister of one of the guests at Toby's wedding. They have now been happily married for eleven years.

Exercise 3: Healing Toxic Shame through Love and Acceptance

This exercise uses reconditioning to rewire old patterns of toxic shame. As always when working with reconditioning, it's important to prepare yourself carefully, to avoid reinforcing negative feelings and patterns.

1. Settle into your own mindful empathy, your willingness to see and your willingness to care. Evoke a sense of your wiser

self. Bring to mind a moment of your own understanding and acceptance when you had deep compassion for someone else's struggles: when someone missed qualifying for a state athletic tournament by two points, or when a colleague left at home the videos he had planned to show at a regional training meeting. Notice the caring compassion of your wiser self flowing from your heart to his.

2. With the resource of your own compassionate acceptance of another in the background, bring to your awareness a memory of a small moment of your own guilt or shame. You forgot to leave the car windows cracked when you dashed into the drugstore, you were delayed, and your new puppy in the backseat almost collapsed from heatstroke. At your daughter's preschool, you blurted out the news of a teacher's cancer diagnosis in front of a group of parents. You got a speeding ticket with a potential client in the car. Shame and guilt can carry such an intense charge that incidents like this may not seem at all small. If that's the case, just bring to mind the first moment or one small piece of the experience. As you light up the networks of this memory, small but vivid, keep the compassionate awareness of your wiser self steady. You want to be *with* your experience but not *in* it, affected but not infected.

3. When this memory is vivid, bring to mind a memory of feeling genuinely seen and deeply loved and accepted by another person (or a pet), of being seen for real. Let yourself receive this love and acceptance and feel it in your body.

4. Hold both the memory of shame or guilt and the memory of love and acceptance together in your awareness at the same time. Or switch between the two, as you have learned to do, always strengthening the memory of love and acceptance.

5. When this simultaneous awareness of the paired memories is steady, bring to the foreground your initial feeling

of understanding and compassion for someone else who was feeling shame or guilt. Begin to direct that same flow of love and acceptance you felt for him toward the shame or guilt in yourself. The memory of shame or guilt is pairing with your love and acceptance of someone else and also pairing with the self-love and self-acceptance of your own wiser self. After a moment, let go of the pairings and let your attention rest solely in the experience of self-love and self-acceptance. Take a few moments to savor the resting in this self-love and self-acceptance.

6. Reflect on your experience. Notice any shifts you experience from doing this exercise. Repeat this process of reconditioning as many times as you need to in order to fully dissolve the shame or guilt connected with a particular memory. The more often you practice this process with specific memories, the more you will be reprogramming those deep neural networks associated with toxic shame.

7. You may share this experience with your gratitude buddy or joy buddy as a way of taking in the good of rewiring your brain toward more emotional competence. Notice any gratitude or joy as you share.

The Neuroscience of Healing Toxic Shame with Love and Acceptance

Just that action of paying attention to ourselves, that I care enough about myself, that I am worthy enough to pay attention to, starts to unlock some of those deep beliefs of unworthiness at a deeper level in the brain.

— ELISHA GOLDSTEIN

As we intentionally work with the memories of feeling bad because of who we are (shame) or because of something we did (guilt), it's helpful to remember that implicit memories can feel completely true in the present, with no sense whatsoever that they are memories from the past. As we recondition, we pair explicit positive feelings of pride or of loving, caring acceptance, recognizing these as experiences in the present, with the negative toxic memories that we recognize as belonging to the past.

This reconditioning can also happen in therapy; in healthy intimate relationships; with an attuned friend, a beloved benefactor, or a devoted partner; and in our imagination. Repeating this process strengthens the neural circuitry until the love and acceptance become the new normal.

Sometimes what's even harder than finding the love is taking it in. If we haven't had enough love and acceptance in our lives, oxytocin receptors may not have fully developed in the brain: it's hard to feel love. The repeated, deliberate calling forth of those positive experiences, even when they are hard to feel at first, helps restore the ability to feel connection, love, and trust. Our growing capacity to evoke and feel love and acceptance becomes the superhighway of resilience; old shame and guilt become the country backroad we don't have to go down anymore.

Pulling It All Together

In this chapter you have learned techniques to:

- broaden and build your repertoire of emotions, thoughts, and actions by evoking and savoring positive emotions like joy, gratitude, and contentment that help you build deeper social bonds and increase insights and perspectives;
- rewire your own brain by spending time with others' emotionally healthy brains;
- dissipate the charge of intense afflictive emotions by pairing them with other, stronger, more affirming emotions and

holding the distressing emotions in a larger field of understanding and compassion.

When you integrate your feelings into all of your communication and decision-making processes, your emotions become powerful allies in rewiring your brain for resilience.

CHAPTER FIFTEEN

Developing Emotional Intelligence

I've learned that people will forget what you said
and people will forget what you did, but people
will never forget how you made them feel.

— MAYA ANGELOU

EMOTIONAL INTELLIGENCE is a phrase used by Daniel Goleman almost two decades ago to describe a range of skillful behaviors that allow us to navigate our peopled world with effectiveness and resilience. Curt used it when he channeled his anger into constructive action, meeting with the school principal and obtaining an apology to his daughter. The two Canadian women put it to work when they decided to trust each other with their cars so that they could get through the snowstorm to their loved ones. Toby used it when he expressed loving acceptance that brought Richard out of his swamp of shame, and it helped Monica hold the grief of her several simultaneous losses with compassion. My brother, Barry, put emotional intelligence to work when he was willing to try a gratitude practice to help get him through a medical crisis.

In this chapter, you will learn to apply the skills you have learned in previous chapters in three broad-reaching exercises that use emotions as gateways to resilient actions and to further develop emotional intelligence. This emotional intelligence continues to move you toward the five Cs of coping. You can trust the calm and deep, intuitive knowledge that arises from that intelligence, which contributes to your overall clarity. You can become more competent in navigating the complex worlds of other people and their decision making, even when their emotions are not well regulated. You can trust your emotional intelligence to inform effective communication with others and to get things handled.

Skill 1: Sustaining and Being Sustained by Love and Appreciation

I first heard this story from the mediation teacher Jack Kornfield, though I've heard variations of it from many other sources since.

When a fifth-grade teacher's class became especially disruptive one day, throwing spitwads, calling each other names, and shoving each other in the aisles, the teacher demanded silence, then instructed everyone to take out one sheet of paper. She told the students to write down the name of every other student in the class, one name per line, down the left-hand side of the paper. Then she asked the students to write a brief description of something they appreciated about each student in the space next to the student's name.

Silence took over as the students concentrated on the task. At the end of the class period, she gathered all the papers and told the students she would give further instructions the next day. After school, the teacher cut apart the comments, reassembling them into one scotch-taped piece of paper for each student. At the beginning of class the next day, she handed each student a list with twenty-three comments of appreciation about him- or herself.

The students read the sheets — most of them quietly, some with giggles, a few wiping tears from their cheeks. Many of them had had no idea that they were regarded positively by their classmates until that moment. The exercise became an important opportunity to take in the good about themselves that their classmates had shared and to know, too, that they were contributing to their classmates' feelings of being nourished by appreciation.

But the story doesn't end there; nor do the lessons about

emotional intelligence. A decade later, one of the students was killed in combat in Vietnam. After the memorial service, the father of the young man came up to the teacher and handed her a neatly folded piece of paper. It was the young man's list with his classmates' comments from that lesson in the fifth grade. His father said, "They found it in the chest pocket of his uniform the day he was killed." Overhearing that, a former classmate came up to them both, opened her purse, and pulled out her sheet of paper. "I've always carried this with me; today was an especially important time to remember."

We all are sustained by the love and appreciation of others. We all need to be reminded regularly of that sustenance. Any time we share our appreciation of another, we are using our emotional intelligence to sustain that person, too.

Exercise 1: Carry Love and Appreciation in Your Wallet

Daniel Goleman cofounded the Collaborative for Academic, Social and Emotional Learning (CASEL) to promote the teaching of skills of emotional intelligence and emotional resilience in the classroom. This simple exercise can help you develop these skills on your own.

1. Identify a group of people who all know each other — your coworkers at the completion of a project, your monthly book club or golfing buddies, family members at Thanksgiving — and suggest everyone send a card or email to everyone else in the group with a sentence or two acknowledging something they appreciate about that person, something positive and true. You can simplify this exercise, if you are comfortable doing so, by asking ten people you know — friends, coworkers, or neighbors, even if they don't know each other — to send you a card or email with a simple phrase or sentence of appreciation. (You may already collect comments like this if you write down what people have written on birthday cards or congratulatory cards.)

2. Assemble the comments sent to you into one piece of paper you can fold and carry in your wallet or tape to the bathroom mirror. Read through this list of emotional nourishment at least once a day for thirty days — a month of steadily resourcing and taking in the good.

3. Each day, after you read through your list, notice how you feel about yourself as you take in and savor the appreciation. Notice where you feel any warmth or glow in your body from reading the list.

4. Set the intention to return to this warm glow of self-appreciation as you move through your day, checking in with yourself periodically. Pause and remember the list (look at it again if you need to) and recall that self-appreciation.

5. At the end of the month, reflect on how reviewing your list of appreciations every day has strengthened your resilience in coping with the new, the difficult, the stressful or hurtful. You may add to the bottom of your own list an appreciation of your growing capacities to create resilience for yourself.

This practice is especially helpful at times when your sense of self-worth is being challenged. You're using your own emotional intelligence to create a resource of support as you remember the appreciation of other people.

The Neuroscience of Sustaining and Being Sustained by Love and Appreciation

Practices of self-appreciation have been shown to diminish bouts of anxiety and depression. Taking in the love of others and cultivating love for ourselves activate the release of oxytocin, creating calm in the body and enhancing the neural receptivity in the brain that allows us to learn more resilient strategies of coping. It also provides all the benefits of cultivating positive emotions: putting the brakes on negativity and deepening the wellsprings of optimism, connections to others, resilience, and fulfillment (see chapter 14).

Skill 2: Using Self-Compassion to Answer the Inner Critic

Kristin Neff, PhD, suggests in her book *Self-Compassion* that self-compassion is the complement of self-appreciation, the other side of the coin. Both are self-nourishing practices of emotional intelligence and resilience and gateways to resilient action. Self-appreciation helps us celebrate our strengths and positive attributes, intentions, and choices. Self-compassion helps us recognize and use our frailties, flaws, and vulnerabilities as opportunities for proactive self-care.

We especially need to practice self-compassion and self-care when our inner critic starts to pummel us with harsh, negative self-talk. "What a goofball! You can't even pay your taxes on time, let alone save ahead!" We tend to feel compassion when we see other people relentlessly beating themselves up or putting themselves down, but we might not be aware how many times a day we do the same thing to ourselves.

Chapter 4 includes an exercise for generating feelings of compassion for someone else's struggles and then directing that same flow of compassionate caring toward yourself. In the exercise below, you learn to use the device of writing letters to yourself to access the wisdom of your wiser self in caring for yourself.

Exercise 2: Using Self-Compassion to Answer the Inner Critic

1. Identify a typical comment or running commentary from your inner critic that causes you to feel bad about yourself: a habitual pattern of self-criticism or self-contempt that derails your resilience or at least tries to drag your efforts to be resilient through the mud. "How come you're still trying to get approval from your dad (or wife, or son)? Don't

you know you're a lost cause? You don't even like yourself half the time!" Write down the comment as you typically hear it.

2. Write a letter to a trusted friend about this comment and your struggles with it. (You won't actually mail the letter.) Describe what usually triggers this self-criticism; your typical reactions — body sensations, feelings, and thoughts — to hearing this inner voice; any fears of a germ of truth in the criticism; your wishes and desires for understanding and support in dealing with this repetitive pattern.

3. Putting yourself in the place of the friend you wrote to, write a letter back to yourself. Writing in your friend's voice, convey empathy for the pain of being pummeled by these repetitive criticisms. Acknowledge how hard it is to be vulnerable to this particular form of suffering. Include an appreciation of your own wholeness and your goodness, all your strengths, all your weaknesses, including the ones your inner critic is currently harping on. Include your friend's love and acceptance of you, exactly as you are, with all of your human imperfections, and her understanding of all the events that created your way of being and your particular flavor of the universally human inner critic. You can include any suggestions you imagine your friend might add in the letter; be sure to include her care for your well-being and her wish that you find your way to wise action and relief from this suffering.

4. After writing this second letter, put it aside for a while. When you read it again, let yourself receive and take in the compassion you have conveyed for yourself to yourself.

5. After you have taken in the self-compassion from the second letter you wrote, write a third letter, this time back to your friend, thanking her for her support and reflecting on what you have learned from her letter. Make a note of any

new behaviors of self-care you can now follow up with, based on the encouragement you have received through these letters.

The Neuroscience of How Self-Compassion Answers the Inner Critic

Mindful, empathic recognition of suffering you're experiencing as you focus attention on the messages of the inner critic allows the neural networks of those repetitive patterns to light up in the brain, making it easier to rewire them and change your relationship to them. Even the beginning step of focusing on a wish or desire for understanding and support activates the parts of the brain that can begin to respond to that wish with compassion. Neuroscientists have observed, using fMRI scanning, that a strong compassion practice activates the left shift to the "approach" mode of the left prefrontal cortex, and areas of the motor cortex prime the brain to act in response to the sense of compassion.

Writing letters as though to and from a good friend is a way to surprise the unconscious. You're evoking the wisdom and compassion of your wiser self, and you're letting yourself hear your own intuitive wisdom.

Skill 3: Compassionate Communication

At times our habitual lenses of perception and reactivity can make responsible speaking and empathic listening almost impossible. Both people in a conversation can be caught in a mind-set of "me versus you," "us versus them," or "always or never." The differences feel intolerable, and frustrations run high. Learning to communicate your fears and wishes to other people, and receiving their communication about their fears and wishes in return, is a practice of emotional intelligence that will sustain resilience for a lifetime.

When two people meet in mindful empathy, their emotions can be expressed in a fairly straightforward way. This honesty opens the door to perceiving another person's needs, even in a conflict, facilitating a mutual understanding or at least a respect for differences.

Exercise 3: Compassionate Communication

This exercise is adapted from a method originally known around the world as nonviolent communication (NVC), developed by Marshall Rosenberg, and now called compassionate communication. To some, the method can feel structured and mechanical, but when a conflict needs to be expressed and dealt with, it can be worth its weight in gold. When both people become adept at the protocol, they can identify the emotional needs that must to be addressed and choose appropriate actions to address them.

1. *Stating the intention.* One person begins the conversation with: "There is something happening that's affecting our relationship. I would like to talk about it. Are you available?" Mechanical! But it does close the exits. If the listener is not immediately available at that moment because he's out the door on the way to work, or needs to be on an important conference call in five minutes, or is simply frazzled for the day, he can say no, but he must agree to be available within twenty-four hours. The speaker never has to nag or pursue once the agreement to meet has been made.

2. *Creating the conditions to be heard.* Choose a time and place where there will be no distractions or interruptions. With the two sitting face-to-face, the speaker states the topic in one sentence, and the listener repeats the topic back word for word. The listener then asks, "Is there more?" That's it. No commentary, no rebuttal, no resistance, no incredulity. This method completely prohibits any shame, blame, or name-calling. Safety and mutual respect are the priorities.

3. *Speaking and listening.* The speaker then begins sharing her experience. The listener agrees to listen respectfully until the speaker is done. The speaker frames the experience along the following lines: "I felt really hurt when I perceived (or thought or believed) you were flirting with Sandy at the block party last night." She acknowledges any of her own subjective impressions or thoughts that may have contributed to the experience. The listener listens, repeats the statement word for word, so the speaker feels heard: "You felt hurt when you thought I was flirting with Sandy at the block party last night." The listener expresses no defensiveness, no editorializing, no retaliating, no sharing of his experience. It can be much harder to be the listener than the speaker!

   The speaker continues until she is done, focusing on the feelings and needs underneath the facts of the events. Rather than express the problem as a thought — "I feel as if you're not interested in me anymore" — she tries to get down to the feeling underneath — "I'm worried, and I'm scared." Getting to the heart of the matter usually takes far less time than one would expect when the focus is placed on the feelings driving the speaker's own behaviors.

4. *Summary of concern.* The listener gives a brief summary of the entire concern, and the speaker clarifies until both can agree on a clear statement of it. In this case, it might be: "When you experience me paying attention to other people and not paying enough attention to you or to us, you're worried that I don't love you as much as I did, that I'm not really there for you."

5. *The request for change.* The speaker articulates the request that would address the emotional need underneath: "I need to hear from you that you still love me; that you're in this 100 percent." She then identifies three things she is willing

to do herself to address her emotional needs, for example: "I will check in with you at least once in the coming week to hear how you feel we're doing as a couple." "I will remind myself that I am loved by you before we go to the football game with Sandy and Jim two weeks from now." "I will pull you aside and speak to you right away the next time I experience any worry about your behavior."

The speaker identifies three things the listener could do that would help address her emotional needs, such as: "I ask that you spend five minutes with me every night this week telling me three things you appreciate about me." "I ask that you include me in at least one conversation you have with Sandy in the coming month." "I ask that you spontaneously give me a big hug and tell me you're glad to see me at least once in the coming week."

The speaker and listener each choose *one* of the three behaviors to do in the specified time period. The requests must be for changes in behaviors (not changing personality or character, but behavior) that are *positive* (specifying what is wanted rather than what is not wanted), *specific*, *measurable*, and *set in a specific time frame*, so that both speaker and listener know when they have been accomplished.

6. *Following through.* As the pair implement the change requests, the speaker is responsible for acknowledging and showing appreciation when a request for change has been met. If the change didn't address her emotional need after all, she can use the method again to get clearer and more on target. The listener then takes his turn, using the same formula that lets him create the conditions to be heard, communicate his feelings and needs, and present his six requests for change. If each person does one new behavior every week for a year, the two will have instituted more than one hundred positive changes in their relationship in that year. Pretty resilient!

The Neuroscience of Compassionate Communication

The mechanical formula of this communication tool prohibits the shaming, blaming, and name-calling that might otherwise activate the threat response in either person and preempts the consequent reaction — either a counterattack or withdrawal and stonewalling. When we're not feeling threatened, the prefrontal cortex is not hijacked by a threat response or by the defenses to that perceived threat. The prefrontal cortex stays active, using the resonance circuit so we can listen to and empathize with the other person in order to reach a resolution. Learning to stay open and respond to requests for changes in behavior strengthens confidence in our ability to resolve complaints and conflicts. That reconditioning in turn further strengthens the functioning of the prefrontal cortex.

Pulling It All Together

The skills of emotional intelligence you have learned and applied in this chapter allow you to relate to yourself and to others through compassionate communication and connection. Operating from this base of emotional well-being allows you to move naturally into the five Cs of coping.

- You can return more quickly to calm and equanimity — to your window of tolerance — no matter what is going on around or within you, and no matter how you initially reacted (following old patterns). You can see more clearly what needs to be done and how to effectively do it.
- As the functioning of your right hemisphere becomes more integrated with the functioning of the left, your feelings are more integrated with your thoughts. You have more gut intuition and the energy of your passions to draw on, as well as more skill at analyzing your situation and planning your actions in response.
- The "left shift" you trigger by cultivating positive and prosocial emotions shifts your brain to an "approach" stance,

making you readier to reach out for help rather than carrying the burden all by yourself.

- As you become more competent at navigating your own emotional storms and dismantling your emotional walls, you also become more skillful at relating to other people's difficulties. You can be affected by other people but not infected. You can apply this resilience immediately in more direct, honest, effective communication to reach understanding and solve problems.
- The growing competency helps you become more confident: whatever storms you face, you can cope.

PART SIX

SHIFT HAPPENS: RECOVERING RESILIENCE THROUGH REFLECTION AND RESPONSE FLEXIBILITY

CHAPTER SIXTEEN

Using Reflection to Identify Options

*Between a stimulus and response there is a space. In that space
is our power to choose our response. In our response lies our
growth and our freedom. The last of human freedoms is to
choose one's attitude in any given set of circumstances.*

> — VIKTOR FRANKL,
> Austrian psychiatrist, survivor of Auschwitz

WHEN A BUDDY at a summer barbecue accidentally spilled a beer
all over Darron's new blue jeans, Darron didn't react with annoyance as he might have done some months before. Instead, he deftly
responded, "No worries! These jeans need a good washing anyway."
For most of us, it takes practice and rewiring of the brain to be this
flexible in our responses, especially when faced with bigger troubles:
To be able to say at the loss of a job, "Maybe I need to look at the
direction my life is heading anyway." Or, if the bank is threatening
to foreclose on the house, "It's time to think through our finances
again." Or, on being told about soaring blood pressure, "It's time I
learned more about taking care of my health." Rather than remaining mired in thoughts that see such life events as disruptive — which
they certainly are — or traumatic — which they certainly can be —
we can choose to take them as cues to learn new responses: to find
ways to respond to a trigger or a stressor with new behaviors rather
than out of automatic, reactive habits, to shift perspectives, create
options, and choose among them wisely.

Researchers have found that people who exhibit high degrees of response flexibility also exhibit high degrees of resilience. Flexibility in the neural circuitry of the prefrontal cortex allows them to vary their responses to life events depending on their judgment of what will work best *now*, not simply on what has worked before. Response flexibility is the essential neural platform from which we can choose to cope differently, more adaptively, and more resiliently. It is the neurobiological basis of resilience.

If you have practiced the skills presented in previous chapters, you have steadily created more neural flexibility in your brain. The exercises in chapters 16–18 teach you skills in reflection: noticing and naming patterns, shifting perspectives, modifying patterns and creating options. They create pathways within the brain that will allow you to greatly enhance your response flexibility.

This chapter focuses on reflection and options. You have to be able to see clearly what's what before you can make wise choices and changes in your behaviors. Exercises in mindful empathy strengthen the prefrontal cortex in its capacities to generate steady awareness, clear reflection, and deep self-awareness, even in the face of all the issues you don't want to look at, the things you don't want to see as true.

Empathic self-awareness allows you to clearly identify your patterns of response *as* patterns of response and to take your reactivity to any moment of experience as a cue to practice rewiring your brain. Chapter 17 explains how to use the processes of new conditioning, deconditioning, and reconditioning to monitor and modify those patterns of response. The rewiring creates more flexibility in your neural circuitry so that you can shift perspectives and challenge your encoded beliefs about the absolute truth of the way things are.

From this fresh vantage point, you can discern options and choices that were invisible before. In chapter 18 you learn to disengage yourself from any conditioned neural circuitry that would automatically send you down the same old pathways and block your resilience. You cultivate the capacity of discernment — considering wisely which choices will work best in the current circumstances. The response flexibility thus created in the brain allows wiser, more creative choices and behaviors.

Using Reflection for Day-to-Day Resilience

It's all well and good to become mindfully aware of moment-to-moment experience when sitting quietly on a meditation cushion at home or at a peaceful meditation retreat, or when we have a few moments at our desk or on the front porch to reflect on our current state of affairs. It's not so easy to maintain that calm awareness when we're in the throes of meeting the unexpected: when our job is suddenly outsourced or our twenty-year-old son is asking us to post bail for his arrest for petty theft.

We practice mindfulness specifically to strengthen the capacities of the prefrontal cortex to reflect and see clearly no matter what is going on. One way to begin is through the practice of noticing and naming, which keeps the prefrontal cortex engaged and allows us to stay calm as emotions flare up. This practice of noticing and naming lays the groundwork for shifting perspectives and discerning options when the going really gets tough.

Skill 1: Noticing and Naming Creates Options

Years and years ago, I was on a two-week vacation with my friend Sara in the Canadian Rockies; we were hiking, biking, and driving the Icefields Parkway through Banff and Jasper National Parks. One sunny morning, I had neglected to fasten my bike securely on the bike rack of the car; ten miles down the road, it flew off onto the highway. Hitting the road at 60 mph, the front wheel was badly skewed, making the bike unrideable. I flipped out.

My friend was calm and patient. No one was hurt; the wheel could probably be fixed; it was a beautiful day in a beautiful part of the world. Sara's steadiness helped me notice, name, and thus manage my own anxiety about the wheel not being fixable and spoiling our trip. I put my hand on my heart; we breathed together deeply, and her steadiness helped bring me back into equanimity. That recovered equanimity helped alleviate my guilt about my carelessness spoiling our day. It also helped me surrender and accept the situation as it was.

The guy at the bike shop wasn't as empathic. "This is just a bump on a pickle," he told me. But he did guarantee he could fix the wheel in four hours. As Sara and I settled ourselves at a nearby lake for a leisurely picnic, I began to reflect on the event more deeply.

Maybe the bike-shop guy was right. In the bigger picture, was this really such a big deal? Would I be upset about this five years from now? Next week? By dinner? Stepping back and reflecting helped me put the whole event into perspective. What was, was just fine.

Coming to an inner peace and acceptance of what was happening allowed me to reengage with Sara. The chance to relax and talk for four hours, rather than racing each other up and down hills on our bikes, was a luxury. By the time we picked up my repaired wheel, we realized it was one of the best times of our trip.

The Neuroscience of Why Noticing and Naming Creates Options

Sara's calm helped me come back into my own window of tolerance. Through my insula I could notice the physiological sensations of the anxiety in my body; through the connection to safety and trust in my friendship with Sara, I could activate the release of oxytocin in my brain and calm myself down. By evoking the mutual compassion in our shared resonance circuits, I could look at the episode with more kindness toward myself.

By calmly focusing my attention on my anxiety in the moment, I activated my anterior cingulate cortex, enabling it to focus on other reactions that were beginning to cascade in response to my initial reactions: the fear that the wheel might not be fixable, my guilt at spoiling our trip. My insula and anterior cingulate cortex were feeding information into my prefrontal cortex. By naming the experience, I was activating the prefrontal cortex to reflect on the meaning of the experience of this bump on a pickle, strengthening my brain's capacity to make sense of it.

My prefrontal cortex could draw on memories explicitly encoded by my hippocampus of previous moments of coping: knowledge of what I had done or what others would do in situations similar to this. Through the shared reflection and brainstorming with Sara, I could begin to discern options and choose how we would cope with the snafu. I was strengthening my response flexibility.

Exercise 1: Noticing and Naming to Create Options

1. Imagine you're walking down the sidewalk of a busy street in your neighborhood. You notice a friend walking toward you on the other side. You wave and call out "Hello!" but the friend does not respond. Notice your own split-second reaction to that lack of response: a contraction in your body, a drop in energy. Notice whatever thoughts might begin to cascade in response to your body's reaction. Maybe you think, "Hmm, that's unusual. I'd better try again." Or, "Whew! He has a lot on his mind. I wonder if I should even bother him?" Notice any reactivity to those thoughts. "Gee, he seems a little stuck-up today." Or "Oh, no! What have I done wrong?" Notice whether your thoughts follow a pattern that you have noticed before, such as feeling bad about yourself or wanting to reach out even more.

2. Now imagine that your friend sees you and, on his own, waves and calls out "Hello!" to you. Again, notice your own split-second reaction to his connecting with you: maybe a smile, an uplift of energy. Bring awareness to any shifts in your body, notice any shifts in your thoughts: "He noticed me!" Or "I'm glad we weren't disconnected after all." As you reflect on your experience, notice whether your

thoughts follow a pattern that you have also noticed before, perhaps of relief or gratitude.

3. Take a moment to name the reactions and the patterns you discovered, with compassion for any reactions that may have been triggered by the noticing. With every moment of practice in noticing and naming, you are strengthening your prefrontal cortex. And by pausing to do this, you are conditioning your brain to create choice points, giving yourself the chance to respond with more flexibility and choose a different response the next time.

Deepening Our Skills in Reflection

When our awareness is steady enough, we can focus our attention on our reactivity as soon as it happens. We can begin to use mindful empathy immediately to notice patterns. This sets the stage for rewiring them, which in turn creates more response flexibility in our neural circuitry. Our brain has already encoded millions of moments of experience into thoughts, ideas, beliefs, and rules about who we are and how the world works. Those encoded beliefs and rules filter our perceptions now, moment to moment. Some of them are accurate and helpful, especially if our early learning from experience was guided toward clear seeing, taking responsibility, and making wise and skillful choices; if we had role models for facing reality without flinching; if we learned from others early on how to acknowledge and face up to our responsibilities and problems; if we saw for ourselves the value of doing one scary thing a day and developing competencies, even through mistakes.

Some of our thoughts, ideas, and beliefs, of course, are not so helpful. Some perceptions can be quite distorted, especially if our early learning from experience was shaped by rules, assumptions, and projections that are not, in fact, representations of who we truly are or reliable guides to how the world actually works. For example, thoughts such as the following are simply not true in any objective sense: "I never finished high school, so no one will ever hire me." Or "My dad was right; I'll never amount to anything." Or "What's the point of trying? The rich only get richer, and the poor only get poorer."

These self-limiting thoughts can completely derail our sense of competence and resilience, leaving us caught in suffering. Negative thoughts can be so self-reinforcing that they can block any new learning, any new choices or options. Identifying our patterns of conditioning leads to the clarity and insight we need to begin to change them.

Skill 2: Naming Patterns as Patterns

Mindful empathy allows us to be present to the experience that is happening in the moment, aware of it but able to step outside it. With practice, we can notice any thought *as* a thought, any pattern of thoughts *as* a pattern. We can notice any feeling *as* a feeling, any cascade of feelings *as* a cascade. The same is true for any state of mind, even multilayered, richly complex (tortuous) states of mind; for any process of the brain — planning, organizing, evaluating, worrying — and for any story that we've told ourselves since we were five, or twelve, or since we got married or divorced. We can know that any view, no matter how forcefully compelling or stubbornly held in this moment, is not — does not have to be — true in all moments. We can be aware of changes and inconsistencies in ourselves: sometimes I think this way, sometimes I don't. I'm thinking or feeling this way now, but I wasn't ten minutes ago or yesterday. We can appreciate the power of the human brain to generate the complex, comprehensive stories that it does and still realize that what we're seeing is not the ultimate truth but tracings, or the entrenchment, of patterns of neural firing in the brain.

Mary, a student in one of my meditation groups, told me this story. The afternoon after her first meditation retreat, she found herself getting into a very spiritually incorrect snit because all the washers in the local Laundromat were full when she wanted to do her laundry on the way home. It took less than a minute to stir herself into a full snarl of "Why can't people do their laundry some other time!" before she remembered to pause, perceive, and reflect. She realized that all the washers were being used because a local Girl Scout troop had just come out of camp, and two of the mothers were valiantly trying to cope with two weeks' worth of laundry for twenty-seven ten-year-olds.

Mary might have gone on home in a less cantankerous but still slightly disappointed funk, but one of the mothers graciously found her an empty washer in the back. Getting to do her laundry after all gave Mary a chance to notice her emerging chagrin at her self-absorption and the time to get curious and explore what had just happened — over nothing! On retreat she had learned a specific form of mindful empathy called the ABCs of mindfulness: to be aware, to be with, with compassion.

As Mary put her clothes in the washer, she applied these ABCs to her snit. She reflected on the response that started the chain reaction. It wasn't even a complete thought, just an internal exclamation of "Oh no! I can't do what I want!" She became aware of her immediate response: a flare of resentment at someone else's laundry getting in her way. So she was able to step back and ask herself, "Since when do I have the right to get angry just because someone else has needs, too, and I might have to wait my turn? What's this anger at feeling thwarted?"

By the time the washer started the first spin cycle, Mary was beginning to see a pattern of getting angry when she felt thwarted: road rage at stalled traffic when she was already late to work; a pissy moment when the store where she always bought fresh pasta had run out and she had to go all the way to another store to get some (as though, she thought, that's a hardship when 10 percent of the world's women have to walk three miles to get drinking water every day).

By the time her clothes had gone through the second rinse and spin cycle, Mary could simply be with her anger and notice that her pattern of experiencing an instant flare of anger at being thwarted was a frequent one. It was a deeply conditioned and often unconscious response by now. Nobody else even had to be involved except as a catalyst to her own reactivity.

As Mary moved her clothes from the washer to the dryer, she found the compassion to see that any pattern of response, including her pattern of responding to being thwarted with anger, *is* only a pattern that can be changed. By the time her clothes were dry and ready to fold, she could let go of exploring the pattern for the time being and return to the simple, calm awareness she had experienced while on retreat.

The Neuroscience of Naming Patterns as Patterns

When we become fully aware of any phenomenon — a feeling, a thought, a mental state, a pattern of behavior, a view, a belief — as Mary became aware of her pattern of response of anger at being thwarted, we light up the entire neural network of that phenomenon: the entire constellation of body sensations and impulses, the pleasantness or unpleasantness of the feelings, thoughts, and the beliefs about ourselves for having that experience. That awareness and lighting up of the network of the pattern allows you to rewire it if you choose. When we shift our full awareness of that integrated state to a full awareness of another integrated state, as Mary did when she shifted back to the calm she had experienced on retreat, we are shifting among entire neural networks of various states of being, not just our conscious thoughts about them. Noticing and naming the various states of being, as well as noticing and naming the shifts among them, keeps the prefrontal cortex of the brain engaged, so that we can step back and reflect on them as patterns or states that can be shifted. We no longer have to be embedded in them or wholly identified with them. When we're not tangled in commentary, we can find a calm center, the eye of the hurricane. We use the process of deconditioning to begin to find the space among the states of being, the choice points where we can choose how we want to relate to these states of being and intentionally shift among them.

Exercise 2: Naming Patterns as Patterns

1. Take ten to fifteen minutes to identify five different states of being that inform your views or perspectives on things. Examples include being lonely, discouraged, down; being friendly, warmhearted, generous in spirit; being exuberant, energized, ready to tackle an army; being thoughtful, contemplative, in a reverie; being interested, curious, open-minded. As you identify these different states, make sure one of the five states of being is your wiser mind or your wiser self. This state of compassionate reflection can help you apply the ABCs of mindfulness to all the other states you are identifying.

   When we first become compassionately aware of our habits and filters of mind, the parade of realizations can seem like one horror show after another. So many ways we've behaved can make us cringe now: the disappointment or hurt we've caused, or the failures we've experienced. It takes great courage and compassion to become aware of relational goof-up 173 or remorse-to-the-core episode 89. Refresh your experience of your wiser self as often as you need to in order to stay steady, able to notice and name.

2. Sometimes it's helpful to think of people who fully embody these states of being in order to evoke them in our awareness more clearly: people we know, literary characters, historical figures, creatures in film or fantasy, ourselves at different ages and stages of development. They may be people who

embody being cantankerous, grouchy, irritable; being playful, delighted, happy; being caring, compassionate, committed; being critical, judgmental, complaining; being focused,
clearheaded, wise.

3. Brainstorm states of being with a friend. The relational resonance creates a mental play space between the two of you
to generate more ideas. You can probably come up with at
least twenty.

4. When you've identified at least five different states of being
that could inform your views or perspectives, practice shifting among them. Just as you can walk around any piece
of furniture in your home and see it from different angles,
you can walk around any phenomenon or event in your life
and see it, and your experience of it, from different angles,
from different states of being that inform different perspectives. Focus on one of these for a few moments, then shift to
another.

5. Notice that you *can* shift your awareness among these different views. Begin to notice different states as you shift among
them throughout your day. Notice them, name them, reflect
on whether they are true and useful to you, and then choose
to shift to another state or view. You're conditioning your
brain to practice that shifting.

This exercise harnesses the capacity of the prefrontal cortex to
see any phenomenon *as* a phenomenon, to help you identify any
state of being that informs your perspectives and views *as* simply
one state of being. With practice, you can identify the perspectives
through which you tend to filter your experience most often and
then choose to respond to life events from perspectives that are more
flexible, more adaptive, and more resilient.

Skill 3: Recognizing Opportunities to Shift Old Patterns and Create Options

My client Shirley told me this story about preparing her taxes last spring. She began early in the morning, and within thirty minutes got caught in an old mind-set: "This is confusing; this is overwhelming; this isn't workable. I don't know what I'm doing; I never was good at numbers; I can't do this!" Because Shirley had been practicing a form of compassionate reflection for more than a year, she noticed her state of mind. That noticing broke the automatic pattern of her reactivity. She noticed her annoyance at her state of mind. She quickly realized that being caught in this state wasn't helpful. She also realized that she didn't have to stay caught in the old mind-set now.

Shirley took a walk around the block to clear her mind, came back to her desk, and took another five minutes to create a different mind-set for herself. Could she use preparing her taxes as an opportunity to practice? Shirley brought her mindful empathy to bear on the issue, noticing every moment that she stayed in her wise mind — open-minded and curious about how her mind was responding to the task of preparing her taxes. She noticed and named moments when she was learning something new — a changed rule about depreciation, a better way to categorize her expenses. She also noticed and named moments when her mind began to contract in the face of something she didn't know. She did call her neighbor Tom, a retired accountant, for advice three times that afternoon, but she managed to finish her taxes by dinnertime. She also noticed her sense of pride in mastering the task that had threatened to overwhelm her that morning, enjoying the deepening trust in herself and her practice; she noticed her gratitude that she noticed her initial patterns of response and took them as a cue to practice. The noticing and naming kept her prefrontal cortex functioning well and brought her out of confusion into clarity.

The Neuroscience of Recognizing Opportunities
to Shift Old Patterns and Create Options

By framing every moment of experience as an opportunity to practice noticing and naming, we are breaking a previously conditioned automatic pattern of response that carries us along in old automatic patterns of behavior. Creating opportunities for awareness and discerning choice points is essential to being able to choose a different response. When we recognize an opportunity to practice mindful empathy, we have activated the capacities of the prefrontal cortex to reflect, to ask, "Is what I'm feeling, thinking, or doing right now skillful or unskillful, effective or ineffective, an efficient or a costly use of resources?" We are conditioning a new habit in the brain of mindful (and compassionate) reflection that enables us to create new options going forward.

Exercise 3: Recognizing Opportunities to Shift Old Patterns and Create Options

1. Identify five situations in which you might be triggered to respond from an automatic conditioned pattern: it's after midnight, and your spouse hasn't called or come home; you receive a notice from the IRS in the mail; you're due for an annual physical checkup or visit to the dentist; you just ran a red light; your boss dismissed as irrelevant a project you had worked hard on and felt was significant.

2. The next three times events like these occur, even though you might be feeling strong emotions at the same time (notice and name those, too!), use the perspective of your wise mind or wiser self to practice pausing, noticing, and naming what's happening. Practice noticing, reflecting, and discerning what you are feeling, thinking, and doing before you decide what to do next. Notice whether viewing this

event through the lens of the wiser self shifts your perspective of the event or creates any choice points for responding differently.

3. Recall the views of the different states of being you identified in exercise 2. Experiment with applying these views to the event. Notice any shifts in your view of the event caused by shifting perspectives. Notice how viewing the event from these different states of being is different from viewing it from the perspective of your wiser self.

4. Experiment with applying the different views or perspectives generated by different states of being to one particularly troubling event in your life: a child custody hearing, accidentally hitting the neighbor's dog as it dashed in front of your car, your luggage being lost at the beginning of a two-week vacation in a foreign country, half of your savings lost in a real estate deal gone sour.

5. As you apply several different states to one particular event, notice any shift in your perceptions, interpretations, feelings, or thoughts about yourself. Notice which states allow your patterns of response to be more open and flexible. Always practice inhabiting your wise mind, or wiser self, as one of the perspectives from which you're viewing the situation.

6. Set the intention to develop a new habit of perceiving life events, especially stressors, as opportunities to practice waking up and growing up, to notice patterns of response and states of being so that you can begin to create choice points and respond differently, more resiliently.

As the Buddhist teacher Pema Chödrön advises:

The Buddhist teachings are fabulous at simply working with what's happening as your path of awakening, rather than treating your life experiences as some kind of deviation from what is supposed to be happening. The more difficulties you have, in fact, the greater opportunity there is to let them transform you. The difficult things provoke all your irritations and bring your habitual patterns to the surface. And that becomes the moment of truth. You have the choice to launch into the lousy habitual patterns you already have, or to stay with the rawness and discomfort of the situation and let it transform you, on the spot.

Your strengthened prefrontal cortex can do that transforming on the spot.

Pulling It All Together

In this chapter you have learned mindfulness skills that allow you to:

- step back and reflect on experiences that are triggering old, reactive responses. When you notice and name those responses, you are strengthening your prefrontal cortex in its function of self-awareness, which is essential to creating new options.
- recognize moments when you can shift your state of mind or behavior and practice the reflection and seeing clearly that will allow you to do so.
- develop response flexibility in your brain — the neurobiological platform of resilience.

In the next chapter you will learn how to use the capacities of your prefrontal cortex to reflect on, shift, and transform any patterns you choose.

CHAPTER SEVENTEEN

Shifting Gears: Modifying Our Patterns of Response

*The truth is that our finest moments are most likely to occur
when we are feeling deeply uncomfortable, unhappy, or
unfulfilled. For it is only in such moments, propelled by
our discomfort, that we are likely to step out of our ruts
and start searching for different ways or truer answers.*

— M. SCOTT PECK

I WAS DEEP in a worrisome thought one day, not paying attention
to where I was walking, when I blithely stepped ankle-deep into the
wet cement of a freshly laid crosswalk. I was startled, then horrified.
Negative reactions started cascading inside me, including, "How
careless! How could you have been so asleep at the wheel!" I was just
about to fall into an all-too-familiar pattern of berating myself for
being so clumsy when another inner voice piped up, "Wait a minute!
So I was preoccupied! I'm sick and tired of winding up feeling lousy
about myself when I was just unconscious for a moment. For once
I'd like to just deal with something and not make it all about my
being clumsy."

I stood there in the cement, noticing all these different reactions cascading. Years of practice helped me realize I *did* have a
choice about how I was going to handle the situation. I lifted my
feet out of my stuck shoes and stepped onto dry ground as construction workers headed over to help me. As I lifted my shoes

out of the cement, I tried for a little bit of compassion for myself. "Shit happens! I'm probably not the only person on the planet who made a mistake today because I wasn't paying attention. Sure, I'm a little embarrassed in front of these guys, but that doesn't mean anything more about me than I just wasn't paying attention."

I walked over to a convenient outdoor faucet on the wall of a nearby apartment building to wash my shoes and feet. As I began to have some hope that I might even save my shoes (I did), I noticed feeling some pride that I was coping well — with the outer event and with my inner reactions to it.

By the time one of the construction workers gave me some paper towels to dry my shoes and feet, my prefrontal cortex got it together and it dawned on me: "Yes, shit happens. Life is happening in this way in this moment. But 'shift' happens, too." I could open to the lesson of the moment: choosing to shift my perspective allowed me to cope resiliently. The experience also taught me, once again, that shifting perspectives and responding resiliently is possible in any moment at all.

One of the hallmarks of resilience is to be able to shift gears and recalibrate our responses quickly. Once we notice the automatic patterns that are filtering our reactions and thus shaping our responses, as Shirley did with her anxiety about her taxes, or as I did with my harsh self-judgment about stepping into the wet cement, we can choose to immediately shift those perspectives in ways that will rewire them. In his book *The Mindful Therapist*, Dan Siegel uses the phrase "monitor and modify" for noticing and then initiating changes in perspective and behavior that will harness our neural plasticity to accomplish that rewiring.

Each of the three exercises below uses one of the three processes of brain change — new conditioning, deconditioning, and reconditioning — to expand the brain's capacity to respond flexibly. As always, use the practice of mindful empathy to safely "hold" and catalyze the rewiring of your brain.

Skill 1: New Conditioning to Shift Perspectives

I saw the movie *The Sound of Music* five times as a teenager. The wisdom of the song "My Favorite Things" appealed to me long before I had ever heard of positive psychology, discerning the wholesome from the unwholesome, cognitive behavioral therapy, or affirmations:

> When the dog bites, when the bee stings,
> When I'm feeling sad,
> I simply remember my favorite things,
> And then I don't feel so bad.

Many of us have learned to think of something positive to redirect our thoughts when we're feeling bad. Sitting in the dentist's chair, we might remember our son's scoring the winning goal in soccer last week. Anxious about stepping out on a stage to deliver a public talk, we redirect our thoughts to the fun we had with our friends on our last vacation.

Almost every day, new findings in neuroscience are published that validate the power of positive thoughts, or even different thoughts, to interrupt automatic, negative thoughts, activate different circuits in our brains, and shift our view. The practice of refocusing our attention, shifting our view, and eventually reframing our experience, over and over, strengthens the brain's capacity for response flexibility and thus resilience.

Exercise 1: Shifting Perspectives by Replacing ANTS with APTS

This exercise uses new conditioning to replace automatic negative thoughts (ANTs) with automatic positive thoughts (APTs).

1. Identify one habitual negative thought you would like to replace. You're sick of it, like I was when I stepped ankle-deep in wet cement and almost fell down the rabbit hole of calling myself clumsy.

2. Brainstorm several alternative thoughts to counter your negative thought. The alternative may be a directly opposite thought: for example, "I'm lazy" can be countered with "I'm motivated when I'm interested." The alternative may be in a different realm of thought entirely: "I'm lazy" may become "I'm so looking forward to Greg and Diane coming over on Saturday; I wonder what I'll cook?" Or it may be simply a thought about someone who loves you that lets you take refuge in feeling that love, or remembering a moment of feeling "Sure I can!"

3. When you notice the habitual negative thought arising, practice using your alternative thought immediately.

The point of this exercise is not to block any future thought of "I'm lazy." It's to interrupt the cascade of self-deprecation that immediately and reflexively follows that thought. Sending the brain in another direction gives it a few moments to recalibrate itself. Cultivating an immediate positive response to a negative thought creates the space to shift perspective, supporting more flexibility and resilience. And, every time we do it, we are conditioning our brain for more resilience.

The Neuroscience of New Conditioning to Shift Perspectives

Harnessing the neuroplasticity of your brain — choosing to learn or condition new, more adaptive patterns of response — is choosing to become more competent at being resilient. The longer you dwell or ruminate on an old, negative thought, the more deeply grooved it becomes in your circuitry. Perseverating usually does not solve the problem; it actually reduces the flexibility in our thinking that could solve the problem. "Switching the channel" by redirecting your attention to more positive, optimistic thinking helps shake the brain loose of the old habit. You can learn examples of more positive thoughts — specific content — from role models, teachers, coaches, therapists, and friends. By repetition and perseverance, your brain learns the process of making the new thoughts the new normal. The new states of mind and thoughts become enduring traits of mind and behavior.

Repeatedly shifting perspectives — regardless of the content — creates more flexibility within your neural circuitry to keep doing so. Choosing to shift becomes the new habit of the brain, and perceiving yourself as making choices not only shifts the content of specific patterns but also shifts your perception of yourself as choice maker.

Skill 2: Deconditioning to Shift Perspectives

The only real voyage of discovery consists not in seeking new landscapes but in having new eyes.

— MARCEL PROUST

This quote from Proust has been one of my favorites for a long time. It points to the necessity of creating new perspectives — learning to see things differently, with new eyes — in order to open our minds and heart to new discoveries. But modern neuroscience shows that one of the best ways to keep our brains open to new learning and new ways of seeing things is, in fact, to seek new landscapes.

All of us have learned to seek new landscapes to clear the cobwebs from our minds: we go on vacations, retreats, weekend hikes, sightseeing trips. The latest findings in neuroscience demonstrate that taking ourselves out of a familiar environment, even temporarily, wakes the brain out of patterns of perception that have become routinized. New scenery and scenarios activate new neural circuits in our brains. New experiences open us up in ways that can lead to new learning and new views, to seeing the "big picture": they can help us shift the processing of our experience to the defocusing network. We loosen the grip on our old ways of thinking and create more flexibility in the brain to more easily shift our perspectives.

We can practice shifting perspectives in small as well as large, life-changing ways. Years ago I was hiking in the backcountry of Yosemite National Park, seeking new landscapes to get a new perspective on some old problems. Seven miles along the trail, I came upon a park ranger with a small group of hikers sprawled on the ground, each of them completely absorbed in observing one square foot of ground from a height of six inches. Each person was simply focusing attention on everything he or she could see in that square — plants, lichens, bugs — and everything that was happening in it for five minutes. The ranger called this an exercise in "belly botany." I was astonished when I tried it myself. I saw life, death, stillness, aggression, and beauty, all on a tiny scale. I was even more astonished when I looked up again and saw the eight-thousand-foot peaks all around us. My view expanded exponentially: every square foot of these hundreds of square miles of wilderness was full of the things I had been present to in my small belly-botany patch. This quantum shift from micro to macro scales can quickly change our view of our place in the larger scheme of things and open our minds to new possibilities. You can try this exercise almost anywhere.

Exercise 2: Using Belly Botany to Shift Perspectives

1. Find a one-square-foot patch on a favorite beach, in a meadow, in a forest, in your own backyard, in a flower box, or in a city park. Lie comfortably on your stomach so that your eyes can focus on your patch from a height of approximately six inches. Come into a sense of presence. Defocus on any sense of self: concentrate your attention on your patch and notice any activity, any stillness, any change of the light and shadows, the relationships of things one to another; notice harmonies of colors and shape; notice oddities.

2. After five minutes (or more), stand up and focus your attention on the larger landscape. Notice the sudden change in scale. Maintain the defocusing on your sense of self in this larger view for a few minutes, noticing the shapes and colors, harmonies, and oddities in what you see.

3. Bring your attention back to yourself and notice any changes in your view of yourself, any new perspective on the place of your life among the small and the vast.

With practice, you can access this tool of shift any time you need to gain a fresh perspective. Focusing attention away from yourself encourages a defocusing in the circuitry in your brain that allows new views and new perspectives to emerge.

The Neuroscience of Deconditioning to Shift Perspectives

When we focus our awareness on things at a small scale and then shift our awareness to the vast, the shift in focus in the visual cortex helps us begin switching between the focusing network in the brain, which engages with experience more concretely by focusing on specific objects, tasks, activities, or perspectives, and the defocusing network, which engages with experience more diffusely from a spacious, "simply being" perspective.

The shift to the defocusing network shifts our processing from the structured and the concrete to the more fluid and unfolding. This creates a neural receptivity that allows new perspectives and new insights to emerge out of a deeper, intuitive knowing. The subjective experience of these moments of insight often feels like an "Oh!" or "Aha!" moment and carries with it a "truth sense": "Oh, now I get it; this is what's true." From our new viewpoint, we can make new choices.

Skill 3: Reconditioning to Shed Old Identities

Development involves giving up a smaller
story in order to wake up to a larger story.

— JEAN HOUSTON

A few years ago my client Karen shared with me a distressing insight about one of her conditioned patterns of relationship, or rather, her lack of pattern. On a rare sunny afternoon over the weekend, she had been reading a book in Golden Gate Park in San Francisco. She noticed a young woman pushing a young girl on the swings. The two of them were laughing and talking and seemed to be having a lot of fun together. Karen assumed they were a nanny and her charge and went back to reading her book.

After fifteen minutes or so, Karen overheard the young girl say, "Mommy, Mommy! Let's go see the puppy!" As the woman and girl skipped away to meet a Dalmatian puppy and its owner, my client saw — with some horror — a huge hole in her understanding of play in relationships. It had never occurred to her that this woman and young girl were mother and daughter. Nothing in her life experience had told her that this kind of playful interaction could happen between a mother and daughter. Her own experience of being with her mother, or even with the mothers of her childhood friends, while adequate in many other ways, hadn't included much lighthearted play or fun.

Karen's distress was acute. She wanted to have her own family someday. But her realization that she was missing this template or internal working model of a healthy parent-child relationship was jarring. What kind of mother would she be if she hadn't grasped that playing with her own child could be fun?

We had to bring a lot of mindfulness and empathy to this dilemma. Karen had to anchor her investigation of what was missing in her experience, and thus in her conditioned view of herself, in the mindful empathy of her wiser self. Her longing to have children was sincere, and her dedication to her own growth was fierce. She had to find ways to create new experiences of herself with children that would supply those missing experiences of play and fun between an adult and a child. She had to choose to repair her conditioned messages about motherhood with the new views and perspectives she would gain from those new experiences. Her wiser self would have to hold both her wholesome yearning to be a loving mother and the deep grief over her missed experiences and conditioning about motherhood and play.

We began to look for ways that Karen could spend time with young children and with adults who knew how to play with them. These included hanging out on play dates with married friends and their own young children; volunteering at a local preschool one afternoon a week; and helping to coach a girls' soccer team. As she engaged in these new experiences, she worked on always allowing the new views of herself that they brought to counter the old views, and always holding the process in the compassionate reflection of her wiser self. It took about a year and a half for Karen to completely recondition her sense of self in relationship to young children and to form the sense that she herself could become a playful, loving mother.

She told me at the end of that phase of our work together, "I didn't even know this piece of the puzzle was missing until that day in the park. But, somehow, I knew I *could* recover it. I mean, I could learn to be playful and enjoy being playful, by doing it over and over and over. I guess somehow it's sunk in, and now... well, now I know I can be playful myself and stay open to being playful with a little child. I'm not afraid anymore that I won't know how to do this with my own kids. It's a miracle."

Exercise 3: Reconditioning to Shed Old Identities

1. Focus your attention on being present in this moment.
2. Call to mind your wiser self: the wise, resourceful, capable embodiment of your truest self. Anchor your awareness

there. Evoke this experience of comfortably inhabiting your wiser self at every level of neural encoding: a visual image; positive states of ease, trust, and well-being that your wiser self embodies; the sensations and movements of your body that help ground the sense of your wiser self; the name you use for your wiser self; the thoughts that arise about yourself as your wiser self. You're lighting up the integrated networks of your wiser self as a resource.

3. Identify a negative perspective you have of yourself that you identify with as "you" and that you would like to change or rewire. (Positive, wholesome beliefs, of course, we strengthen as resources.) Recall a specific experience that embodies this perspective. After you identify the perspective or belief or identity, park that identity in the background of your awareness.

4. From the perspective of the wiser self, imagine yourself in a new identity, embodying the desirable new views and beliefs. Begin to imagine the thoughts you would think and the actions you would take from this new identity. Imagine the emotions you would feel; let yourself feel them now in your body. You're lighting up the neural networks of the new identity you will embody.

5. Parking both the wiser self and the new identity on the periphery of your awareness, take a moment to evoke the felt sense of the old identity you have chosen to rewire. Light up as many of the neural networks as you can by remembering the thoughts, the feelings, and the states of being of this old identity.

6. Evoking the mindful empathy of the wiser self, bring both the old remembered identity and the newly imagined identity into your awareness simultaneously.

7. Either steadily hold both the old and new views of self in your mindful and empathic awareness at the same time, or

mindfully alternate between the two many times. Whenever you need to, you can take a moment to refresh your awareness of your wiser self. Refresh the sense of the new identity too, as many times as you need. When it seems as if the sense of the new identity, is consistently stronger than the old, let go of the old identity and rest your awareness solely in the new identity, held in the larger awareness of the wiser self.

8. After a few moments of anchoring your awareness only in the new identity, reevoke the old identity once more, and notice whether that network lights up as strongly as before.

Sometimes we can notice a significant difference, sometimes only a slight one. With enough practice and repetition, the old identify will fade. Experiencing success in rewiring an old identity, even once, empowers us to practice this reconditioning again and again.

The Neuroscience of Reconditioning Old Identities

When we deeply believe any idea about ourselves, we can become so closely identified with that belief that we don't even see it as a construct: we see it as an integral part of our nature, not a choice or pattern that was learned and can be unlearned. Sometimes a pattern is established so early that it gets encoded only in implicit memory; we don't even know we believe it. That view of the self has become invisible to us.

When we create new experiences that evoke a new perspective of ourselves and then pair that new view with an old one, as Karen did, and as we continue to create new experiences that evoke and reinforce the new view, the neural encoding of both the old view and the new view repeatedly falls apart and reconsolidates. Over time, the new view completely rewires the old. Eventually we may even have trouble remembering the old view of ourselves, or remembering the power that identity once had in determining our behavior.

The practice of separating from old identities, dismantling the neural encoding that underlies them, is crucial for increasing our capacity for flexible response. We can identify so strongly with old, less resilient coping strategies that relinquishing them feels like losing ourselves. We need to recondition or rewire the old view so that we can shift to a more empowered, more resilient sense of self. That shift generates the neural flexibility we need in order to create more options of response.

The psychologist and philosopher Jean Piaget distinguished between *assimilation* — adding new experiences to an old construct of ourselves without disturbing the construct — and *accommodation* — rewiring the circuitry so that we dismantle the original construct. What we're attempting here is accommodation through reconditioning. The process is not always comfortable: we often don't bother to try it until some pain or anguish compels us to. Rachel Naomi Remen testifies to this truth:

> Crisis, suffering, loss, the unexpected encounter with the unknown — all of this has the potential to initiate a shift in perspective. A way of seeing the familiar with new eyes, a way of seeing the self in a completely new way. The experience that I have in watching people with cancer is that the more overwhelmed someone is at the beginning, the more profound the transformation that they undergo. There's a moment when the individual steps away from the former life and the former identity and is completely out of control and completely surrenders, and then is reborn with a larger, expanded identity.

The more practiced and competent we become at using our tools and resources to transform our sense of self through reconditioning, the more courageously we can tolerate the growing pains of this process of brain change and rewiring for resilience.

Pulling It All Together

In this chapter you have learned that:

- once we've experienced the confidence that we can monitor and modify our perspectives, our beliefs, our patterns, our behaviors — that we can intentionally shift an entire state of being, even once — we create the most significant shift of all, from a helpless "poor me" to an empowered "I" that knows it can generate options and choose among them wisely;

- this empowered "I" can move more fully toward the five Cs of coping, as when I stopped my slide into my habit of self-criticism over stepping into the wet cement and chose to shift my perspective toward a healthy pride in how well I was coping;

- the same thing can happen as you become more empowered and competent at replacing an automatic negative thought that threatens to disempower you with an automatic positive thought, or when you skillfully connect to resources, as Karen did when she empowered herself to connect to new experiences with children in order to rewire her old, sabotaging beliefs about herself.

This empowered "I" allows you to find the calm and the courage to discern wise choices and respond flexibly. We use our calm, clarity, and connections to generate the competence and courage of resilience.

CHAPTER EIGHTEEN

Discerning Wise Choices and Responding Flexibly

Autobiography in Five Short Chapters

I
I walk down the street.
There is a deep hole in the sidewalk.
I fall in.
I am lost . . . I am helpless
It isn't my fault.
It takes me forever to find a way out.

II
I walk down the same street.
There is a deep hole in the sidewalk.
I pretend I don't see it.
I fall in again.
I can't believe I'm in the same place
But, it isn't my fault.
It still takes a long time to get out.

III
I walk down the same street.
There is a deep hole in the sidewalk.
I see it is there.
I still fall in . . . it's a habit.

My eyes are open,
I know where I am.
It is my fault.
I get out immediately.

IV
I walk down the same street
There is a deep hole in the sidewalk.
I walk around it.

V
I walk down another street.

— PORTIA NELSON

NEW PERSPECTIVES HOLD THE KEYS to our growth and freedom. Choosing to harness our brain's neuroplasticity and rewire our conditioned responses and perspectives toward flexibility and resilience means we get to walk down another street. We don't have to, but we can choose to. Now we have the neural capacity to perceive options where we saw none before, discern which options might be most productive, and choose wisely among them what course of action to take.

Skill 1: Creating Options, Discerning Choices, Choosing Wisely

Every moment brings a choice; every choice has an impact.

— JULIA BUTTERFLY HILL

We have already learned to refrain from shame and blame about resilience gone awry or about past decisions gone awry. Here we teach ourselves to refrain from self-critical faultfinding about that past. The acknowledging of fault in stanza 3 of "Autobiography in

Five Short Chapters" entails taking responsibility. We take responsibility for past experiences to learn what options might make the most sense now, not to derail our resilience by judging ourselves harshly for them, or to unthinkingly continue them in order to avoid negative judgments about ourselves if we change course now.

Rather than beating ourselves up, as I began to do about my bicycle flying off the back of the car or blithely stepping into wet cement, we open up a reflective inquiry: "Well, why *did* this happen? What do I need to pay more attention to here?" Shifting the perspective from "How *could* I?" to "Well, actually, why *did* I?" allows us to come to a clear comprehension of what's happening and what needs to change. In this sense, good judgment means forming an opinion objectively, based on learning from past experiences, and staying open to new experiences without shutting ourselves down by devaluing, criticism, or condemnation.

A couple of months after Darron demonstrated his response flexibility at the party by calmly realizing he could simply wash the beer out of his jeans, the bank notified him that he was two months behind on his mortgage payments and that it would begin proceedings to foreclose on his home if he didn't send in the amount he owed within thirty days.

Darron had been laid off from his job as a foreman on a big condominium construction project six months before, when the downturn in the economy sent shock waves through the housing industry. He and his family had responded flexibly enough at first: they were getting by on savings, his wife's income from working at the local deli, and Darron's picking up small remodeling jobs here and there. When Darron's mom needed emergency dental surgery a few months later and his parents couldn't pay for it, to Darron the only choice seemed to be to foot the bill and figure out later how to keep up with the mortgage payments. By the time Darron came in to see me after he got the foreclosure notice, he realized he needed to walk down another street.

Darron and his wife looked over their finances for the past twelve months and projections for the next twelve months. Darron met with a mortgage broker at the bank and, with the help of a financial planner, began to educate himself about options. With me, he explored his own history of putting his parents' needs above his own and the effect of that conditioning on his decision making.

Darron, his wife, and two brothers met one Saturday afternoon to brainstorm ways to come up with the mortgage payments in the next thirty days. Even impossible-seeming solutions, like giving up the house and moving in with Darron's parents, were on the table. As more options were put forward than Darron could have come up with on his own, he began to have more confidence that the dilemma could be solved.

In sessions with me, Darron came to realize that he had developed a strategy of giving to his parents — in the forms of time, attention, work on their house, and money for bills when times were hard — in order to "earn" their time, attention, and love in return. When his mom asked for help in paying for her dental surgery, Darron agreed out of habit, without thinking through the effect on his own finances.

We had to dig deeper to find the root causes of his decision to skip two mortgage payments in a row. What became clear was Darron's deeply implicit expectation that, after all he had done for his parents, they should know when he needed help without his having to ask for it. Darron's unconscious hope that his parents would pay back the money for the dental surgery without his having to ask overrode his own common sense about asking for repayment so that he could pay his own debts.

We examined Darron's core values, the moral compass that had helped guide him to these choices and actions. Darron told me that among his core values were being kind to other people, being helpful, and being generous. He came to see that there was no need to change those values, but he needed to refocus those values more on himself and his own family, not exclusively on his parents. We also framed his reluctance to assert himself and let his parents know when he needed help as an old, conditioned survival strategy — if I don't bother you, I'll get to stay on your good side — masquerading as a core value. Darron began to realize that taking care of his own family was also a core value and that he could begin to act accordingly.

I asked Darron to review the various options he had generated in his family brainstorming, while keeping in mind his value of taking better care of his family and breaking his old habit of not asking for help. When we came to the possibility of asking his parents to repay the money he had given them for the dental surgery within thirty days so that he could square up his mortgage payments, he burst into such a spontaneous grin that we both laughed at the suddenness and the sureness of it.

Darron later told me that he had felt so sure of this decision that he went to his parents' house the next afternoon, taking along both of his brothers for moral support, and made his request for repayment politely but assertively. To his surprise, his parents actually seemed relieved and anxious to help. Darron had not only changed his own behaviors; his certainty that he was doing the right thing catalyzed change in his parents, too.

Exercise 1: Creating Options, Discerning Choices, and Choosing Wisely

1. *Assess what is happening* as clearly as you can. This includes getting all the facts about the situation you are being asked to cope with; getting expert opinions and perspectives from competent, resilient others; seeing clearly the circumstances and past decisions that contributed to the situation; and assessing your own patterns of resilience to see what's helpful and unhelpful to you now — where you are open to new learning and where you might be defended against new information or in denial.

   Assessment requires resources — of time, help from other people, open-mindedness. Assessment is essential to cultivating response flexibility; without it, we have no options except to react as we have reacted before.

2. *Identify options.* Brainstorming is a useful tool of deconditioning that can free our brains temporarily from old rules and preconceptions. Creating neural receptivity within the

brain allows new associations or linkages to form spontaneously and come to consciousness. Here's one approach:

(a) Ask a small group of friends to meet with you to
identify options. The open-minded exchange of ideas, and
the associations they lead to, will spark more ideas than
brainstorming by yourself or with just one other person.

(b) All of you generate as many ideas as you can as
quickly as you can, without any judgments or evaluations
allowed. You may notice that the intuitive side of your brain
can generate ideas as quickly as the analytical side. Let
your brain generate new ideas by association with what has
already been suggested.

(c) Once your group runs out of steam for generating
new ideas, categorize the ideas by topic, still without judgment or evaluation.

3. *Identify holes in the sidewalk and walk around them.* Identify
any self-limiting beliefs or automatic patterns of response
(see exercises 2 and 3 in chapter 16) that might have contributed to the situation you find yourself in or that might be
derailing your ability to generate and choose among options
now. When you can clearly see these habits of belief, these
inner saboteurs, take the clarity as a cue to walk down
another street — to adopt new perspectives, especially the
perspective of your wiser self, that can approach the situation with optimism and courage.

4. *Identify the core values* that will guide you in choosing among
the options. We all live by a moral compass, conscious or
unconscious, that guides our choices of behavior. It is part
of the conditioning we get from our parents, peers, teachers,
coaches, role models, and culture and society at large about
what's right or wrong. Your wiser self, for now, embodies
the highest values of that moral compass.

5. *Consult your wiser self.* Find a time and place where you can

come into a sense of presence and have a heart-to-heart talk with your wiser self. State your dilemma and the options you have generated by yourself or with your friends. Simply listen to the deep wisdom of your wiser self speaking to you — not necessarily yet about which options to choose, but about which values matter to you most in choosing. It's this "truth sense" that will guide you in choosing options. Bring your awareness back to the present moment; register this guidance from your wiser self in your awareness as you make your choices.

6. *Discern which options best serve your values.* With a clear understanding of your core values to guide your choices, you can begin to discern which of the options you've generated best fit those values: which ones feel right and which feel "off," are a less ideal match, or don't fit at all. As strange as it may sound after this long, mindful process, sometimes you can help your brain figure out which option is best by tossing a coin. It's not that the coin toss makes the decision for you, but in the split second when you realize which way up the coin is landing, you can experience a quick gut reaction: "Uh-oh; this isn't what I wanted," or "Phew! I'm glad it turned out this way." That is the voice of your intuitive wisdom.

7. *Choose wisely.* This is the natural culmination of the steps above. There's always the possibility that you would choose differently if you had more information or if circumstances changed and opened up more options. You are aiming for the wisest choice possible in the current circumstances.

Whatever choice you make and whatever the consequences, you have created more response flexibility in your brain. That is the neurobiological platform of resilience that will allow you to make wiser and wiser choices in the future.

The Neuroscience of Creating Options, Discerning Choices, and Choosing Wisely

The prefrontal cortex makes its decisions by integrating input from many parts of the brain. It uses both the processing of the focusing network, which can focus on facts and details, and the processing of the defocusing network, which can link old ideas together in new ways. The prefrontal cortex has to weigh input from the rational left hemisphere of the brain with input from the emotional and intuitive right. The prefrontal cortex draws on many different explicit memories encoded by the hippocampus with the intuitive wisdom or gut sense of the wiser self. It may even use social support to activate the release of oxytocin to create enough safety and trust in the brain to make a decision possible. The stronger the functioning of the prefrontal cortex, the more thoroughly we can assess all the elements of what is happening, understand what needs to happen, identify options and blocks to those options, identify the values that we want to shape our decision, and then decide what is the best thing to do.

Pulling It All Together

You have now completed a series of exercises that train your brain to respond more flexibly to life events. The new neural flexibility allows you to:

- reflect with awareness on habitual behavior patterns and perspectives;
- use the three processes of brain change to monitor and modify those perspectives; shift or rewire them for more resilient responses;
- assess what is happening, identify options, identify and shift blocking beliefs (that is, to walk around the holes in the sidewalk), identify core values you want to inform your choices, decide which options best serve those core values, and then choose among your options wisely.

This new response flexibility in your neural circuitry is the neurobiological platform of resilience. When you learn that you can be flexible, you move steadily toward the five Cs of coping: remaining calm in a crisis, as I learned to do with my bent-out-of-shape bike; seeing clearly, as Mary learned to see her pattern of anger in response to threat; staying connected to resources to create options, as Darron did with me, his family, with experts; becoming competent, as Shirley did when she took getting caught in an old mind-set as a cue to practice; and deepening courage, as Karen did to give up an old identity and grow into a new one.

Having developed your capacities for response flexibility and strengthened this neurobiological platform of resilience, you have just one more step to take on the journey to rewire your brain for more resilience. In the next chapter, you will learn tools to integrate the entire brain more fully, creating an enduring, stable platform for lifelong resilience.

PART SEVEN

RECOVERING RESILIENCE THROUGH SIMPLY BEING

CHAPTER NINETEEN

Resting in the Wisdom of Being

Wisdom tells me I am nothing.
Love tells me I am everything.
Between the two, my life flows.

— Sri Nisargadatta

In 1971, the Apollo 14 astronaut Edgar Mitchell became the sixth human being to walk on the moon. On the return flight to Earth, this MIT-trained aeronautical engineer experienced a radical shift in consciousness. As Mitchell watched the Earth "rise" from behind the moon into the black emptiness of space, he suddenly saw the preciousness of this blue jewel of a planet we call home and the oneness of everything living on it. Mitchell's epiphany about the interconnectedness of all life on Earth led to his founding the Institute of Noetic Sciences two years later to research how shifts in consciousness such as the one he experienced — the *noesis*, or deep inner knowing, that comes in the form of epiphanies, revelations, and sudden insights into the true nature of reality — could be cultivated.

Neuroscientists are now beginning to unlock the mystery of what happens in the brain in these moments of epiphany and what could explain the radical shifts in consciousness that they lead to. They are also beginning to see that extraordinary states of consciousness can lead to a greater neural integration, greater harmony, and greater synchrony in the physical brain. This deeper brain integration can create a platform of resilience that is almost unshakable. It gives the brain the flexibility and bandwidth to cope with anything at all.

Much remains to be learned. The neurological mapping of shifts in states of consciousness is very new. But techniques for shifting consciousness, drawn from the Buddhist contemplative tradition, have been validated through thousands of years of practitioners' experience, and related practices are used in contemporary Western psychology. In this chapter you will learn to use tools that help create the conditions for epiphanies, allowing you to experience insights into your own true nature and to move toward the deeper brain integration that rewires the brain for maximum resilience.

First, you use the awareness you have cultivated through all the exercises in this book to notice how the five Cs of coping are being integrated into your behaviors of your personal self — resilient behaviors that you used the focusing network of your brain to condition or recondition. Then you use the defocusing network of the brain, used in the process of deconditioning, to temporarily suspend the prefrontal cortex's guardianship of that personal self and open your awareness into a state of reverie that allows new ideas and new associations about the self to emerge. That state of reverie creates opportunities for "Aha!" moments, epiphanies or intuitive insights about yourself and your patterns of coping. Those insights can radically alter the ways you think about yourself.

You then open your awareness through the defocusing network and the process of deconditioning even further, to an experience of the *unconditioned*, as though you were dropping below all the layers of conditioning into what Dan Siegel calls a "plane of open possibilities." The insights and epiphanies you experience in that plane, which many people experience as the *nonself* (see chapter 3), can radically rewire or recondition your established patterns of self, especially negative ones. Using the prefrontal cortex not just to switch between the focusing and defocusing networks, between the self and nonself, but also to fully integrate the experiences of self and nonself can rapidly integrate all the levels of functioning of the entire brain.

Brain scans of people who have experienced this process of neural integration confirm that radical changes take place in the specific patterns of neural firing that encode a particular response. The scans also show that neurons all over the brain fire at a higher frequency (processing signals more rapidly) and in greater synchrony (with greater coordination). The whole brain itself becomes more resilient.

Awareness of the Whole Self

We learned in chapter 3 to develop the awareness that all emotions and sensations of the body are transient, as are all contents, processes, states, and traits of mental activity. Awareness — the state of mind that observes all of that coming and going as coming and going — is itself not coming and going. Our awareness of that greater awareness may come and go; most of us lose awareness of awareness in our busy daily lives. But the awareness itself is ever present, always ready to be rediscovered any time we choose to focus our attention. When we find the space between the stimulus and the response, we alter the rhythm of our doing; we wake up and create space for being.

Awareness is the knowing, not the contents that are known. We can experience it as a vast sky that can hold all the clouds and storms moving through it. We usually pay more attention to the contents of clouds and storms than to the sky that contains them. As the Zen teaching tells us, when we are in a contracted state of mind, it's like looking at the sky through a pipe. With mindfulness of awareness, we become adept at putting down the pipe and looking at the whole sky again.

In this chapter you will learn to alternate between the awareness of the self managed by the prefrontal cortex and the awareness of that spacious, unconditioned nonself that allows you to see the sky whole again. When the experiences of self and nonself are mindfully integrated, we enhance the integration of the whole brain and tap into the deep, intuitive wisdom of our whole self.

Exploring the Contents of the Personal Self

We begin the process of shifting from the focusing network to the defocusing network, and from the focusing on the self to the defocusing of nonself, by using the prefrontal cortex to focus our awareness on our experience of the moment, basic mindfulness and acceptance of what is, including our basic sense of self.

We know that all snowflakes share the same basic, six-sided crystalline structure, yet no two snowflakes are identical. We know that human thumbprints share the same basic whorl patterns, yet no two human thumbprints are identical. Human brains share the same neural structures and mechanisms for processing experience and information, yet no two human brains are identical, either. All human selves share elements of personality style, roles, identities, beliefs, and values, yet no two selves are identical, ever.

The prefrontal cortex is instrumental in maturing the sense of a unique self as the brain develops, recognizing patterns of self as "I," even as those patterns evolve over time. With the reflective self-awareness of the prefrontal cortex, we can begin to notice and name the patterns of memory that constitute our personal history, patterns of coping that underlie our style of personality, and patterns of conditioning — some chosen, some circumstantial — that inform our identities and our values.

Exercise 1: Exploring the Contents of the Self Even as They Evolve

1. Settle into a sense of presence and stillness in your body, a sense of calm and ease in your mind. Evoke a sense of mindful empathy to create a state of awareness and acceptance of any contents of self, any pattern of conditioning, any facet of your personality that may emerge. For this exercise, you are focusing your awareness on aspects of your resilient self, but other aspects may come into consciousness as well.

2. Begin by recollecting moments when you experienced each

of the five Cs of coping, in turn. Start with calm: call to mind a moment when you remained calm in a crisis or were able to return to a state of calm after a crisis. Perhaps your building was burgled or your car was stolen. You were able to connect to your resources, see the situation clearly, feel competent in how you were handling things, and return to your window of tolerance fairly quickly. Savor this moment of calm: let yourself really feel it in your body for a minute or two.

3. Next, recollect a moment of clarity, when you saw clearly what was happening and what needed to happen next. This memory could be a recent one — from this morning or this past week — or it could be a memory from last year or in your early twenties or back in the third grade. Perhaps it was a moment when you saw a disaster coming — financial or relational — and were able to see right away what needed to be done to avert it. Again, light up the networks of this moment of clarity: let yourself savor it fully in your body for a minute or two.

4. Repeat this process with each of the remaining three Cs in turn. Recall a moment of being connected to resources — either people or other resources — and calling on people who knew better than you did how to handle a situation, such as dealing with a belligerent customer. Recall a moment of competence — the sense of "Sure I can!" or "Wow, I just did!" Maybe you drew on the skills you've cultivated for setting boundaries and negotiating change to handle the disruptive customer yourself. Recall a moment of courage facing a difficulty while remaining anchored in calm, clarity, connection, and competence. That might mean simply showing up day after day to do what needs to be done. You always have at least one memory of each of these capacities to draw on: it doesn't matter how small, only that it is genuine.

5. As you light up the network of each memory in turn, savor the sense of it in your body for a minute or two. For each of these memories of your resilient self, notice how the brain creates associations to additional memories on its own. You don't have to make those associations happen: in fact, you probably can't keep them from happening. These associations may give you even more information about yourself and how you cope.

6. If you wish, cycle through memories of your five Cs of coping a few more times. Notice how easily your brain can shift from the contents of one memory to the contents of another. Notice your awareness shifting from the contents of the self to the flow among those contents, which you experience as your "self." Notice how the sense of self evolves: it's fluid, not fixed. Notice how the sense of self emerges: it's multiple, not monolithic. You can ask certain aspects of the self to step into the background and other aspects, like your wiser self, to step forward. Notice your brain's neuroplasticity in action as you do this. You can choose how to focus your awareness; you can choose how to modify and shift your sense of self.

The Neuroscience of Exploring the Contents of the Self

The mature prefrontal cortex uses the focusing network of the brain to hold the sense of self together — the brain structures of "selfing." A stable, secure sense of self is essential to our well-being; a neural swamp is a flimsy basis for building resilience. But with the steady practice of mindfulness, we see that experiences of self may also be fluid. The self is an ever-changing flow of patterns, none of which are, or should be, fixed forever. (Neural cement is not a good platform for building resilience, either.) As the American architect, inventor, and futurist Buckminster Fuller said, "I seem to be a verb." That is a more accurate description of our "self."

Gaining Insights into the Self through Reverie

When we feel stable and secure enough in the flow of ourselves, we can safely relax the mind's grip on the self and shift into a mode of consciousness in which the sense of selfing temporarily dissolves. We do this fairly regularly in daydreams or in a reverie, where our awareness can just float. We similarly let go when we relax and fall asleep. The state of reverie arises from the brain's defocusing mode of processing. In this state, rather than being occupied with analysis and problem solving, the brain is free to meander and wander: to dream if we're asleep, to play if we're awake. The metaphorical, holistic right hemisphere of the brain in particular is free to find new associations between one idea and another, or one memory and another, to connect the dots in a new way. The state of reverie creates the conditions for new insights — "Aha!" moments — to pop up into consciousness out of the blue.

Exercise 2: Relaxing in a Reverie; Gaining Insights into the Self

1. Find a place where you can settle into a calm state of body and mind. Resting on the sofa is fine; a walk in the woods or along a beach works, too.

2. Allow your brain to let go of the constant constructing of your sense of self that we do through planning, remembering, worrying, and comparing. Let yourself relax into the awareness of simply being, into a sense of having nowhere to go, nothing to do, no one to be.

3. Allow yourself to stay absorbed in this reverie for anywhere from ten to thirty minutes.

4. When you feel stable in the defocusing mode of the reverie, you may choose to bring into this reverie a mishap in

coping, a moment of less-than-resilient response to a situation. Simply notice and name that moment, and then let it percolate in the reverie. Your brain is not solving problems, just playing.

5. With practice and growing trust in the process, you may suddenly gain a new insight into that mishap — a new angle, a new perspective, a new take. Notice both the content of this insight and the phenomenon of the epiphany itself. Notice the "truth sense" that accompanies it: "Oh, that's right!" or "Of course!" It's the intuitive rightness of the insight that lets us know an epiphany has occurred.

6. When you come out of your reverie, jot down some notes about it. Writing down the experience shifts the processing of the insight from the right hemisphere of the brain, where it was generated, to the left hemisphere, where it can be articulated in words, and helps integrate it into your circuitry.

As you relax into this state of reverie, you need not fear losing yourself completely. None of the hard work we've done to establish a resilient sense of self is ever lost. (Unfortunately, we can't so easily lose an unresilient sense of self, either.) If there's any sense of alarm, the brain will reconstitute your sense of self, resilient or unresilient, literally in a heartbeat. If your brain doesn't generate an epiphany during your first practice reverie, be patient. Cultivating a sense of openness, curiosity, and interest, without judgment, is helpful.

The Neuroscience of Relaxing into Reverie, Gaining Insights into the Self

Neuroscientists have discovered that even when the brain is not focusing on anything at all, neural activity does not cease. Neurons are still firing all over the brain in what is called a default network. The default mode of operation of our brain seems to be to search for something new to focus on, something to play with, something to make associations to. This is why daydreaming can be such a wellspring of creativity: the defocusing creates a mental play space where new ideas and associations can link up.

By defocusing, we deflect the attention of the left hemisphere of our brain from analysis of a problem and shift into the processing mode of the right hemisphere, which specializes in creating original associations, connecting the dots in new ways. This creates the conditions for a new insight to emerge in our awareness, for our own deep knowing to come to consciousness.

Through fMRI scanning, neuroscientists have discovered that the anterior superior temporal gyrus, a small fold of brain tissue located in the same part of the right hemisphere that connects the dots, is unusually active just seconds before an epiphany. It's possible that this activity is the neural correlate of insights occurring in the brain.

Dissolving the Self into the Nonself of Simply Being

We join spokes together in a wheel,
but it is the center hole
that makes the wagon move.

We shape clay into a pot,
but it is the emptiness inside
that holds whatever we want.

We hammer wood for a house,
but it is the inner space
that makes it livable.

We work with being,
but nonbeing is what we use.

— LAO-TZU
Translation by Stephen Mitchell

Exercise 1 involves using our awareness to explore the contents of the personal self and how those contents can come and go, shift and evolve. Exercise 2 offers practice in coming into a state of reverie that creates a mental play space where we can "dissolve" the grip of our conditioned patterns and generate new insights into the self. The exercise below offers a technique for shifting into the defocusing mode of consciousness again, to allow our awareness to expand further, free of the limitations of any conditioning, into an experience of the unconditioned. In this state, a sense of nonself or simply being can arise. This vast, unconditioned consciousness is not a philosophical concept but an embodied experience. In the steady experience of spaciousness or formlessness, we experience the plane of open possibilities. Nothing is formed; anything can be imagined; anything can happen. The experience of nonself or simply being can catalyze powerful epiphanies about the true nature of the self. It can also generate a frequency of brain waves that can help integrate the entire brain and lead to more resilient functioning.

By focusing our awareness on awareness, we are giving the brain something to do as we gently encourage it to do less and less. As awareness approaches nondoing, only being, the mind can come to rest in unconditioned awareness, with only awareness happening. Focusing attention on breathing in this exercise gives the brain an anchor in reality, even as everything else disappears. There is only being, and our awareness of being.

A note of caution: Using the process of deconditioning to dissolve the self into the realm of the unconditioned involves repeated deconsolidation and reconsolidation on a large scale. As in other exercises that use these processes, it is important to create a safe context for them. In this exercise, we first come to an awareness of our internal secure base (see chapter 8). From this inner base of resilience and security, letting go of the carefully constructed, hard-won personal self doesn't drop us into an existential void but leads us into wholeness.

A second note of caution: The defocusing network involved in this large-scale deconditioning tends to be more active in the right hemisphere of the brain than the left. It's important to pay attention to your experience to avoid being overwhelmed by the negativity bias of the right hemisphere.

If you do experience a sense of being dropped into a void or black hole, bring your awareness back to connecting with a true other or your true self, with your wiser self, or with your own innate goodness. Shift your attention to what is stable and supportive to bring you back into your window of tolerance; draw upon your refuges and resources, as described in chapter 5. When you feel stable in your awareness of your experience in the present moment, and reassured and comfortable, it's safe to resume the practice.

Exercise 3: Dropping into the Unconditioned: Dissolving the Self into the Nonself

1. Sit comfortably. Allow your eyes to gently close. Focus your awareness on your breathing, gently in and out. As you follow your breathing, notice your own awareness of your breathing, the awareness that allows you to know that you are breathing.

2. When that awareness of your breathing is steady, begin to notice the breathing of any people around you, or people you imagine being around you. There's no need to do anything; just notice or imagine other people breathing as you are breathing, and notice your awareness of that. Notice what you are aware of in your own being as you rest in this awareness.

3. Staying anchored in an awareness of your own breathing, expand your awareness of breathing to include the breathing of more people you know, who are not necessarily physically near you. Notice your awareness of your awareness of everyone breathing. Notice your awareness of your own being as you remain aware.

4. Still anchored in an awareness of your own breathing, expand your awareness further to include people you don't know, outside the building you are in, perhaps elsewhere in the neighborhood, throughout the city, across the region. Become aware of all of them breathing together. Notice your awareness of your awareness: you are simply being, being aware.

5. Continue to expand your awareness to include people all over the country, all over the planet, all breathing. Expand your awareness to include all living creatures breathing in the parks, the forests, underground, in the lakes and rivers, in the oceans, the sky, of all sentient beings breathing together. Notice your awareness of your awareness of existence, and your awareness of simply being.

6. Expand your awareness to include all forms of existence, some breathing, some not — the air, the water, the rocks. And notice your awareness of your awareness of the breathing, and your awareness of simply being.

7. Expand your awareness beyond our planet to other planets, other stars, other galaxies, and the space between the planets and stars and galaxies. Expand your awareness as far as you can possibly imagine; notice your awareness of your awareness expanding. Rest comfortably, safely, in this vast spacious awareness, in this vast simply being, for as long as you choose. Take your time.

8. Gently bring your awareness back to your awareness of sitting in the room you are in, in this moment, breathing. Focus your awareness on simply breathing. Take a moment to shift gears and reflect more fully on your experience of simply being. You may experience a lightness, a spaciousness, or an openness in your being.

This is the spaciousness where new insights can occur spontane-ously. Even if they don't occur right away, this vast, open aware-ness of the unconditioned creates the conditions for revelation. We can reliably access this defocused, diffuse mode of conscious-ness through awareness practice. We can also refocus our attention on our immediate situation in an instant. On the human plane, it's essential to be able to do that. As the spiritual teacher Ram Dass cautioned, even in a bliss state, it's important not to forget your ZIP code.

The Neuroscience of Dissolving the Self into the Nonself

Scans of the brain waves of meditators adept at achieving states of transcendental awareness, such as the awareness of awareness that is possible to achieve in the exercise above, reveal a dramatic increase in gamma waves in their brains as they meditate. This is the high-est brain-wave frequency, indicating high levels of concentration, a unity of consciousness, even bliss. Other researchers have observed a measurable spike in gamma waves just milliseconds before an insight breaks through into consciousness. When we concentrate our awareness on awareness, we are actually creating the conditions in the brain for revelation.

Reflections on Experiencing the Unconditioned

I am larger and better than I thought.
I did not think I held so much goodness.

— WALT WHITMAN

Neuroscientists have not yet fully mapped the brain activity that occurs in the silence and stillness of unconditioned awareness, but consciousness researchers report with consistency and accuracy the phenomenon of epiphanies, or insights into the deep meaning and nature of reality. Epiphanies carry with them the profound "truth sense" that Isaac Newton experienced when the bonk on the head by an apple led to his sudden understanding of the force of gravity, or the certainty that led the Greek mathematician Archimedes to leap from his bathtub to run through the streets of Athens crying, "Eureka!" (I've found it!) when he suddenly understood the physics of volume and displacement.

Epiphanies vary from person to person and from tradition to tradition. They are often characterized by a sense of awe or mystery that has been referred to by many different names in many traditions over the ages: a perception of essence, spirit, the divine, the sacred. People often describe feeling a profound sense of benevolence, or loving presence, a feeling of the self being at one with all of existence, similar to the sensation Edgar Mitchell experienced on his return trip from the moon. Of particular value for building resilience is a deeply felt realization of the innate goodness of our own true nature.

This sense of innate goodness is validated by 2,500 years of training and practice in the Buddhist wisdom tradition. There is a sense of coming home to the true nature of our being, a sense of abundant enough-ness, a profound sense of well-being — the spiritual platform of resilience. We don't have to seek this sense of innate goodness: it comes when the mind and brain are quiet, when everything else falls away. This experience carries with it the truth sense of an epiphany. We know it to be true in the heart, in the gut, at the cellular level. It becomes a powerful resource for rewiring any conditioned patterns, including less-than-resilient patterns of coping.

If we try to skip this stage of awakening to and aligning with true nature as our true home, if we bypass simply being and escape into doing, we lose the freedom that this mental, emotional, and relational play space offers us to create something entirely new. We miss out on a huge opportunity to wake up and grow up; it's all too easy to repeat the conditioned patterns we have learned before.

Integrating the Self and Nonself

There is a natural and inviolable tendency
in things to bloom into whatever they truly are
in the core of their being.
All we have to do is align ourselves with
what wants to happen naturally and put in the
effort that is our part in helping it happen.

— DAVID RICHO

Steadily experiencing the unconditioned, abiding in the spacious formlessness of the unconditioned, could bring a person very close to a state of ultimate enlightenment if one persevered in the practice.

Here on the human plane, the brain's capacity to access the defocused state of mindful presence, get the big picture, be open to and comfortable with the unknown and the uncertain, and then shift between defocused and focused processing allows us to radically rewire patterns of self. This change can be described as a quantum shift in our understanding of self. It creates deeper integration in the brain: our mental activity becomes less scattered, less fragmented, more interconnected and whole. As we alternate between a very coherent, individual self and a self dissolved into the oneness of existence, we come to a deeper knowing of our own true nature as a unique individual expression of the universal energy that sustains all of existence. From this integration and alignment with our true nature we gain more mental capacity to handle the vicissitudes of life, to solve problems without hesitation or floundering, to be creative and innovative, to come to terms with a situation that may seem unresolvable. Our consciousness has opened up. We create a resilient connection with life in general, facing it with awareness, acceptance, and emergent wisdom.

Exercise 4: Integrating the Self and Nonself

When the extraordinary consciousness of the true nature of your unconditioned nonself is strong enough, you can use it to reconsolidate the ordinary consciousness of your conditioned personal self, rewiring many old, conditioned stories and beliefs about yourself. Who you understand yourself to be and how you respond to life's events are now informed and guided by this deep knowing. In this exercise, this expanded consciousness becomes a tool you use to transform your sense of self.

1. Evoke the awareness of awareness you experienced in exercise 3. Try to evoke the sense of the true nature of your being that you might have experienced through that exercise as well. If this seems too much of a stretch at first, simply evoke your sense of your wiser self, your personal manifestation of this true nature.

2. Bring to mind a pattern, a belief, an identity of your personal self that you might like to rewire: an old sense of inadequacy, a lack of trust in your competence or creative potential. Light up the networks of this pattern by evoking all the layers of neural firing associated with it: body sensations, feelings, thoughts about yourself.

3. Try to bring this sense of your personal self into the spacious awareness of awareness, or into the sense of wellbeing or wholeness of your true nature. If that's too much of a stretch, begin by alternating between these two modes of consciousness, always strengthening or refreshing the sense of awareness of true nature. When the sense of true nature seems stronger, let go of the sense of personal self and rest in your awareness of your true nature.

4. After a moment, reevoke the pattern or sense of personal self you were attempting to rewire. Notice any changes in that sense of personal self now that it is held, informed, and guided by your true nature.

My mentor Diana Fosha reminds us: "People have a fundamental need for transformation. We are wired for growth and healing, and we're wired for self-righting and resuming impeded growth. We have a need for the expansion and liberation of the self, the letting down of defensive barriers, and the dismantling of the false self. [We stretch] toward maximal vitality, authenticity, and genuine contact. In the process of radical change we become more ourselves than ever before, and recognize ourselves to be so."

Exercise 5: Experiencing the Whole Self

We can now use the integrative capacities of the prefrontal cortex to help us experience our whole self. The following exercise involves recognizing the multiple, complex layers of self we want our prefrontal cortex to integrate. Sometimes I imagine these layers of self nesting inside one another like the Russian wooden dolls my grandmother kept on the mantelpiece.

1. Go through the list of layers of self below. For each one, remember a moment or incident that exemplifies it. (Your example of the last layer, the unconditioned, may come from exercise 3 above.)

2. Allow your awareness to flow among all five layers of self. All of these layers make up your whole self and define who you are at any given moment, whether or not you are always fully conscious of them.

   (a) *Inner child.* This is the realm of early implicit and explicit patterns of coping that become encoded as parts, facets, aspects, and states of ourselves. Some of these we admire and are proud of; some we don't like and may even loathe; some we may be too ashamed of to identify with; some, whether they were resilient or not, may have become lost or forgotten.

   (b) *Adult.* This is our grown-up personal self, doing the

best it can to navigate the world with what it has learned about how the world works, how people work, and who the self is. The adult self is the personal self that chooses how to use the strengthened prefrontal cortex to rewire the patterns of the inner child; the stable yet flexible personal self that harnesses the neuroplasticity of the brain to experience, embody, and express the five Cs of coping; and the ever-evolving self that calls on the resources of the wiser self to inform and guide its actions.

(c) *Wiser self.* This is the imagined resource of our strongest, most loving, most compassionate, most generous, most resilient self, our own personal flavor of the innate goodness and well-being of universal true nature. It is the part of us that has kept persevering in our intentions and our choices to recover resilience. It guides the choices of the adult self with wise, intuitive knowing. When we align the adult self with the qualities and virtues of our wiser self, our capacities for resilience are infused with greater energy. The adult self becomes more confident about its capacities to cope.

(d) *True nature.* This is the realm of the sacred into which we dissolve the adult self. We experience universal qualities such as kindness, gratitude, joy, generosity, and equanimity as our true home. Our true nature is the reservoir of universal goodness and well-being expressed by the wiser self, and the gateway to the larger awareness that holds all the nouns and verbs of existence. Aligning our adult self with our true nature anchors all of our resilience in integrity and courage and gives us a moral compass to guide our course of action.

(e) *The unconditioned.* This is the vast spaciousness of awareness itself, the nothingness that all things arise from and pass away into. It is the realm of the mental play space we access through deconditioning, where there's space and flow for new choices to emerge.

When we begin to skillfully flow among these five layers of self, we are free, not caught in a particular role or identity or in the patterns of response encoded at five years of age, or twelve, or twenty-seven. The flexibility of navigating these layers of self sustains flexibility in our coping. At any given moment, we can recognize which layer we are inhabiting; we can choose where we want to focus; we can change our response to life events.

The Neuroscience of Integrating the Self and Nonself

The brain operates differently with focused attention than with open, spacious awareness. The tasks are different and the outcomes are different; we carefully cultivate and integrate both to maximize our resilience. So far, neuroimaging has shown that focused attention most fully activates the ventral medial (forward and central) part of the cortex. (The prefrontal cortex is located in this region.) This is the part of the brain that constructs and holds the sense of self together. Through neuronal pathways connecting to the motor cortex of the brain, it also sends signals to take action.

When we allow our awareness to relax or dissolve into a more spacious, bare awareness, by contrast, we activate the dorsal lateral part of the cortex (toward the rear and both sides). With this increased neural receptivity, the brain can create new associations more readily. The brain organically rewires and reorganizes itself.

We have been reconditioning patterns of response in the brain, or conditioning new patterns, through the focused (self) mode of processing; we have approached the experience of the unconditioned or nonself through the defocused mode of processing and deconditioning. We can switch between these two networks of processing and two modes of consciousness. As we become more grounded, more centered in the unconditioned true nature of who we are, we can learn to return to this state of awareness whenever we lose our way, when we become hijacked by an unresolved trauma or befuddled by the new territory we're moving into. The more familiar we become with this sense of loving presence as our true home, the sooner we can notice when we're off course and bring ourselves back. Eventually we become so attuned to the state of our inner state that we can do this in the space of a breath.

Deeper Brain Integration

When we integrate the patterns of neural firing we use in the focusing network with the patterns of neural firing we experience in the defocusing network, we set in motion a radical process of transformation within the brain.

Using the defocusing network to access the unconditioned helps the brain fire at its highest frequency of brain waves — gamma waves. Gamma waves are produced when many parts of the brain are firing rapidly and in synchrony. This activity creates new, complex neural networks and greater neural harmony in the brain.

We have learned to use tools to harness the brain's neuroplasticity to strengthen the prefrontal cortex to manage our emotions and calm our nervous system when we're startled or frightened, quelling the fear response of the amygdala; to tune into the inner experience of others and ourselves; to see clearly our reactions to any experience, internal or external; to generate options of response; and to choose wisely and flexibly among them. Through this learning process, the brain productively rewires old, conditioned patterns of response to stress and trauma. New experiences in relationships, in our body, in our emotions, and in our thoughts and perceptions can increase the flexibility of our responses to stressors and traumas. As we rewire old patterns, those patterns become more adaptive and resilient; therefore, we experience greater health and well-being.

This neural harmony supports increased integration by the prefrontal cortex at all levels of the brain. The prefrontal cortex integrates our bodily sensations and emotions with our thoughts, reflections, and conscious decisions about them; it also integrates the right hemisphere's felt sense of our emotions with the left hemisphere's rational assessment of them. It integrates our conscious and unconscious memories; it integrates various ego states or parts of the personal self to create a coherent narrative of the self that supports our resilience.

What Deeper Brain Integration Makes Possible

Mastering the art of resilience does much more than
restore you to who you once thought you were.
Rather, you emerge from the experience transformed
into a truer expression of who you were really meant to be.

— CAROL ORSBORN

As we learn to navigate between the spaciousness of simply being (nothing to do, nowhere to go, no one to be) and our sense of self (I have things to do! I'm expected to show up and be responsible! I am somebody!), we continue to let go of habitual patterns of coping that simply don't work well, and we intentionally practice skills that will help us create the life we want for ourselves and our loved ones, with many, many repetitions so that they do actually create new brain circuitry. As we continue to rewire internally, we can generate more authentic, creative, wholesome options for ourselves and develop the internal integrity and alignment that will help us realize our dreams.

Pulling It All Together

Learning to work skillfully with the brain's defocusing mode allows you to:

- experience the awareness that holds all the constructs of the self as stable and coherent, yet ever changing and ever evolving;
- create the conditions of reverie — the mental play space of deconditioning — and an expanded awareness in which epiphanies, insights, and revelations can occur;

- use that expanded awareness to enter a mental "plane of open possibilities" where you can more easily experience the phenomenon known as nonself — the unconditioned nature of reality prior to any conditioning;
- recognize this state of simply being as your true home;
- integrate the experiences of nonself or true nature into a sense of whole self, experiencing a flow among the inner child, the adult self, the wiser self, your true nature, and unconditioned awareness. This integration can create greater neural integration, harmony, and synchrony within the brain itself, strengthening the resilience you need to handle all the vicissitudes of life.

Take a deep breath and acknowledge to yourself how much good work you've done to recover your birthright capacities of resilience and well-being. Completing the experiential exercises in parts 3–7 helps you develop a brain better prepared to respond well to life's ongoing stressors. These practices can help you rewire a variety of old, conditioned responses to trouble and trauma and strengthen your prefrontal cortex. They can help you boost your relational, somatic, emotional, and reflective intelligence and recover the innate capacities of your brain to respond skillfully and adaptively to life's storms and struggles. You can now reliably experience more calm, more clarity, stronger connections to resources, increased competence, and greater courage, all of which will allow you to cope with anything, anything at all.

PART EIGHT

LAUNCHING INTO A
MORE RESILIENT LIFE

CHAPTER TWENTY

Moving Resilience beyond the Personal Self

A ship is safe in harbor, but that's not what ships are for.

— GRACE HOPPER

HAVE WE ARRIVED? In a way, yes. The wise effort we have already put into using self-directed neuroplasticity to rewire our brains, and the more complex neural integration that results from that effort, has set us up for the continued learning, growth, and transformation that are fulfilling in themselves as well as beneficial for our resilience. The neural platform of resilience gives the psyche a kind of safety net: the brain is now rewired and primed to meet the unpredictable but inevitable challenges of life adaptively, with courage, optimism, and creativity.

Even when difficulties threaten to overwhelm our expanded capacities to cope, the brain itself is more resilient and better prepared to meet them. More complex integration of brain circuits and structures means more channels of communication within the brain, more synchrony in neural firing patterns, and calmer frequencies of brain waves. There's more give and flex in the entire body and mind system.

Thus prepared, we can be realistically optimistic. We will always face uncertainties and unknowns, and sometimes we will encounter true catastrophes. But as we become more skillful in facing them, our resilience becomes more effortless.

Jon Kabat-Zinn, developer of mindfulness-based stress reduction, describes our strengthened capacities for resilience this way: "We all accept that no one controls the weather. Good sailors learn to read it carefully and respect its power. They will avoid storms if possible, but when caught in one, they know when to take down the sails, batten down the hatches, drop anchor and ride things out, controlling what is controllable and letting go of the rest. Training, practice, and a lot of firsthand experience in all sorts of weather are required to develop such skills so that they work for you when you need them. Developing skill in facing and effectively handling the various 'weather conditions' in your life is what we mean by the art of conscious living."

This conscious, resilient living requires that we continue learning from experience, keep experimenting. The "use it or lose it" principle applies to our brains, especially our prefrontal cortex, as well as our muscles: we need to work on maintaining the brain cells, neural circuits, and capacities to respond flexibly in our brains throughout our lives. We also have to keep challenging our brains by taking on new and difficult tasks that draw on and extend all our capacities for learning. Challenges such as learning to play a musical instrument, learning to speak a foreign language, and memorizing poetry are often recommended by brain-fitness experts because they require the integration of functions in both hemispheres of the higher brain. Problem solving, which requires input from our intuitive, holistic right hemisphere as well as from our rational, analytical left hemisphere, is another excellent way to push the brain to maintain its capacities of resilience.

Years ago my friend Ted worked as an electrical engineer at SRI International (Stanford Research Institute International), a large engineering consulting firm. A plaque at the entrance to the electrical engineering lab read:

We have not solved your problems.
In fact, we have more questions than when we started.
But we believe we are confused at a higher level
and about more important things.

Recovering resilience can feel a bit like that. We set our intentions, draw on our resources, learn the tools and techniques, and then wonder why this is taking so long. Am I doing it right? Would something else work better? Rest assured, the tools and techniques presented here are exactly the tools you need to keep rewiring your brain for resilience. Developing and maintaining resilience requires that we continue to cultivate qualities and behaviors that support it. We can choose to make resilience a central organizing principle of our lives — not just an interesting hobby or occasional lifesaver, but the core that everything else aligns around, that increases our happiness and well-being.

Learning Model for Resilience

The following model is taught all over the world to cultivate qualities and behaviors that particularly support resilience. In this model, we move through four phases of competence and awareness of that competence, from a complete lack of the competence or even knowledge of our need for it to full knowledge and mastery of it.

1. *Unconscious incompetence.* We don't know how to do something, and we don't even know that we don't know. We're innocent or clueless; the brain is in homeostatis. This was the situation for my client Karen (see chapter 17) when she initially failed to grasp that a young woman and child playing together could be mother and daughter. This is the "ignorance is bliss" phase of learning — except, of course, when it isn't.
2. *Conscious incompetence.* This is an "Oh shit!" circuit. We

don't know how to do something, and we suddenly realize we don't know. Becoming aware of this may cause chagrin and horror, as it did for Karen. If ever our resilience is going to derail, it's right here. Old patterns of fear of failure, passivity, or shame may resurface. We can get past any denial or blocks to learning by reframing this step as the beginning of gaining competence, as Karen did. When we harness the innate drive for mastery — to recover any missing competencies and to learn new skills — we can be proud of taking steps to recover our resilience.

3. *Conscious competence.* This is the phase in which we know how to do something, and we know that we know. Through all of our new experiences, resources, tools, and techniques, we are learning. New patterns of response are being rewired in the brain. We are becoming masterful and competent. We spend a lot of our adult lives in this phase, of course. We are confident that we know, in spite of old, negative stories about ourselves that might linger. We don't go back to the old stories; we persevere in the new, taking in the good as Karen did with her comment, "Now I know I can be playful... I guess somehow it's sunk in." We are deepening and solidifying the circuits of the competency and of learning.

4. *Unconscious competence.* Once we know how to do something well and practice doing it again and again, the new skill becomes wired into our implicit procedural memory. Our wise effort becomes increasingly effortless. It's like learning to ride a bicycle: we don't even have to think about it anymore. Once playing with kids became second nature, Karen could let go of her worries about motherhood once and for all.

Exercise 1: Learning Resilience

1. Identify one attribute of resilience you would like to cultivate or a behavior that your resilience is now strong enough

to support your growing into: assertiveness, determination, purposefulness, collaboration. Assertiveness is used as an example here, but you can focus on any attribute of your choice.

2. Identify areas of your life where assertiveness seems to be lacking; maybe it hasn't even occurred to you that being assertive in these areas would be useful. They could include negotiating with your spouse over household chores; talking to the bank manager about financing a car purchase; persuading the city council to install a needed stop sign in your neighborhood; or writing to your congressional representative about health-care reform.

3. Identify moments in your life when you could and should have been assertive but had no clue how to do that. Maybe you still don't. Hang in there: don't retreat or procrastinate. Now is the moment to set the intentions to master this useful life skill. Set the intention to learn assertiveness by practicing and experimenting with it. Set a second intention to see yourself, and feel proud of yourself, as someone who intentionally cultivates capacities of resilience.

4. Whatever means you use to develop your assertiveness — attending workshops, practicing with friends, putting it to use in real-life situations — notice your skills steadily developing. The awareness of competence is essential to wiring that knowledge of your assertiveness into your sense of yourself.

5. Recall a moment when you realize you were assertive, this morning or last week. Take in the fact that you exercised that skill without even thinking about it. Congratulations. You've mastered another competency supporting your resilience.

You can repeat this exercise as many times as you wish, with as many qualities you wish to cultivate for more resilience. You are learning from experience rather than concepts, from experiments rather than instructions. That's what keeps rewiring the brain in the most integrated and resilient fashion, lifelong.

What Resilient Learning from Experience Opens Up

As an irrigator guides water to his fields,
as an archer aims an arrow, as a carpenter
carves wood, the wise shape their lives.

— BUDDHA

Shaping our brains to be increasingly resilient and, beyond that, shaping our lives to be increasingly fulfilled and meaningful can take people in many different directions. Whatever direction we choose, we rely on the skillful use of our prefrontal cortex — and the brain integration it makes possible — to seek, discern, and settle into what gives meaning and purpose to our lives, to move beyond coping and surviving to creating change and thriving.

Big Organizing Principles (BOPs)

How we live our days is, of course, how we live our lives.

— ANNIE DILLARD

We've learned that one capacity of the prefrontal cortex is to create a coherent narrative of our sense of self. Another way of describing that coherence is to say that we come to see clearly the big organizing principles (BOPs) that guide our actions: the wholesome patterns of coping we choose to live by, or what philosophical traditions call values and virtues. Among my clients, Betty, a single mother of three, identified her BOPs as patience, faith, and planning. Neil, a retired surgeon, chose curiosity, gratitude, and awe. David, a car mechanic learning computer skills at the local community college, steered his course by hope, steadiness of purpose, and the love of his family.

Exercise 2: Identifying Your BOPs

1. Identify three principles from this list that resonate with you as BOPs.

accountability	focus	kindness	patience
commitment	forgiveness	knowledge	prudence
cooperation	frugality	love	purposefulness
courtesy	helpfulness	loyalty	reliability
creativity	honesty	magnanimity	resourcefulness
dependability	humility	mercy	respect
determination	idealism	modesty	reverence
discipline	industriousness	obedience	simplicity
faithfulness	joyfulness	orderliness	tolerance

2. Identify three arenas where you are able to manifest these BOPs (or others that you choose) regularly: For example, helping kids with homework calls for patience; working with customers takes courtesy; volunteering at the homeless shelter once a week calls on your selflessness. Acknowledge your conscious competence or even your unconscious competence in applying these principles.

3. Identify one more BOP from the list, or another quality from your own list of values, that you would like to cultivate and that would be a stretch for you to cultivate. Set the intention to look for opportunities to manifest this BOP every day for the next month.

4. As you manifest this BOP more in your daily life, notice how your view of yourself as an agent of change in your own life develops as you wisely shape your life and become competent.

Finding Keys for Cracking the Code of Life

All truly wise thoughts have been thought already
thousands of times; but to make them truly
ours, we must think them over again honestly,
until they take root in our personal experience.

— JOHANN WOLFGANG VON GOETHE

We can find guidance about which BOPs lead to the deepest happiness and meaning for each of us, the greatest sense of fulfillment and well-being, through many different models and paradigms. These are systems that help us crack the code of life, showing us how to move through suffering and struggle to strength and well-being.

One such paradigm is the eightfold path of the Buddhist tradition, which influences many of the practical tools and techniques offered here. Understanding what causes suffering and what leads to the end of suffering leads to wise intention (one of the practices that accelerates the rewiring of the brain), which leads to wise mindfulness (seeing clearly, always with empathy and compassion rather than judgment) and wise concentration (steadiness of mind, steadiness of purpose, perseverance). These practices in turn lead to wise effort (letting go of the unwholesome, cultivating the wholesome, deconditioning and reconditioning coping strategies that don't work, conditioning new strategies that do) in learning practices that lead to wise action, wise speech, and wise livelihood — the ways we engage and thrive in the world. Sylvia Boorstein adds wise relationships as a ninth step on this path — her deep wisdom reverently reshaping an ancient and revered path of practice.

In addition to the Buddhist model, many other models can help us find our moral compass: other spiritual traditions, modalities of therapy and personal growth, philosophies of politics and business, customs of culture. It matters that we find a set of values or principles to live by so that we don't drift, get lost, or sink. It matters that we settle ourselves into living those values and principles, experimenting to see how they really work and how they might need to evolve.

Exercise 3: Finding Keys for Cracking the Code

Finding your key for cracking the code, or finding an organized system of BOPs to live your life by, is similar to finding a path of practice (see chapter 5).

1. Identify the core values you already live by and seek out role models or paradigms of practice that can lead beyond them to something even more truthful and useful.
2. Ask friends, colleagues, and mentors whose lives exemplify the qualities you would like to cultivate more in your life what paths and practices they follow and how you might experience them for yourself.
3. Approach any model with a sense of openness and curiosity. Apply the teachings to the needs and circumstances of your life with a sense of exploration and excitement. See what works, what fits, and leave the rest. You can choose for yourself whether to follow the entire model to the last dotted *i* and crossed *t* of its teachings.

Here's the way I remember a lovely Aesop's fable from my childhood that illustrates this practice of applying what's useful from a model to your own life. A magpie announces that she is giving a free seminar on nest building to all the birds of the forest. So the birds gather. The magpie lays a bowl of twigs on a branch in a tree, and the oriole says, "Oh! That's how nests are built!" and goes off. That's how orioles have been building their nests ever since. The magpie then daubs the bowl of twigs with some mud to seal the cracks, and the jay says, "Oh! That's how nests are built!" and flies off, and that's how jays have been building their nests ever since. The magpie then lines the caulked bowl of twigs with some soft downy feathers, and the robin says, "Oh! That's how to build a nest!" And that's how robins have been building their nests ever since. The magpie continues teaching throughout the day, and various birds continue to fly off until the end of the day, when the only birds left to learn how the magpie is building a nest are the other magpies.

I used to think the moral of that fable was that if you didn't stay until the very end, you wouldn't learn everything there was to learn about building a nest, and that would be a failure. But now I think it shows that every single species of bird did learn how to build a nest, and what they learned was good enough for them to survive and thrive as a species. You decide when you've learned what you need to from a model or paradigm, when it's enough to help you to survive and thrive as the unique individual that you are.

The crafting of a resilient and meaningful life doesn't stop with crafting "more" for the personal self. Researchers have found that practices that move the concerns of our resilience beyond our personal self immeasurably enrich our own lives and the lives of others when we maintain our intention to practice them.

Altruism

In every community there is work to be done.
In every nation, there are wounds to heal.
In every heart, there is the power to do it.

— MARIANNE WILLIAMSON

Patti Quigley and Susan Retik were "ordinary" suburban Boston housewives, both pregnant, when their husbands were killed on the planes that were flown into the World Trade Center on September 11, 2001. In interviews, both Patti and Susan stressed how important it was to them to respond to the tragedy of 9/11 and their husbands' deaths "out of love rather than hate." They channeled their anguish into a three-day fund-raising bike ride from Ground Zero in Manhattan to Boston, raising $140,000, which was distributed to economic development projects to benefit Afghani women through Care International: women widowed by decades of conflict in Afghanistan, from the Russian invasion through the Taliban occupation to the American military presence. Three years after

9/11, Patty and Susan traveled to Afghanistan to meet with some of the women who had used these funds to start their own businesses. This personal statement of international reconciliation continues to ripple outward still.

Altruism — an unselfish concern for the welfare of others — is one of those qualities that we can express when we feel resilient. A natural outcome of mindful empathy, altruism is also fueled by the release of oxytocin. When we feel the plight of another through our resonance circuit and are moved to act, our behavior is partly motivated by the "tend and befriend" function of oxytocin. And when we have come into earned secure attachment, we can maintain a balanced focus on self, other, and the world. Moving flexibly between independence and interdependence, between autonomy and affiliation, allows us to act generously and compassionately in this world.

We can find inspiring examples of altruistic behaviors through books, magazines, film and television, the Internet, and the stories we pass on to each other: American schoolchildren who contribute pennies to buy paper and pencils for schoolchildren in rural India; a Canadian teenager who researched the effect of unclean water on health for a school science project and then spent three years raising money to build 272 wells in rural Africa; high school students in America who ran half marathons to raise funds to build a girls' high school in Nicaragua; a church group from England that spends one week every spring rebuilding homes around the world destroyed by hurricanes, earthquakes, and tornadoes.

My grandmother became blind from glaucoma when I was two years old. I grew up learning to "read" Braille with my eyes as my grandmother and I sat on the living-room couch and she read the pages with her fingers. I learned to set aside the sharp knives as we did the dishes together and learned how she kept bills of different denominations in separate compartments in her wallet so that she could know how much money she was handing to the store clerk.

After my grandmother died, I found a way to contribute to the restoration of people's vision that has brought me deep satisfaction for more than thirty years. I save all my receipts from dining out during the year, and at the end of the year I contribute the same total amount to Seva, a nonprofit organization that trains doctors in developing countries to perform cataract surgery, saving the eyesight of more than 3 million poor people to date. Could I do more? Probably. And sometimes I do. But this steady practice is one of the ways altruism has become one of the big organizing principles of my life.

Exercise 4: Practicing Altruism

1. Take five minutes to identify an opportunity for your resilience to move beyond your personal self in an act of generosity or altruism: participating in an environmental cleanup day at a local park; becoming a counselor at a summer camp for children with life-threatening illnesses; tutoring in an adult literacy program.

2. Notice any changes in your experience of yourself as you decide which action to take, prepare to do it, and implement your plan. Notice changes as you take in the feeling of your own generosity, simply knowing that you acted out of compassionate caring, whether or not you learn of the outcome of your efforts. Notice how you feel if you learn of the ripple effects of your action from someone's email or card. Let the experience of altruism broaden and build your resources of resilience.

Compassionate Action: Becoming an Agent of Change

I long to accomplish great and noble tasks, but it is my chief duty to accomplish humble tasks as though they were great and noble. The world is moved along, not only by the mighty shoves of its heroes, but also by the aggregate of the tiny pushes of each honest worker.

— HELEN KELLER

Our mature resilience — the ability to courageously meet challenges and solve problems as they arise — supports us in taking compassionate action in the world. We become agents of change who evoke changes in others. Our resilience fuels the generativity that can change the world. And we change the world one person, one program, one committed action at a time.

One colleague, after coming to terms with her own grief at being diagnosed with bipolar disorder, found a way to apply her research skills to improve services at the mood disorders clinic of the local medical school. Another colleague, the mother of a son with autism, offered free weekend workshops every month for a year to other parents of children with autism, sharing what she had learned about coping lovingly and skillfully with her own child and about reducing her burnout through self-compassion and self-care. The son of yet another colleague chose to celebrate his thirty-fifth birthday by recruiting his buddies to spend one exhausting but exhilarating weekend building a home in a neighboring county for a family of five displaced by a recent flood. But it's also possible to share compassion and effect change in small ways.

Exercise 5: Becoming an Agent of Change

1. Take a moment to identify a cause or purpose that stirs your sense of caring and your willingness to act: protecting the environment, volunteering in an after-school art program.
2. Either in a moment of reverie on your own or brainstorming with friends, begin to imagine ways in which you can create change in the world through your own resilient efforts. In the coming weeks and months, find a way to express that intention as a part of your resilient growth, and treasure your growth and fulfillment as you do.

Pulling It All Together

Resilience is your birthright. Throughout *Bouncing Back* you have learned to use tools and techniques that enable you to:

- improve the moment-to-moment functioning of your brain;
- use three proven processes of self-directed neuroplasticity to change old patterns of coping and create new, more resilient ones;
- create the conditions, resources, and practices that help you rewire your neural circuitry most reliably and most safely;
- choose the new experiences — in interactions with other people, in reflections and imagination, in simply being — that rewire your neural circuitry most efficiently and effectively;
- develop confidence in your own competence to return to calm in a crisis, to see clearly what needs to happen to resolve the crisis or to come to terms with it, and to connect to the resources that give you the courage to carry on.

You'll notice your strengthened capacities to bounce back operating everywhere as you adjust to challenging situations, make tough decisions, and embark on new adventures. To bring all of these teachings back down to earth as you continue to maximize your resilience and well-being, here's a final teaching, from the cartoon beagle Snoopy. It is printed on a flag that hangs in my garden — a gift from my brother, Barry, who practiced gratitude with me while he was in the hospital:

Live well, laugh often, love much.

ACKNOWLEDGMENTS

I BEGAN WRITING A DECADE AGO, to reconcile the paradox I was living at the time of simultaneously strengthening the self in my role as a licensed psychotherapist and letting go of the self as a dedicated practitioner of *vipassana*, or insight meditation. Neuroscience helped me build the bridge between Buddhist mindfulness practice and Western relational psychology.

I have been blessed to be guided by many skillful mentors and teachers, people whose brains I've been privileged to interact with along the unfolding path, wise elders who taught me how to rewire my brain for resilience and well-being, who profoundly shaped and guided my thinking, and who themselves embody aliveness and wholeness: Bonnie Badenoch, James Baraz, Sylvia Boorstein, Tara Brach, Lou Cozolino, Janina Fisher, Diana Fosha, Ron Frederick, Christopher Germer, Daniel Goleman, Rick Hanson, Sue Johnson, Jon Kabat-Zinn, Dacher Keltner, Jack Kornfield, Jonah Lehrer, Ben Lipton, Marsha Lucas, Kristin Neff, John O'Donohue, Pat Ogden, Mary Oliver, David Richo, Candyce Ossefort-Russell, Frank Ostaseski, Stephen Porges, Kim Rosen, Richard Schwartz, Dan Siegel, Ron Siegel, Rich Simon, David Wallin, David Whyte, Danny Yeung.

I've learned lessons of resilience — showing up and saying yes to life in the face of adversity — from many patients, students, workshop participants, interns, and readers of the monthly e-newsletter *Healing and Awakening into Aliveness and Wholeness*. Although they are not named here, their contributions to the transformations in my own thinking and being have been profound. I deeply bow.

There are those who, in their own wisdom and compassion, have helped me craft a life in alignment with all I have learned and seek to teach: Peter Baumann, Judith Bell, Dan Clurman, Andy Dreitcer, Daniel Ellenberg, Patricia Ellsberg, Terri Hughes, Alice Jacobsen, Bonnie Jonsson, Daniel Lappin, Richard Miller, Rose Saint John, Charlotte Siegel, Terry Trotter, Cassi Vieten.

Three places served as refuges and resources for much of my writing and mulling: Wilbur Hot Springs in Northern California — a "sanctuary for the self" whose respectful staff and fellow guests made rejuvenating in the mineral waters and writing away on the deck pure joy; Spirit Rock Meditation Center in Woodacre, California, a refuge for letting go of the self, where the teachings of wisdom, compassion, and liberation from suffering are deeply lived and celebrated; and my own beloved garden, where every string that trains the wisteria has been a prayer for a friend — a peaceful sanctuary that helps me balance the creative flow with focused productivity.

I deeply thank Shoshana Alexander and Caroline Pincus, experienced editors whose deep faith nurtured this book from before the beginning, who could hear my voice more clearly than I could, who patiently translated the Latin of my neuroclinical jargon into clear, everyday English. I'm also grateful this book landed in the capable hands of Jason Gardner at New World Library, as well as those of copyeditor Erika Büky. Both provided skillful editing and polishing of the entire manuscript. I also thank Marilynne Chophel and Gaylene Newquist, readers who early on brought sparkle and wisdom to the stories and exercises, and Brad Reynolds, whose illustrations of the brain brought a much needed clarity to the concepts in the text.

I thank dear friends and family, including my beloved brother,

Barry, who gave me the title of the book — "Resilience. What's that? Oh, I know. It's bouncing back from the terrible" — and others who provided daily encouragement: Margaret Deedy, Michael Goldberg, Karuna Graham, Barb and Bob Hirni, Cherry and Emma Jones, Phyllis Kamrin and Elijah Goldberg, Rhea Loudon, Katherine Mapes-Reznik, Steve McKiernan, Lorrie Norby, Marianne and Stan Stefancic. And from the depths of my heart, I express my gratitude for the love and support of my Gourmet Poets' Society: Dina Zvenko, William Strawn, Eve Siegel, Lynn Robinson, Lynne Michelson, Cariadne MacKenzie-Hooson, Phyllis Kirson, Gary Horvitz, Marilynne Chophel, Paul Basker — and Bette Acuff, who gave me the small figurine that sits by my computer, a Buddha with a laptop.

ENDNOTES

Introduction

xix *Researchers have found*...Philip Moeller, "Happier People Deal Better
with Hardships," *Huffington Post*, April 11, 2012, citing research of
George Bonanno at Columbia University, www.huffingtonpost
.com/2012/04/11/happiness-and-hardships_n_1417944.html.

xix *"Blessed are they"*...Debra McKnight-Higgins, yoga instructor, Fairfax,
CA, class instructions, April 29, 2011.

xx *capacities for resilience*...Louis Cozolino, *The Neuroscience of Human
Relationships: Attachment and the Developing Social Brain* (New York:
W. W. Norton, 2006), 21–33.

xx *Only in recent years*...Daniel J. Siegel, *The Mindful Brain: Reflection and
Attunement in the Cultivation of Well-Being* (New York: W. W. Norton,
2007), 31–32.

xxii *"Based upon everything we know"*...Richard Davidson, "Project
Happiness," *Common Ground*, August 2012.

Chapter 1

4 *Resilience, like all innate capacities*...Daniel J. Siegel, "Awakening the
Mind to the Wisdom of the Body," paper presented at conference "The
Embodied Mind: Integration of the Body, Brain and Mind in Clinical
Practice," Lifespan Learning Institute, Los Angeles, CA, March 4, 2006.

4 *When our conditioning*...Bonnie Badenoch, *Being a Brain-Wise Therapist:
A Practical Guide to Interpersonal Neurobiology* (New York: W. W. Norton,
2008), 52–75.

6   *The human brain*...Cozolino, *The Neuroscience of Human Relationships*, 10–14.

6   *a human infant*...BabyCenter, "Milestone Charts: What You Can Expect from Birth to Age 3," www.babycenter.com/milestone-charts-birth-to-age-3, accessed October 1, 2012.

6   *Interactions in the early environment*...Cozolino, *The Neuroscience of Human Relationships*, 37–47.

6   *prefrontal cortex*...Cozolino, *The Neuroscience of Human Relationships*, 21–30.

7   *John Bowlby proposed*...John Bowlby, *A Secure Base: Parent-Child Attachment and Healthy Human Development* (New York: Basic Books, 1988), 3.

7   *The parents' response*...David Wallin, *Attachment in Psychotherapy* (New York: Guilford Press, 2007), 26–28.

8   *"permanent psychological significance"*...Cozolino, *The Neuroscience of Human Relationships*, 146–48.

8   *"Secure attachment is the strongest inoculator"*...Pat Ogden, "Integrating the Body in Trauma Treatment: A Sensorimotor Approach," transcript of interview by Ruth Buczynski, National Institute for the Clinical Application of Behavioral Medicine, May 16, 2012, p. 4, www.nicabm.com/trauma-therapy, accessed May 16, 2012.

8   *When a parent*...Wallin, *Attachment in Psychotherapy*, 86–88.

9   *An ancient Chinese proverb*...Jon R. Stone, ed., *The Routledge Book of World Proverbs* (New York: Routledge, 2006), 394.

10   *Focusing our attention*...Daniel J. Siegel, *The Developing Mind: How Relationships and the Brain Interact to Shape Who We Are* (New York: Guilford Press, 1999), 23–31.

10   *neuroscientist Donald Hebb*...Siegel, *The Developing Mind*, 26.

11   *Conditioning*...Cozolino, *The Neuroscience of Human Relationships*, 81–93.

13   *neuroplasticity*...Siegel, *The Mindful Brain*, 31–32.

13   *All mental activity*...Rick Hanson and Richard Mendius, *Buddha's Brain: The Practical Neuroscience of Happiness, Love and Wisdom* (Oakland, CA: New Harbinger Publications, 2009), 8.

14   *"If you want to lift a hundred pounds"*...Norman Doidge, "Neuroplasticity: The Possibilities and Pitfalls," transcript of interview with Ruth Buczynski, National Institute for the Clinical Application of Behavioral Medicine, March 30, 2011, p. 13, www.nicabm.com /thebrain2011, accessed March 30, 2011.

14   *Getting to Know the Brain*...Siegel, *The Mindful Brain*, 29–50; Cozolino, *The Neuroscience of Human Relationships*, 50–62; Hanson and Mendius, *Buddha's Brain*, 6–7.

15   *The brain learns to be resilient from both the bottom up*... Pat Ogden,
      Trauma and the Body: A Sensorimotor Approach to Psychology (New York:
      W. W. Norton, 2006), 21–25.

15   *"downstairs"*... Daniel J. Siegel, *The Whole-Brain Child: 12 Revolutionary
      Strategies to Nurture Your Child's Developing Mind* (New York: Bantam,
      2012), 37–65.

15   *The lower brain controls*... Siegel, *The Mindful Brain*, 29–50; Cozolino, *The
      Neuroscience of Human Relationships*, 50–62.

16   *Figure 1.* Based on Rick Hanson and Richard Mendius, *Buddha's Brain:
      The Practical Neuroscience of Happiness, Love and Wisdom* (Oakland, CA:
      New Harbinger Publications, 2009), 54; Bonnie Badenoch, *Being a Brain-
      Wise Therapist: A Practical Guide to Interpersonal Neurobiology* (New York:
      W. W. Norton, 2008), 15; Daniel Goleman, *Social Intelligence: The New
      Science of Human Relationships* (New York: Bantam Books, 2006), 81;
      Louis Cozolino, *The Neuroscience of Human Relationships: Attachment and
      the Developing Social Brain* (New York: W. W. Norton, 2006) 52–53.

17   *Table 1.* Based on Louis Cozolino, *The Neuroscience of Human
      Relationships: Attachment and the Developing Social Brain* (New York:
      W. W. Norton, 2006), 51–62; Bonnie Badenoch, *Being a Brain-Wise
      Therapist: A Practical Guide to Interpersonal Neurobiology* (New York:
      W. W. Norton, 2008), 12–28; Daniel Goleman, *Social Intelligence: The
      New Science of Human Relationships* (New York: Bantam Books, 2006),
      64–70, 352.

18   *Figure 2.* Based on Louis Cozolino, *The Neuroscience of Human
      Relationships: Attachment and the Developing Social Brain* (New York:
      W. W. Norton, 2006), 67; Bonnie Badenoch, *Being a Brain-Wise
      Therapist: A Practical Guide to Interpersonal Neurobiology* (New York:
      W. W. Norton, 2008) 17.

19   *It integrates information coming from the lower brain*... Badenoch, *Being a
      Brain-Wise Therapist*, 28–33.

19   *As a result of its integrative capacities*... Siegel, *The Mindful Brain*, 42–44.

19   *enable us to efficiently rewire our brains*... Cozolino, *The Neuroscience of
      Human Relationships*, 199–209.

19   *All of these executive, top-down functions*... Cozolino, *The Neuroscience of
      Human Relationships*, 66–75.

20   *Table 2.* Based on Bonnie Badenoch, *Being a Brain-Wise Therapist: A
      Practical Guide to Interpersonal Neurobiology* (New York: W. W. Norton,
      2008) 28–41.

22   *Table 3.* Based on Louis Cozolino, *The Neuroscience of Human
      Relationships: Attachment and the Developing Social Brain* (New York:
      W. W. Norton, 2006), 41, 66–75; Bonnie Badenoch, *Being a Brain-Wise*

Therapist: A Practical Guide to Interpersonal Neurobiology (New York: W. W. Norton, 2008), 12–22.

23   *hippocampus*...Badenoch, *Being a Brain-Wise Therapist*, 16.

23   *childhood amnesia*...Cozolino, *The Neuroscience of Human Relationships*, 57.

24   *the discovery of mirror neurons*...Cozolino, *The Neuroscience of Human Relationships*, 59.

25   *focusing network*...Norman A. S. Farb, Zindel V. Segal, Helen Mayberg, Jim Bean, Deborah McKeon, Zainab Fatima, and Adam K. Anderson, "Attending to the Present: Mindfulness Meditation Reveals Distinct Neural Modes of Self-Reference," *Social Cognitive and Affective Neuroscience* 2 (August 2007): 313–22; Rick Hanson, "Dual Mode Theory," paper presented at neurodharma study group, San Rafael, CA, October 5, 2009; Jonah Lehrer, *Imagine: How Creativity Works* (New York: Houghton Mifflin Harcourt, 2012), 29–32. Despite difficulties with quoted sources in *Imagine*, Lehrer still provides an accessible presentation of well-researched, cutting-edge neuroscience.

25   *This defocusing network*...Farb et al., "Attending to the Present"; Hanson, "Dual Mode Theory."

Chapter 2

30   *Insecure-avoidant, insecure-anxious, and disorganized attachment styles*... Wallin, *Attachment in Psychotherapy*, 88–91, 91–93, 93–96.

33   *The first 2½ years*...Louis Cozolino, "The Social Brain," paper presented at conference "The Wholeness of Mind, Brain, Body and Human Relatedness," Lifespan Learning Institute, Los Angeles, CA, March 7, 2010.

33   *four general styles of attachment and coping*...Cozolino, "The Social Brain."

36   *80 percent of the neural instructions*...Siegel, *The Developing Mind*, 28–34.

38   *Researchers know that the coping styles we learn*...Cozolino, *The Neuroscience of Human Relationships*, 57.

38   *At the same time*...Cozolino, *The Neuroscience of Human Relationships*, 66–72.

39   *The negativity bias*...Rick Hanson, "Taking In the Good," seminar, Greater Good Science Center, University of California, Berkeley, October 15, 2011.

41   *As Eleanor Roosevelt said*...Eleanor Roosevelt, *You Learn by Living: Eleven Keys for a More Fulfilling Life* (New York: Harper Perennial, 2011), 29.

41   *Trauma is different*...Francine Shapiro, *EMDR: The Breakthrough "Eye*

Movement" Therapy for Overcoming Anxiety, Stress and Trauma (New York: Basic Books, 1997), 23–25.

42   *Repeated traumas, if left unresolved*... Bessel van der Kolk, "Clinical Implications of Neuroscience Research in PTSD," paper presented at conference "Healing Moments in Trauma Treatment," Lifespan Learning Institute, Los Angeles, CA, March 13, 2011.

43   *Neuroplasticity has always existed*... Cozolino, *The Neuroscience of Human Relationships*, 81–93.

Chapter 3

50   *"self-directed neuroplasticity"*... Jeffrey M. Schwartz and Sharon Begley, *The Mind and the Brain: Neuroplasticity and the Power of Mental Force* (New York: HarperCollins, 2002), 21–53.

50   *All mental activity creates new neural structure*... Hanson and Mendius, *Buddha's Brain*, 5.

51   *Mindfulness — the steady, nonjudgmental awareness*... Jon Kabat-Zinn, *Coming to Our Senses: Healing Ourselves and the World through Mindfulness* (New York: Hyperion, 2005), 24.

51   *Empathy — a wholesome practice of connection*... Cozolino, *The Neuroscience of Human Relationships*, 203–4.

51   *Research is increasingly showing*... Sara Lazar, "The Mindful Brain: Reflection and Attunement and the Neuro-plasticity of Mindful Practice," paper presented at conference "Mindfulness and Psychotherapy," Lifespan Learning Institute, Los Angeles, CA, October 6, 2007.

52   *The practice of mindfulness*... Jack Kornfield, presentation at conference "The Wise Heart and the Mindful Brain: Buddha Meets Neurobiology," San Francisco, CA, June 8–9, 2007.

53   *Mindfulness of Breathing*... Sara W. Lazar, Catherine E. Kerr, Rachel H. Wasserman, Jeremy R. Gray, Douglas N. Greve, Michael T. Treadway, Metta McGarvey, et al., "Meditation Experience Is Associated with Increased Cortical Thickness," *NeuroReport* 16 (2005): 1893–97.

53   *Taxi drivers*... Eleanor A. Maguire, David G. Dadian, Ingrid S. Johnsrude, Catriona D. Good, John Ashburner, Richard S. J. Frachowiak, and Christopher D. Firth, "Navigation-Related Structural Change in the Hippocampi of Taxi Drivers," *Proceedings of the National Academy of Sciences* 97 (2000): 4398–4403.

53   *Research also shows that mindfulness*... Lazar et al., "Meditation Experience Is Associated with Increased Cortical Thickness."

54   *Exercise 1.* Based on teachings of Sylvia Boorstein, Spirit Rock Meditation Center, Woodacre, CA.

55   *"That which is aware of fear"*...James Baraz, meditation retreat, Spirit Rock Meditation Center, Woodacre, CA, September 1–5, 2005.

57   *Guy Armstrong*...Guy Armstrong, training in loving kindness practice, Spirit Rock Meditation Center, Woodacre, CA, September 18, 2004.

58   *Exercise 2.* Linda Graham, created for course "Deepening Joy," March 12, 2010.

58   *when our minds contract*...Cariadne MacKenzie-Hooson, personal communication, April 23, 2004.

60   *This true nature*...Kornfield, presentation at "The Wise Heart and the Mindful Brain."

60   *Neuroscientists* have *begun*...Farb et al., "Attending to the Present."

60   *A second circuit*...Farb et al., "Attending to the Present."

62   *tools of self-reflection*...Christopher Germer, Ronald Siegel, and Paul R. Fulton, *Mindfulness and Psychotherapy* (New York: Guilford Press, 2005), 28–51.

62   *attention training*...See, for example, The Mindfulness in Schools Project, http://mindfulnessinschools.org, accessed November 21, 2012.

62   *stress-reduction*...See, for example, Center for Mindfulness in Medicine, Health Care, and Society, University of Massachusetts Medical School, "Stress Reduction Program," www.umassmed.edu/cfm/stress/index.aspx, accessed November 21, 2012.

62   *take it all seriously,*...Andy Dreitcer, presentation on centering prayer, neurodharma group, San Rafael, CA, May 6, 2012.

65   *Exercise 3.* Linda Graham, created for workshop "The Neuroscience of Resilience and Renewal," Esalen Institute, Big Sur, CA, September 1, 2012.

66   *Marianne Williamson*...Marianne Williamson, *A Return to Love: Reflections on the Principles of "A Course in Miracles"* (New York: HarperCollins, 1992), chap. 7, section 3.

Chapter 4

69   *Research shows that five elements of that empathy*...Badenoch, *Being a Brain-Wise Therapist*, 52–75.

69   *Resonance*...Cozolino, *The Neuroscience of Human Relationships*, 200–201.

71   *Frank Ostaseski*...Frank Ostaseski, training in compassionate caregiving, Zen Hospice Project, San Francisco, CA, April 1998.

72   *Exercise 1.* Adapted from Daniel J. Siegel, seminar "Attachment and Interpersonal Neurobiology," Summit Medical Center, Oakland, CA, October 14, 2001.

72   *Attunement*...Cozolino, *The Neuroscience of Human Relationships*, 201–3.

72   *55 percent of all emotional meaning is conveyed*...Albert Mehrabian, *Silent Messages: Implicit Communication of Emotions and Attitudes* (Belmont, CA: Wadsworth, 1972), 44–45.

73   *Exercise 2.* Linda Graham, training on the neuroscience of attachment, Marina Counseling Center, San Francisco, CA, February 28, 2006.

74   *Empathy works through the prefrontal cortex*...Cozolino, *The Neuroscience of Human Relationships*, 203–4.

75   *The English novelist Dinah Craik*...Dinah Craik, *A Life for a Life* (London: Hurst and Blackett, 1985), 264.

76   *Self-empathy entails understanding*...Cozolino, "The Social Brain."

77   *Exercise 3.* Linda Graham, "Neuroscience and the Art of Self-Care," workshop at *Psychotherapy Networker* symposium "Creating a New Wisdom: The Art and Science of Optimal Well-Being," Washington, DC, March 22, 2012.

78   *empathy requires a capacity*...Cozolino, *The Neuroscience of Human Relationships*, 195–98.

79   *As compassion keeps the mind and heart open*...Kristin Neff, *Self-Compassion: Stop Beating Yourself Up and Leave Insecurity Behind* (New York: HarperCollins, 2011), 9–13.

80   *Exercise 4.* Based on Rick Hanson, *Just One Thing: Developing a Buddha Brain One Simple Practice at a Time* (Oakland, CA: New Harbinger Publications, 2011), 22–25.

81   *Neuroscientists haven't fully mapped the function of self-acceptance*... Daniel J. Siegel, *Mindsight: The New Science of Personal Transformation* (New York: Bantam Books, 2010), 188–89.

82   *William James, pioneer of American Psychology*...Robert I. Fitzhenry, ed., *The Harper Book of Quotations* (New York: HarperCollins, 1993), 17.

83   *Exercise 5.* Adapted from John Freedom, individual training in emotion freedom technique, San Rafael, CA, July 22, 2005.

84   *Wiser Self and True Nature*...Kornfield, "The Wise Heart and the Mindful Brain."

84   *Exercise 6.* Adapted from Coaches Training Institute training, San Rafael, CA, August 19, 2005.

87   *Practitioners of each paradigm*...Jack Kornfield, *Bringing Home the Dharma: Awakening Right Where You Are* (Boston: Shambhala, 2011), 245–49.

Chapter 5

90   *The brain learns and rewires itself best*...Janina Fisher, training in sensorimotor psychotherapy, Sensorimotor Psychotherapy Institute, Berkeley, CA, January 25–27, 2008.

90   *Becoming present means*...Tara Brach, "Opening Our Heart in the Face of

Fear," paper presented at conference "Mindfulness and Psychotherapy: Cultivating Well-Being in the Present Moment," Lifespan Learning Institute, Los Angeles, CA, October 5, 2007.

90   *Exercise 1.* Linda Graham, "Deepening Joy" course, February 12, 2010.

91   *Intention*... James Baraz and Shoshana Alexander, *Awakening Joy: 10 Steps That Will Put You on the Road to Real Happiness* (New York: Bantam Books, 2010), 7–28.

92   *more than half the time*... Marilyn Mandala Schlitz, Cassandra Vieten, and Tina Amorok, *Living Deeply: The Art and Science of Transformation in Everyday Life* (Oakland, CA: New Harbinger Publications, 2007), 34–40.

92   *Adopting the stance that we should*... Wray Herbert, "The Willpower Paradox," *Scientific American Mind*, July 2010, www.scientificamerican .com/article.cfm?id=the-willpower-paradox.

93   *Exercise 2.* Linda Graham, "Deepening Joy" course, February 12, 2010.

94   *By persevering in the use of new tools*... Siegel, *The Developing Mind*, 26.

94   *A reporter interviewing Thomas Edison*... Baraz and Alexander, *Awakening Joy*, 19.

95   *Exercise 3.* Linda Graham, created for workshop "Neuroscience and the Art of Resilience," CorStone, Sausalito, CA, September 11, 2010.

97   *Modern neuroscience confirms*... Wallin, *Attachment in Psychotherapy*, 86–88.

97   *"resettle our molecules"*... Phyllis Kirson, personal communication, January 17, 2004.

99   *Neuroscientists have discovered*... Daniel J. Siegel, "Awareness, Mirror Neurons, and Neural Plasticity in the Development of Well-Being," paper presented at conference "The Healing Power of Emotion: Integrating Relationships, Body and Mind," Lifespan Learning Institute, Los Angeles, CA, March 10, 2007.

99   *Exercise 4.* Linda Graham, "Neuroscience and the Art of Self-Care."

100 *The Peace of Wild Things*... Wendell Berry, *Collected Poems* (New York, Northpoint Press, 1984), 69.

101 *Exercise 5.* Based on Francine Shapiro, EMDR Institute training, South San Francisco, CA, July 14, 2000.

103 *Exercise 6.* Based on Jack Kornfield, *A Path with Heart: A Guide through the Perils and Promises of Spiritual Life* (New York: Bantam Books, 1993), 228–43.

105 *Exercise 7.* Linda Graham, "The Neuroscience of Resilience and Renewal" workshop.

107 *Exercise 8.* Linda Graham, "The Neuroscience of Resilience and Renewal" workshop.

109 *Exercise 9.* Linda Graham, "Deepening Joy" course, November 12, 2010.

109   *"To see a world in a grain of sand"*...William Blake, "Auguries of
      Innocence," in *The Oxford Book of English Mystical Verse*, ed. D. H. S.
      Nicholson and A. H. E. Lee (Oxford: Clarendon Press, 1917), 57
110   *Virginia Woolf wrote*...Virginia Woolf, *A Room of One's Own* (New York:
      Harcourt Brace Jovanovich, 1929), 172.

Chapter 6

113   *New conditioning*...Based on Siegel, *The Developing Mind*, 24.
114   *Deconditioning*...Based on Farb et al., "Attending to the Present"; Lehrer,
      Imagine, 31–36, 44–52.
114   *Reconditioning*...Based on Bruce Ecker, "The Brain's Rules for Change:
      Translating Cutting-Edge Neuroscience into Practice," *Psychotherapy
      Networker*, January–February 2012, 35–38.
117   *Exercise 1.* Linda Graham, "The Neuroscience of Resilience and
      Renewal" workshop.
118   *Exercise 2.* Linda Graham, "Deepening Joy" course, November 12, 2010.
119   *Reconditioning depends on*...Goleman, *Social Intelligence*, 78.
122   *Exercise 3.* Linda Graham, "Neuroscience and the Art of Self-Care"
      workshop.
125   *"use the brain"*...Gerald Huther, *The Compassionate Brain: How Empathy
      Creates Intelligence* (Boston: Shambhala, 2004), 17.

Chapter 7

130   *If your earliest experiences*...Siegel, *The Developing Mind*, 89–92.
131   *Past Relationships*...Diana Fosha, *The Transforming Power of Affect: A
      Model for Accelerated Change* (New York: Basic Books, 2000), 71–88.
132   *True others*...Fosha, *The Transforming Power of Affect*, 169–71.
133   *As Wilde was walking*...Oscar Wilde, *De Profundis* (Los Angeles, CA:
      IndoEuropean Publishing, 2010), 1.
134   *The process of being seen*...Siegel, *The Developing Mind*, 101–3.
134   *Among my favorite stories*...Jack Kornfield, Spirit Rock Meditation
      Center, Woodacre, CA, February 1998.
135   *As Henry David Thoreau said*...Henry David Thoreau, "Life without
      Principle," *Atlantic Monthly*, October 1863, v. 12, 484.
136   *When we shift*...Mark Brady and Jennifer Austin Leigh, *The Little Book
      of Listening Skills: 52 Essential Practices for Profoundly Loving Yourself and
      Other People* (Grand Rapids, MI: Paideia Press, 2008).
136   *Exercise 1.* Based on training with Jon Kabat-Zinn on mindful parenting,
      Spirit Rock Meditation Center, Woodacre, CA, March 4, 2000.

137   *The anterior cingulate cortex*...Cozolino, *The Neuroscience of Human Relationships*, 55.

138   *Exercise 2*. Linda Graham, "Neuroscience and the Art of Self-Care" workshop.

139   *This exercise brings the vagus nerve into play*...Steve Porges, "Neuroception: A Subconscious System for Detecting Threats and Safety," paper presented at conference "The Healing Power of Emotion: Integrating Relationships, Body and Mind," Lifespan Learning Institute, Los Angeles, CA, March 10, 2007.

140   *As you remember experiencing a moment of kindness*...Cozolino, *The Neuroscience of Human Relationships*, 186–98.

140   *When your partner shares*...Daniel A. Hughes, "Psychological Treatment through Relationships: Attachment and Inter-subjectivity," paper presented at conference "The Wholeness of Mind, Brain, Body and Human Relatedness," Lifespan Learning Institute, Los Angeles, CA, March 6, 2010.

141   *Exercise 3*. Based on Sylvia Boorstein, *metta* retreat, Spirit Rock Meditation Center, Woodacre, CA, January 6–13, 2006.

143   *"know the song of your heart"*...Contributed by Shoshana Alexander, personal communication, July 18, 2008.

144   *Loving kindness practice*...Farb et al., "Attending to the Present."

146   *Exercise 4*. Based on Jack Kornfield, training on the Brahma Viharas, Spirit Rock Meditation Center, Woodacre, CA, July 2003.

147   *The steady eye contact*...Allan Schore, "Relational Trauma," paper presented at conference "Current Approaches to the Treatment of Trauma: The Shift from Cognitive to Affect Regulation, EMDR, Sensorimotor and Other Evidence-Based Treatments," Lifespan Learning Institute, Los Angeles, CA, March 7, 2009.

148   *We may "smallify"*...Daniel Ellenberg, personal communication, October 11, 2008.

148   *Exercise 5*. Linda Graham, based on individual study with James Baraz, May 2004.

150   *When we intentionally evoke the sense*...Wallin, *Attachment in Psychotherapy*, 76–77.

150   *The psychological self*...Jerry Lamagna, "Of the Self, By the Self and For the Self: Internal Attachment, Attunement and Psychological Change," *Journal of Psychotherapy Integration* 21, no. 3 (2011): 280–307.

151   *Exercise 6*. Based on Virginia Satir, training at Marina Counseling Center, San Francisco, CA, January 1992.

154   *"The Guest House"*...Rumi, *The Essential Rumi*, trans. Coleman Barks (San Francisco: HarperCollins, 1995), 109.

Chapter 8

157 *you missed out*...Bowlby, *A Secure Base*, 11–12.

157 *FACES*...Siegel, *The Mindful Brain*, 78.

157 *This base of inner security is a vital protection*...Ogden, "Integrating the Body in Trauma Treatment."

157 *locates the neural substrate*...Siegel, *The Mindful Brain*, 164.

158 *specific relational capacities*...Phil Shaver, "Secure Attachment Primes Secure Relationships," paper presented at conference "Anatomy of Intimacy: Desire, Monogamy and the Neurobiology of Intimate Attachments," Lifespan Learning Institute, Irvine, CA, November 9, 2008.

158 *The findings of the research*...His Holiness the Dalai Lama, *Ethics for the New Millennium* (New York: Penguin Putnam, 1999), 17.

159 *Exercise 1.* Linda Graham, "Deepening Joy" course, August 13, 2010.

160 *When we seek out new experiences*...Daniel J. Siegel, "An Interpersonal Neurobiology Approach to Psychotherapy," paper presented at conference "Toward a New Psychology of Interpersonal Relationships," Lifespan Learning Institute, Los Angeles, CA, March 9, 2012.

161 *Rick Hanson*...Hanson and Mendius, *Buddha's Brain*, 67–77.

162 *Exercise 2.* Based on Hanson, *Just One Thing*, 17–21.

162 *If we are so busy*...Hanson and Mendius, *Buddha's Brain*, 67–77.

164 *Exercise 3.* Based on Jack Kornfield, training in wise speech, Spirit Rock Meditation Center, Woodacre, CA, February 2001.

165 *Relaxing into the defocusing mode*...Farb et al., "Attending to the Present"; Lehrer, *Imagine*, 31–36, 44–52.

166 *A teaching story in the Buddhist tradition*...Sylvia Boorstein, *metta* retreat.

167 *Exercise 4.* Based on Diana Fosha, immersion course in accelerated experiential dynamic psychotherapy, Adelphi University, New York, July 28–August 1, 2003.

Chapter 9

171 *these bonds provide us*...Daniel Gilbert, *This Emotional Life*, PBS series, January 4, 2010, available online at www.pbs.org/thisemotionallife.

172 *more predictive of our success*...Goleman, *Emotional Intelligence*, 42–45.

172 *Researchers at the University of Michigan*...James Coan, "Our Social Baseline: How Healthy Relationships Increase the Efficiency of Our Thoughts and Actions," paper presented at conference "Toward a New Psychology of Interpersonal Relationships," Lifespan Learning Institute, Los Angeles, CA, March 9, 2012.

173 *Our nervous systems have evolved*...Robert J. Neborsky, "Brain, Mind and

Dyadic Changes Processes," paper presented at conference "The Healing Power of Emotion: Integrating Relationships, Body and Mind," Lifespan Learning Institute, Los Angeles, CA, March 10, 2007.

173 *Exercise 1.* Linda Graham, "The Neuroscience of Resilience and Renewal" workshop.

174 *When we reach out...* Porges, "Neuroception."

175 *Developmental psychologists...* BabyCenter, "Milestone Charts: What You Can Expect from Birth to Age 3."

175 *Theory of mind...* Cozolino, *The Neuroscience of Human Relationships,* 195–98.

176 *Exercise 2.* Linda Graham, "The Neuroscience of Resilience and Renewal" workshop.

177 *Theory of mind is a complex mental capacity...* Cozolino, *The Neuroscience of Human Relationships,* 195–98.

179 *Exercise 3.* Linda Graham, "The Neuroscience of Resilience" workshop.

181 *even in "good enough" close relationships...* Ed Tronick, "Rupture in Relationships," paper presented at conference "Toward a New Psychology of Interpersonal Relationships," Lifespan Learning Institute, Los Angeles, CA, March 11, 2012.

182 *Exercise 4.* Linda Graham, "The Neuroscience of Resilience" workshop.

184 *Most of us will experience injury, injustice...* Jack Kornfield and Fred Luskin, "The Science and Practice of Forgiveness," Greater Good Science Seminar, University of California, Berkeley, May 15, 2010.

185 *Exercise 5.* Based on Kornfield and Luskin, "The Science and Practice of Forgiveness."

187 *Forgiveness is a powerful practice...* Farb et al., "Attending to the Present."

188 *every resilient behavior...* Gilbert, *This Emotional Life.*

Chapter 10

193 *window of tolerance...* Siegel, *The Developing Mind,* 253–258.

195 *Exercise 1.* Linda Graham, "Deepening Joy" course, November 12, 2010.

198 *Because of the efficiency...* Porges, "Neuroception."

198 *Exercise 2.* Linda Graham, "The Neuroscience of Resilience and Renewal" workshop.

199 *Dyadic regulation...* Fosha, *The Transforming Power of Affect,* 61–66.

200 *One is the vagus nerve...* Porges, "Neuroception."

200 *The other structure...* Schore, "Relational Trauma."

200 *Losing Our Equilibrium...* Porges, "Neuroception"; Cozolino, *The Neuroscience of Human Relationships,* 88–93.

201 *Table 4.* Adapted from Janina Fisher, training in sensorimotor

psychotherapy, Sensorimotor Psychotherapy Institute, Berkeley, CA, January 25–27, 2008.

204   *Fast-Track Survival Responses*...Cozolino, *The Neuroscience of Human Relationships*, 317–19.

204   *The prefrontal cortex operates on a slow track*...Cozolino, *The Neuroscience of Human Relationships*, 317–19.

206   *Stress Responses Can Knock the Prefrontal Cortex*...Fisher, training in sensorimotor psychotherapy.

207   *Cortisol also destroys new brain cells*...Sharon Begley, "The Emotional Styles of the Brain," transcript of interview with Ruth Buczynski, National Institute for the Clinical Application of Behavioral Medicine, April 18, 2011, p. 17, www.nicabm.com/thebrain2011.

Chapter 11

209   *The hormone oxytocin is the neurotransmitter*...Goleman, *Social Intelligence*, 164.

210   *Stephen Johnson*...Stephen Johnson, *Mind Wide Open: Your Brain and the Neuroscience of Everyday Life* (New York: Scribner, 2004), 107.

210   *a single exposure to oxytocin*...Sue Carter, "Oxytocin in Prairie Voles; Oxytocin in Humans," paper presented at conference "Anatomy of Intimacy: Desire, Monogamy and the Neurobiology of Intimate Attachments," Lifespan Learning Institute, Irvine, CA, November 7, 2008.

211   *Any warm, loving touch*...Dacher Keltner, *Born to Be Good: The Science of a Meaningful Life* (New York: W. W. Norton, 2009), 182.

211   *Exercises 1a and 1b.* Based on Keltner, *Born to Be Good*, 187.

212   *Exercise 1c.* Adapted from Stan Tatkin, "Bottom Up Techniques to Use with Your Couples," presentation at conference "Intimacy and Couples," Lifespan Learning Institute, Irvine, CA, November 7–9, 2008.

212   *Safe touching with loved ones*...Keltner, *Born to Be Good*, 205.

213   *We can give our brains baths*...Goleman, *Social Intelligence*, 244.

213   *As Dan Goleman says,*...Goleman, *Social Intelligence*, 216.

213   *Exercise 2.* Linda Graham, "Neuroscience and the Art of Self-Care" workshop.

215   *Breathing deeply*...Hanson and Mendius, *Buddha's Brain*, 81.

215   *Breathing positive emotions*...Institute of HeartMath, "Science of the Heart: Exploring the Role of the Heart in Human Performance," www.heartmath.org/research/science-of-the-heart/emotional-balance-health, 5, accessed October 1, 2012.

215   *Neural pathways from the heart to the brain*...Institute of HeartMath, "Science of the Heart."

215   *In evoking a memory or image*...Badenoch, *Being a Brain-Wise Therapist*, 156.

216   *The autonomic nervous system*...Badenoch, *Being a Brain-Wise Therapist*, 20.

216   *When we intentionally slow down*...Hanson and Mendius, *Buddha's Brain*, 81.

217   *Exercise 3a.* Based on personal study with Terry Trotter, Albany, CA, May 14, 2009.

218   *Exercise 3b.* Adapted from Frank Ostaseski, training in compassionate caregiving, Zen Hospice Project, San Francisco, CA, April 1998.

218   *The body stores somatic memories*...Ogden, "Integrating the Body in Trauma," 3.

219   *Exercise 4a.* Based on Mark Williams, John Teasdale, Zindel Segal, and Jon Kabat-Zinn, *The Mindful Way through Depression: Freeing Yourself from Chronic Unhappiness* (New York: Guilford Press, 2007), 104–6.

220   *The anterior cingulate cortex*...Cozolino, *The Neuroscience of Human Relationships*, 104–9.

221   *Exercise 4b.* Adapted from Marsha Davis, Elizabeth Robbins Eshelman, and Matthew McKay, *The Relaxation and Stress Reduction Workbook* (Oakland, CA: New Harbinger Publications, 2008), 41–46.

222   *Exercise 4c.* Based on Natalie Rogers, training in expressive arts therapy, San Francisco, CA, April 15–17, 2004.

224   *The body has its own wisdom*...Fisher, training in sensorimotor psychotherapy.

224   *Our resilience can be thrown*...Fisher, training in sensorimotor psychotherapy.

225   *Exercise 5.* Based on Peter Levine, training in somatic experiencing, University of California, Berkeley, October 15–16, 2004.

Chapter 12

229   *A master monk*...Sylvia Boorstein, Spirit Rock Meditation Center, Woodacre, CA, January 2006.

230   *An excellent example*...Coan, "Our Social Baseline."

231   *Phil Shaver discovered*...Shaver, "Secure Attachment Primes Secure Relationships."

231   *Sue Carter*...Carter, "Oxytocin in Prairie Voles; Oxytocin in Humans."

232   *Exercises 1a–c.* Linda Graham, "Neuroscience and the Art of Self-Care" workshop.

234 *the greatest predictor of success*...Moeller, "Happier People Deal Better with Hardships."

235 *Research also shows that for purposes of somatic resourcing*...Moeller, "Happier People Deal Better with Hardships."

235 *Exercise 2.* Linda Graham, "The Neuroscience of Resilience and Renewal" workshop.

236 *A baby can*...BabyCenter, "Milestone Charts: What You Can Expect from Birth to Age 3."

236 *it can send an inhibitory transmitter*...Badenoch, *Being a Brain-Wise Therapist*, 31.

237 *My meditation teacher*...Sylvia Boorstein, *metta* retreat.

237 *Exercise 3.* Linda Graham, "The Neuroscience of Resilience and Renewal" workshop.

238 *A sense of incompetence*...Fisher, training in sensorimotor psychotherapy.

239 *When we're about*...Bill Bowen, training in somatic resourcing, John F. Kennedy University, Pleasant Hill, CA, June 13, 2008.

239 *Dopamine is the neurotransmitter*...Jonah Lehrer, *How We Decide* (New York: Mariner Books, 2010), 34–39.

240 *The insula*...Lehrer, *How We Decide*, 40–42.

240 *Read Montague, professor*...Lehrer, *How We Decide*, 41.

240 *Bill Bowen*...Bowen, training in somatic resourcing.

241 *"Do one thing every day"*...Eleanor Roosevelt, *You Learn by Living: Eleven Keys for a More Fulfilling Life* (New York: Harper Perennial, 2011), 23–42.

241 *"About to grow!"*...Jack Kornfield, "The Wise Heart and the Mindful Brain."

241 *Exercise 4.* Linda Graham, "The Neuroscience of Resilience and Renewal" workshop.

242 *one of the best tools*...Moeller, "Happier People Deal Better with Hardships."

242 *Our brain rewires*...Lehrer, *How We Decide*, 42, 48.

243 *Exercise 5.* Linda Graham, "Deepening Joy" course, May 14, 2010.

244 *One of the major functions*...Badenoch, *Being a Brain-Wise Therapist*, 35–37.

Chapter 13

250 *The desire to get rid of*...Daniel Goleman, *Destructive Emotions: How Can We Overcome Them?* (New York: Bantam Books, 2004) 49.

250 *neuroscientists who study feelings*...Lehrer, *How We Decide*, xiv–xvii.

250 *According to Daniel Goleman*...Goleman, *Emotional Intelligence*, 28.

251 *our emotions are unparalleled mechanisms of human connection*...Diana

Fosha, "Attachment, Emotion, Integration and Healing in Experiential Action," paper presented at conference "The Healing Power of Emotion: Integrating Relationships, Body and Mind," Lifespan Learning Institute, Los Angeles, CA, March 9–11, 2007.

251   *These sensations are filtered...* Badenoch, *Being a Brain-Wise Therapist,* 24–28.

252   *A few winters ago...* Heather Martin and Sylvia Boorstein, *metta* retreat, Spirit Rock Meditation Center, Woodacre, CA, January 6–13, 2006.

252   *All emotions are...* Goleman, *Emotional Intelligence,* 5–8.

252   *Once we learn...* Fosha, *The Transforming Power of Affect,* 115–17.

253   *The prefrontal cortex is the manager of emotions...* Badenoch, *Being a Brain-Wise Therapist,* 30, 33–35.

255   *Developing the Prefrontal Cortex...* Badenoch, *Being a Brain-Wise Therapist,* 57–75.

259   *Exercise 1.* Linda Graham, "Neuroscience and the Art of Self-Care" workshop.

260   *repeated noticing and naming...* Lazar et al., "Meditation Experience Is Associated with Increased Cortical Thickness."

260   *Exercise 2.* Linda Graham, "The Neuroscience of Resilience" workshop.

262   *We all rely...* Schore, "Relational Trauma."

263   *people don't always know...* Diana Rico, "Prelude to Courage," *Ode,* June 2011, 17.

263   *computer programs available that train the brain...* See, for example, Paul Ekman, "F.A.C.E. Training: Interactive Training by Dr. Paul Ekman," http://face.paulekman.com, accessed November 21, 2012.

263   *A wave of emotion...* Daniel N. Stern, *The Present Moment in Psychotherapy and Everyday Life* (New York: W. W. Norton, 2004), 31–40.

264   *Exercise 3.* Linda Graham, based on training in *tonglen* by Don McLeod, Spirit Rock Meditation Center, Woodacre, CA, June 2000.

266   *Depression, which is...* National Institute for Mental Health, "Depression," www.nimh.nih.gov/health/publications/depression, accessed November 21, 2012.

266   *many ways besides medication...* Michael Yapko, "Treating Depression: An Experiential Approach," presentation at *Psychotherapy Networker* symposium "Creating a New Wisdom: The Art and Science of Optimal Well-Being," Washington, DC, March 25, 2012.

268   *Exercise 4.* Linda Graham, "Deepening Joy" course, May 14, 2010.

270   any *emotion can be managed and borne...* Diana Fosha, "Metatherapeutic Processes and Their Transformational Affects," paper presented at conference "The Healing Power of Emotion: Integrating Relationships, Body and Mind," Lifespan Learning Institute, Los Angeles, CA, March 10, 2007.

Chapter 14

273 *cultivating positive emotions*...Barbara L. Frederickson, "The Broaden-and-Build Theory of Positive Emotions," *Philosophical Transactions of the Royal Society of London B, Biological Sciences* 359 (September 29, 2004): 1367–78.

273 *Positive emotions that broaden habitual modes of thinking*...Frederickson, "The Broaden-and-Build Theory."

274 *Even more compelling data*...Keltner, *Born to Be Good*, 235–49.

274 *In over one hundred studies*...Robert Emmons, *Thanks! How Practicing Gratitude Can Make You Happier* (New York: Houghton Mifflin, 2008), 27–46.

275 *Exercise 1.* Based on Robert Emmons, "The Science of a Meaningful Life: Gratitude," seminar, Greater Good Science Center, University of California, Berkeley, October 22, 2010.

277 *Neuroimaging has revealed*...Richard J. Davidson, "Well-Being and Affective Style: Neural Substrates and Biobehavioural Correlates," *Philosophical Transactions of the Royal Society of London B, Biological Sciences* 359 (2004): 1395–1411; Antoine Lutz, Lawrence L. Greischar, Nancy B. Rawlings, Mattieu Ricard, and Richard J. Davidson, "Long-Term Meditators Self-Induce High Amplitude Synchrony during Mental Practice," *Proceedings of the National Academy of Sciences* 101 (2004): 16369–73.

277 *Positive emotions strengthen the capacity*...Frederickson, "The Broaden-and-Build Theory."

278 *Jack Gilbert counsels us*...Jack Gilbert, *Collected Poems* (New York: Knopf, 2012), 213.

278 *Dan Siegel*...Siegel, "Awakening the Mind."

278 *Neuropsychologists know that resonant interactions*...Louis Cozolino, *The Healthy Aging Brain: Sustaining Attachment, Attaining Wisdom* (New York: W. W. Norton, 2008), 67–85.

279 *Paul Ekman*...Paul Ekman, "Darwin and the Dalai Lama, United by Compassion," seminar, Greater Good Science Center, University of California, Berkeley, June 11, 2010.

281 *The poet and anthologist*...Roger Housden, *Ten Poems to Change Your Life* (New York: Harmony Books, 2001), book jacket.

281 *Exercise 2.* Adapted from Baraz and Alexander, *Awakening Joy*, 75–76.

283 *Healthy shame*...Ken Benau, shame-pride-psychotherapy @yahoo.groups.com, online forum post, April 6, 2012.

283 *no one could survive*...Hanson, "Taking In the Good."

284 *Learning to be resilient*...Badenoch, *Being a Brain-Wise Therapist*, 52–63.

284 *Toxic shame takes root*...Ken Benau, shame-pride-psychotherapy
     @yahoo.groups.com, online forum post, February 19, 2012.
284 *neural cells around the heart*...Badenoch, *Being a Brain-Wise Therapist*,
     105–10.
284 *"trance of unworthiness"*...Brach, *Radical Acceptance*, 5–23.
284 *Researchers have identified four processes*...Ken Benau, shame-pride
     -psychotherapy@yahoo.groups.com, online forum post, April 15, 2012.
286 *As my colleague Ken Benau says*...Ken Benau, shame-pride-psychotherapy
     @yahoo.groups.com, online forum post, May 5, 2012.
287 *Exercise 3*. Linda Graham, "Neuroscience and the Art of Self-Care"
     workshop.

Chapter 15

293 *Emotional intelligence*...Goleman, *Emotional Intelligence*, ix.
294 *I first heard this story*...Jack Kornfield, Spirit Rock Meditation Center,
     Woodacre, CA, June 22, 1998.
295 *Exercise 1*. Based on Barbara Frederickson, *Positivity: Groundbreaking
     Research Reveals How to Embrace the Hidden Strength of Positive Emotions,
     Overcome Negativity, and Thrive* (New York: Crown Publishers, 2009),
     215–22.
295 *CASEL*...See www.casel.org.
296 *Practices of self-appreciation*...Neff, *Self-Compassion*, 267–83.
297 *Kristin Neff suggests*...Neff, *Self-Compassion*, 267–283.
297 *Exercise 2*. Based on Neff, *Self-Compassion*, 16–17.
299 *Neuroscientists have observed*...Davidson, "Well-Being and Affective
     Style."
300 *Exercise 3*. Based on Marshall Rosenberg, *Non-violent Communication: A
     Language of Life* (Encinitas, CA: Puddle Dancer Press, 2005), 6–7.

Chapter 16

308 *people who exhibit*...Moeller, "Happier People Deal Better with
     Hardships."
308 *neurobiological basis*...Badenoch, *Being a Brain-Wise Therapist*, 30.
309 *We practice mindfulness*...Siegel, *Mindsight*, 79–101.
310 *Sara's calm*...Porges, "Neuroception."
310 *through the connection*...Goleman, *Social Intelligence*, 244.
310 *By calmly focusing*...Siegel, *The Mindful Brain*, 108–33.
311 *Exercise 1*. Based on Stuart Eisendrath, meditation on mindfulness and
     depression, Spirit Rock Meditation Center, Woodacre, CA, November 15,
     2008.

312   *These encoded beliefs*...Wallin, *Attachment in Psychotherapy*, 133–44.

315   *When we become fully aware*...Siegel, *The Mindful Brain*, 164–88.

316   *Exercise 2*. Linda Graham, "The Neuroscience of Resilience and Renewal" workshop.

319   *By framing every moment*...Siegel, *The Mindful Brain*, 109–10.

319   *Exercise 3*. Linda Graham, "Deepening Joy" course, May 7, 2010.

320   *The Buddhist teachings*...Pema Chödrön, transcript of conversation with Pema Chödrön and Jack Kornfield, San Francisco, CA, May 26, 2005, available at http://archive.thebuddhadhamma.com/web-archive /category/winter-2005, accessed July 1, 2012.

Chapter 17

324   *One of the hallmarks of resilience*...Moeller, "Happier People Deal Better with Hardships."

324   *"monitor and modify"*...Daniel J. Siegel, *The Mindful Therapist: A Clinician's Guide to Mindsight and Neural Integration* (New York: W. W. Norton, 2010), 44–50.

325   *"When the dog bites"*...Richard Rodgers, "My Favorite Things," *The Sound of Music* (1959). Lyrics available at STLyrics, www.stlyrics.com /lyrics/thesoundofmusic/myfavoritethings.

325   *the power of positive thoughts*...Siegel, *The Mindful Brain*, 109–10.

325   *Exercise 1*. Linda Graham, "The Neuroscience of Resilience and Renewal" workshop.

326   *The longer you dwell*...Frederickson, *Positivity*, 163–66.

327   *taking ourselves out of a familiar environment*...Lehrer, *Imagine*, 29–32.

328   *Exercise 2*. Linda Graham, created for e-newsletter "Shifting Perspectives Leads to Resilience," March 18, 2008, archived at www.lindagraham -mft.net.

329   *When we focus our awareness*...Robert Hirni, personal communication, June 28, 2012.

329   *The shift to the defocusing network*...Lehrer, *Imagine*, 29–32.

331   *Exercise 3*. Linda Graham, "The Neuroscience of Resilience and Renewal" workshop.

333   *When we deeply believe*...Wallin, *Attachment in Psychotherapy*, 133–66.

334   *The psychologist and philosopher Jean Piaget*...Linda Graham, "Accommodating Zebras: Healing and Awakening into Aliveness and Wholeness," e-newsletter, April 2011, www.lindagraham-mft.net /newsletters-and-quotes/newsletters/newsletter-april-2011.

334   *"Crisis, suffering, loss"*...Rachel Naomi Remen, in Schlitz, Vieten, and Amorok, *Living Deeply*, 37.

335   *from a helpless "poor me"*...Wallin, *Attachment in Psychotherapy*, 133–66.

Chapter 18

337   *Autobiography*...Portia Nelson, *There's a Hole in my Sidewalk: The Romance of Self-Discovery* (New York: Atria Books, 2012), xi–xii.

341   *Exercise 1.* Linda Graham, created for this book, 2012.

344   *The prefrontal cortex makes its decisions*...Siegel, *The Mindful Brain*, 288–320.

Chapter 19

349   *In 1971*...Schlitz, Vieten, and Amorok, *Living Deeply*, 4, 45–47.

349   *Neuroscientists are now beginning*...Lehrer, *Imagine*, 13–19.

350   *That state of reverie creates opportunities*...Lehrer, *Imagine*, 29–33.

350   *"plane of open possibilities"*...Siegel, *The Mindful Therapist*, 8–17.

350   *Using the prefrontal cortex*...Siegel, *Mindsight*, 71–76.

351   *Brain scans of people who have experienced this process*...Marc Kauffman, "Meditation Gives Brain a Charge, Study Finds," *Washington Post*, January 3, 2005.

352   *Exercise 1.* Linda Graham, created for this book, 2012.

354   *The mature prefrontal cortex*...Farb et al., "Attending to the Present."

355   *"I seem to be a verb"*...Buckminster Fuller, Jerome Agel, and Quention Fiore, *I Seem to Be a Verb: Environment and Man's Future* (New York: Bantam Books, 1970).

355   *rather than being occupied with analysis*...Lehrer, *Imagine*, 29–33.

355   *Exercise 2.* Linda Graham, "Deepening Joy" course, November 11, 2011.

356   *even when the brain is not focusing*...Damien A. Fair, Alexander L. Cohen, Nico U. F. Dosenbach, Jessica A. Church, Francis M. Miezin, Deanna M. Barch, Marcus E. Raichle, Steven E. Petersen, and Bradley L. Schlaggar, "The Maturing Architecture of the Brain's Default Network," *Proceedings of the National Academy of Sciences* 105 (March 11, 2008): 4028–32.

357   *a small fold of brain tissue*...Lehrer, *Imagine*, 17–19.

357   *We join spokes together*...Lao Tzu, *Tao Te Ching*, trans. Stephen Mitchell (New York: Harper and Row, 1988), 11.

358   *The defocusing network involved in this large-scale deconditioning*...Farb et al., "Attending to the Present."

359   *Exercise 3.* Linda Graham, "Deepening Joy" course, November 11, 2011.

361   *even in a bliss state*...James Baraz, personal communication, January 13, 2010.

361   *Scans of the brain waves of meditators*...Marina Watson Pelaez, "'Oneness' Feeling Experienced by Monks, Explained," *Time*, April 27, 2011.

361   *measurable spike*...Lehrer, *Imagine*, 17.

362   *This sense of innate goodness*...Jack Kornfield, *The Wise Heart: A Guide to the Universal Teachings of Buddhist Psychology* (New York: Bantam Books, 2008), 11–21.

364   *Exercise 4.* Linda Graham, created for this book, 2012.

365   *My mentor Diana Fosha reminds us...* Diana Fosha, "Transformance, Recognition of Self by Self, and Effective Action," *Existential-Integrative Psychotherapy: Guideposts to the Core of Practice,* ed. K. J. Schneider (New York: Routledge, 2008), 290–320.

365   *Exercise 5.* Linda Graham, created for presentation "The Personal Self and Its Relationship to True Nature," Spirit Rock Meditation Center, September 8, 2010, available at www.lindagraham-mft.net/resources /dharmatalks.

367   *The brain operates differently...* Farb et al., "Attending to the Present."

368   *Using the defocusing network...* Antoine Lutz et al., "Long-Term Meditators Self-Induce High Amplitude Synchrony."

368   *This neural harmony...* Siegel, *Mindsight,* 71–76.

Chapter 20

373   *Even when difficulties...* Daniel Siegel, "Mindful Awareness," paper presented at conference "The Wholeness of Mind, Brain, Body and Human Relatedness," Lifespan Learning Institute, Los Angeles, CA, March 6, 2010.

374   *Jon Kabat-Zinn, developer...* "The Art of Conscious Living," *VHL Family Forum,* September 1993, www.vhl.org/newsletter/vhl1993/93/cazinn.

374   *"use it or lose it"...* Judith Horstman, *The Scientific American Brave New Brain* (New York: Jossey-Bass, 2010), 15.

374   *We also have to keep challenging our brains...* Horstman, *The Scientific American Brave New Brain,* 17.

375   *"We have not solved your problems"...* Ted Swift, personal communication, June 11, 1994.

375   *Learning model for resilience...* training in fundamentals of coaching, Coaches Training Institute, San Rafael, CA, August 19–21, 2005.

376   *Exercise 1.* Linda Graham, created for this book, 2012.

378   *"As an irrigator guides water"...* Buddha, Dhammapada 6, translated by Thanissaro Bhikkhu, www.beliefnet.com/quotes/Buddhist/General/D /Dhammapada-6-translated-by-Thanissaro-Bhikkhu.

378   *create a coherent narrative...* Siegel, *The Mindful Brain,* 307–11.

379   *Exercise 2.* Linda Graham, "The Neuroscience of Resilience and Renewal" workshop.

380   *Sylvia Boorstein...* Sylvia Boorstein, personal communication, March 29, 2011.

381   *Exercise 3.* Linda Graham, created for this book, 2012.

382   *Patti Quigley... Beyond Belief,* documentary film by Beth Murphy (2006).

383   *altruism is also fueled...* Goleman, *Social Intelligence,* 50–62.

384   *Exercise 4.* Linda Graham, created for this book, 2012.

385   *Exercise 5.* Linda Graham, created for this book, 2012.

INDEX

of relational intelligence skills,
174–75, 177–78, 180–81,
183–84, 187
of resonant relationship skills,
137–38, 139–40, 144–45, 147,
150, 153–55
of response flexibility, 326–27,
329, 333–34, 344
of self-awareness, 354–55, 356–57,
361
of somatic intelligence, 196–97,
236–37, 238, 244
of somatic resources, 215–16,
220–21, 224, 226
Newton, Isaac, 362
Nin, Anaïs, 91
Nisargadatta, Sri, 349
noesis, 349
nonself, 60–61, 86, 350–51, 352,
357–61, 363–68, 370
nonviolent communication (NVC),
300
noticing, 309–12, 313, 315
Noticing and Naming to Create
Options (exercise), 311–12
Noticing and Regulating Your
Emotions (exercise), 259

observing ego, 62, 64–67, 87
Ogden, Pat, 8
organizing principles, 378–85
Orsborn, Carol, 369
Ostaseski, Frank, 71
others
disconnection from, 172
emotionally healthy, connection
with, 278–83, 290
innate goodness of, 141–47
love from, and inner security,
159–61

positive views of self from,
148–50
reading emotions of, 260–62
as resources, 106–8, 140
sharing with, 138–40
supportive recognition from,
134–35
as support network, 98–100,
172–75
true, 132–34, 155, 158, 359
Out with the Old, In with the New
through Reconditioning (exercise),
122–24
oxytocin, 192
activating release of, 210–16
altruism and, 383
brain priming and, 230–32
calming effects of, 209–10,
230–32, 239, 245, 296, 310
receptors for, in brain, 290
self-appreciation and, 296

parasympathetic nervous system
(PNS), 201, 203, 208, 215, 216, 222,
238, 285
"Peace of Wild Things, The" (poem;
Berry), 100
Peck, M. Scott, 323
pendulation, 226
perseverance, 233
cultivation of, 89, 94–96, 111
new conditioning and, 326–27
perspective, shifts in, 324–29, 338–39
Piaget, Jean, 334
places, as refuges, 100–102
Plato, 141
poetry, 280–81
positive psychology movement, 273
positivity, rewiring brain for, 161–63
Practicing Altruism (exercise), 384

ABOUT THE AUTHOR

LINDA GRAHAM, MFT, is a licensed psychotherapist and meditation teacher in full-time practice in the San Francisco Bay Area. She
integrates her passion for neuroscience, mindfulness, and relational
psychology through trainings, consultations, workshops, and con-
ferences nationally. She publishes a monthly e-newsletter, *Healing
and Awakening into Aliveness and Wholeness*, and weekly e-quotes on
resources for recovering resilience, archived at www.lindagraham-mft.net.

HELPING TO PRESERVE OUR ENVIRONMENT

New World Library uses 100% postconsumer-waste recycled paper for our books whenever possible, even if it costs more. During 2011 this choice saved the following precious resources:

3,147 trees were saved

ENERGY	WASTEWATER	GREENHOUSE GASES	SOLID WASTE
22 MILLION BTU	600,000 GAL.	770,000 LB.	225,000 LB.

www.newworldlibrary.com

Environmental impact estimates were made using the Environmental Defense Fund Paper Calculator @ www.papercalculator.org.